Ups and Downs
of a Wandering Life

By

Walter Seymour

stockcero

Seymour, Walter
Ups and downs of a wandering life.-
1ª. ed.– Buenos Aires : Stock Cero, 2003.
300 p. ; 23x15 cm.

ISBN 987-1136-03-X

1. Latinoamérica-Relatos de Viajes I. Título
CDD 909.8

Fecha de catalogación: 03-11-03

Copyright © 2003 Stockcero

1º edición: 2003
Stockcero
ISBN Nº 987-1136-03-X
Libro de Edición Argentina.

stockcero.com
Viamonte 1592 C1055ABD
Buenos Aires Argentina
54 11 4372 9322
stockcero@stockcero.com

Ups and Downs
of a Wandering Life

By

Walter Seymour

Ye who listen with credulity to the whispers of fancy, and pursue with eagerness the phantoms of hope; who think that age will perform the promises of youth, and that the deficiencies of the present day will be supplied by the morrow: read the story of the writer of these pages

First published in 1910 by
JOHN LONG, LIMITED
NORRIS STREET, HAYMARKET - LONDON

Contents

Yours truly

Walter Seymour

Chapter I

EARLY LIFE AND SCHOOL

One of the greatest of English writers, for whom I have the pro-
foundest veneration, Herbert Spencer, considered that a man's
progenitors had great influence on his character and impulses, so my
readers - if there are any - must forgive my mentioning one or two
facts about mine, which may account for my wandering propensities
and curious ways of life.

My father belonged to a branch of the Seymour family settled in
Ireland, and my grandfather, Admiral Sir Michael Seymour, was one
of the fighting captains in the war with France. My uncle Sir Michael,
my cousin Sir Michael, and brother Sir Edward, have continued the
family propensity for the sea.

There was an Admiral Seymour commanding against the Spanish Armada. Among my forbears was John Hampden, also Sir
Humphrey Gilbert; while General Monk, Duke of Albemarle, was
first cousin, and blood-relation to an ancestor.

The Rhett family of South Carolina, whose ancestors were the
first three Governors of Carolina, are distant cousins, and they, while
being rather remarkable in a fighting generation for their duelling
tastes, are considered by many to have been almost the greatest insti-
gators of the American Civil War.

I have also a well-authenticated descent from Edward the First,
though I don't quite know which of his great qualities I have any frac-
tion of. There have been no family wounds from poisoned arrows
since then.

Having done with them, I may state that my father, Richard Seymour, was a Canon of Worcester, and that I was born at Kinwarton, in Warwickshire, where he was Rector, on the 9th December, 1838. After having pretty well worn out the patience of a long-suffering governess, I and my brothers had the tuition of two tutors, who were also successively my father's curates, and with them we often differed, but, having the advantage of superior strength, and the possession of a cane, they came off best.

Close to our garden was a small river, our delight in every way, as we could bathe, hunt rats with the dogs, and catch fish and eels, with the result that even in floods none of us were drowned, and that we boys and my sisters turned out good swimmers.

We had, of course, our share of pet animals. Dogs large and small: Dido, a fierce retriever, in her youth would take any one of us by the leg and drag us round the lawn in spite of howls, to the amusement of the others. Pip, a rough grey terrier, would stand on his hind-legs and growl defiance in the ear of any dog he could reach like that, and was nearly killed more than once. My brother Albert took him to Oxford, where he was supposed to live out of college, but he frequently evaded the porter when he happened to be loose, and made straight for the rooms he wanted.

Ferrets and guinea-pigs, of course, succeeded rabbits. We had a shower-bath in the house, and all the animals had to take their turn of that bath, to their great disgust.

That ferrets were not affectionate my youngest brother Jack found a painful proof. I and one of my brothers were crossing to the ferret-house, and found there Master Jack castigating a large white one. We asked him what he did that for. He pointed to his bleeding lip, and said: "I was only kissing the beast!"

We learned to ride early on a donkey, who was knowing enough to brush us off under the bough of a tree when she had enough of us, and ponies followed, my first fox-hunt being when eight or nine.

In due course I went to school at Radley, the monastic system of which was not welcome-rise at six; a cold schoolroom, for the heating apparatus got out of order, and there were no fires for weeks. The small boys used sometimes to say: "Ha, ha! I am warm: I have seen the fire!" Chapel at eight; then tea and bread-and-butter; plenty of school; a remarkably plain dinner; chapel again, and more tea and bread-and-butter. The head-master was the "Warden", and the under-masters were called "Fellows"; and there were many fads in the early system which were modified till it is now a most excellent public school. I fell under the displeasure of William Sewell, the Warden, over some silly nonsense, which he chose to make a great fuss about, and he treated me, as I still think, with much injudiciousness, and also injustice, which was the verdict of all the school. I think that, except in his own mind, he knew as much about ruling boys as he did about governing the Mormon City. It ended in my father transplanting me to Charterhouse, then in the middle of London, where he had been.

The corporal discipline system at Radley was like that of Jack Easy's school-no flogging, or very rarely, but a plentiful use of the rat-tan-cane. Like Jack, after enough experience of both, I personally much prefer the classic birch to the common cane. As to which causes most personal annoyance there can be no difference of opinion among those who have been experimented upon.

I learnt about as much Latin and Greek as the average boy does, which means that, under the English public-school system, having been taught Latin for eleven or twelve years, I wrote it very badly, and read it with great difficulty, needing a dictionary up to the end. All because it was called a "dead language" and a doggerel form of learning, it was therefore used; whereas, if I had not learnt more of a live modern language in two years, I should have been called an idiot. Of Greek I learnt, of course, less, and the absurd rule of trying to write verses in each was the fancy form of teaching, when the amount of verse-writing of most boys would hardly have arrived in English at, "A was an Archer, who shot at a frog; and B was a Butcher, who had a big dog". The French master, a clever gentleman, was made a joke of, and the boys who cheeked him to his face were never punished. Such was the regard the masters had for any learning, however useful, of which they were ignorant. I soon got to the end of Colensoe's "Arithmetic", and then, as nothing higher was taught, my arithmetic hours were wasted in doing old sums, and the same with the four books of Euclid. The drawing-lesson was equally a farce, and waste of time and money, as it was an extra.

Hullah, the well-known, popular singing-master, drilled us into the "Hardy Norseman" and "Ye Mariners of England", sound being as much a requirement as harmony, and voice-production, beyond being told to open your chest and mouth, was a needless detail.

Angelo taught fencing, and we thrashed each other with single-sticks, and punched the noses of our mates with boxing-gloves by the light of Nature to our hearts' content.

Masters were not always of the wisest. My brother Dick was a boy not easily repressed. One day, when he was making the other boys laugh, the master said to him: "Seymour, you are a fool". "You have no right to call me a fool, sir!" "Solomon would have called you a fool". Yes, sir; but you are not Solomon".

Cricket we worked hard at, and, in spite of the limited extent and roughness of the ground, were very keen about it, and turned out some good cricketers.

Football, of course - though that was long before the rules of "Soccer" and "Rugger" were invented - filled up the winter play-hours but our speciality was football in the cloisters - a rough and very violent form of sport.

I arrived at the sixth form, and got through its requirements with too much facility to learn as much as I ought to have done.

English verse I wrote easily, and got a medal for some strange lines on the Crimea, which I concocted during our holidays. I remember that I followed this success up by writing for the Newdigate at Oxford; and a friend of mine, who really could write, some years later came across my poem among some papers, and remarked that it was almost bad enough to have won the prize. The subject was the Indian Mutiny, and when he came to the lines –

> "The sun was setting, and the bugle peal
> Called the tired soldier to his evening meal!"

he fairly roared with laughter.

As a small boy, it took great labour to teach me to read, so much so that my nearest sister, who was far sharper, thought I was deficient; but at Charterhouse I dipped deeply into an excellent library, and read insatiably, especially poetry.

I remember an "exeat" one Saturday to go down to Sheerness to see my brother Edward, a midshipman on board the Terrible, just returned from the Crimea, where she had seen a good deal of service.

I was asked with him into the wardroom, where I had to take wine with most of the hospitable heroes at table, after which the ceremony was repeated in the midshipman's berth in rum, with effects rather disastrous to a young schoolboy. And the hammock in which

I passed the night seemed to me at first to have brought the movement of an Atlantic swell with it.

The holidays spent in the wilds of the country after London were delightful. We had the kindest and most hospitable of neighbours near us in Mr. Darwin Galton, a country squire of the best sort, to whose kindness I owe much of my early knowledge of shooting and riding. He had no boys of his own, and was kindness itself to us. I remember one day in his room looking at a print of the celebrated Barclay of Ury, and asking him: "Mr. Galton, who is that rat-catcher-looking man?" He roared with laughter, and said: "That rat-catcher-looking man is my uncle, the celebrated Barclay of Ury, who walked a thousand miles in a thousand hours, and trained Tom Cribb for his great fight with Molyneux!"

Mr. Galton was a most practical man in every way, and on his farm and estate had many dodges of his own.

One, I remember, was in the kitchen-garden on the newly-sown beds, or to guard strawberries, where three or four cats, each with its little kennel and a long string to range about, were kept to frighten the birds.

He said to us one day when we had been cleaned, and had ridden over there: "Now, boys, next time you come, don't come dressed up smart; come in your 'pig clothes', then you can have some fun with the keeper, fishing or ferreting". And so we did after that, learning much about ferrets and other animals.

Another neighbour was Sir Francis Goodricke, of Studley Castle, where we were always welcome, and spent many happy days, his family being our greatest friends, and one of his sons was later on my partner in the wilds. His name was Holyoake before he took that of Goodricke.

His was a curious history. Of an old Warwickshire family-squires and bankers at Wolverhampton-he was the celebrated Frank Holyoake at Melton and Newmarket.

Sir Harry Goodricke, his great friend, died young, and left him Ribstone Hall in Yorkshire, and Cleremont in Norfolk.

He also succeeded him as Master of the Quorn, where he had a short and glorious reign. He built Studley Castle on the old Holyoake property, and married the sister of that most popular and charming man, Mr. George Payne.

Lord George Bentinck was a great ally of his, and a frequent visitor at Studley; and at one time Sir Francis, Mr. Payne, and Mr. Charles Greville were partners in racing.

Sir Francis later became serious, and gave up racing and society, and eventually sold Studley. His eldest son Harry, my dear old friend, got a bullet through him at the Redan, within an inch of his heart, a wound from which he seemed to recover. He was very strong and active, and a very good cricketer, but he died young from the effects of his wound.

Our only other near neighbours were the Throckmortons of Coughton - that quaint old house where their relatives the Catesbys, Treshams, etc., used to meet early in James the First's reign - and as they were active Roman Catholics, had no friendly feeling for the King. Vide Guy Fawkes!

Sir Robert was a charming gentleman of the world of manners now, alas! passed away, most courteous and kind to everyone. Many a pleasant day's shooting I had at Coughton, and at Buckland in Berkshire, and his sons Willie, Dick, and Jack were among my dearest and most intimate friends in those happy days of youth and enthusiasm.

The free hospitality of those days is in some ways moderated, and strong temperance people would say, "Thank God for it!" In those days beer was always on tap for everyone who could make an excuse to call at an open-handed house. One of Sir Robert's sons told me that when they lived at Coughton Court the consumption of beer in a year was ten thousand gallons - about twenty-seven gallons a day, so that a hundred people would drink a quart each. But, then, two quarts a day was not much for stablemen, footmen, gardeners, keepers, and all who could make any excuse to call at the house.

When one knows that in old days at Wynnstay there were three men in uniform called "drawers", one wonders less. We may presume that the drawers brewed also, as all beer was brewed at home, and capital stuff it nearly always was! No salt and tobacco put in it by the publicans.

Though Warwickshire was not then among the known cricketing counties, we had a good eleven, and far more enjoyable matches, to my mind, than the present professional affairs. I and my two brothers played, and we had the Mordaunts (John and Osbert), David Bucannon, Tom Ratliff, Beau Featherstone, Kenny, etc.

Beau Featherstone was a very good boxer, as my nose bore witness for ever after. One evening during a two-days' match someone threw out of a window to us below a set of boxing-gloves, which he and I put on. He presently landed me one smartly on the nose, and the glove, when thrown out, had picked up a small, sharp stone, and this split the bridge of my nose. Everyone laughed, and all declared afterwards that it had improved its shape.

A French lady at Leamington amused us by asking "What for do they call him Beau? Is it because he is so handsome?" And he was mighty good-looking!

With a small local club at Kinwarton we generally managed to win our matches, over which party spirit occasionally ran high. When going to play in the Birmingham part, it used to be remarked: "You had better bring a fighting umpire with you!" I remember an amusing incident: A big man was in. "How's that, umpire?" "Out". The big man: "Hout be dommed; oi be the biggest mon in this here bonk, and here oi boid!"

But the decision of the umpire was sometimes of the quality of the local man: "No ball! Wide! Hout, by gum!"

I have lively recollections of the system of medicine both at Radley and at Charterhouse. If a boy at Radley complained of illness, the inflexible matron administered to him a most searching remedy called a "black dose"; made, we believed, chiefly of senna. I know it was the nastiest compound I ever put inside my unlucky mouth; and its strength!

There was an infirmary of which I was twice an inmate, once with mumps, and again from an accident.

Tree-climbing was one of our delights, and I had a nasty fall from a bough breaking, and I came down on my head. All I could remember of it was being given a leg up into the tree by Lord Walter Ker, so well known afterwards in the Navy and at the Admiralty. Then I found myself in the schoolroom, and then in chapel. I was overhauled and sent to the infirmary, where were two other boys with some complaints - possibly none, only "shamming".

I don't think we were very bad, as we kicked up such a row that we were tried and condemned. My companions were severely caned, and sent back to the schoolroom. I got off, as it was thought that caning might be bad for my head, though that was not the part on which the punishment was inflicted.

At Charterhouse our medico was a great character - Dr. Myles. I think I may say that he belonged to the old school of drastic-remedy doctors. Though he could supply many things, he had a sad deficiency of "h's" in his talk.

One of the senior boys came to him, and was examined, and the doctor said: "My boy, you over 'eat yourself!" "Oh no, sir! I beg your pardon, I have lately been most careful in food". "I don't mean you eat too much, but you get too 'ot!"

They told a story in the hall, where the authorities had their mess, that one day, being asked what he would take, he said to the master, Dr. Hale, who had before him a calf's head: "Well, master, I will 'ave some of your 'ead".

In all ordinary complaints there were two remedies, the white mixture and the brown mixture, the latter being the most powerful; and one or other was ordered according to symptoms.

The birch was then in daily use, sometimes, one may say, whole-sale. One might see six or eight sad-looking youths following the head-monitor into the room of execution, and someone would at once give the cause as a "bedroom row" - a bolster-fight, probably - the noise of which had brought up the house-master. No questions were asked, but the whole roomful was birched.

I remember a small, funny little boy, who was a frequent suffer-er. He rejoiced in the appropriate name of Rodwell. A mischievous, cheeky urchin, he was a day-boy, and we heard one day that he had suffered under his father, the Rev. Rodwell, who had caught him in his surplice baptizing the kitten.

We used sometimes to prig the old birches, and in one house, whoever got a "duck's egg" as his share in a house cricket match was summarily birched by the rest of the eleven.

I was at Charterhouse under three head-masters. Dr. Saunders, quite an old-fashioned Head who birched his way to the Deanery of Peterborough.

Can anyone say why the castigation of boys has so frequently led to high places in the Church?

Dr. Elder succeeded him - a very clever and good master - but his health soon broke down, much to our regret, and he was succeeded by Dr. Elwyn, a first-rate scholar, though not a master of great per-sonal influence.

Chapter II

CHRIST CHURCH

My next experience was that of an undergraduate at Christ Church.

The "House", as we called it - for it was infra dig. to call it "College" - was a paradise for a man - for we suddenly ceased to be boys - who was active and cheerful, and had a good-sized allowance.

That the air of the place was conducive to reading I can hardly say; but many did read, and they had every opportunity.

My lot took me first into the most charming, elegantly furnished rooms in Canterbury; then, when the owner of them, who had been down for a term, came back, I ascended to garrets in Peckwater, later on descending to ground-floors in the same quadrangle.

In such rooms, if you wanted to be quiet, it was useless to "sport your oak", for the window was always there for a wandering friend to enter by, and, as glass is fragile and cheap, it was useless to fasten it.

My career there was much like that of many others. I could easily get through examinations, and thoroughly enjoyed the many diversions of the undergrad.

We men of the House looked down with supercilious contempt on out-college men, and called them Squills. If one was entertaining any such, whatever his learning, rank, or relationship, it was necessary to apologize for such want of loyalty by saying that, although a Squill, he was a "good" Squill.

My ground-floor rooms got me into a scrape one 5th of November, as they were used for a magazine of fireworks.

There was a pile on the table, and refreshments as well, chiefly the excellent malt liquors from our famous buttery, both light and strong.

There was a bonfire blazing, outside in the middle of quad; there were twenty or thirty persecutors of Guy Fawkes in the room, and the host, with his face black from the bursting of a roman candle, the shots from which he had been aiming at the legs of the Dean's footman, who was looking on.

In walked the Censor like a cat among the mice, and names were taken down.

I was duly court-martialled before the Dean, and "gated" for the rest of the term - i.e., confined to college after "hall". Dinner in those days was at five, but as it was winter there was not much temptation to remain out.

I was rather badly burnt in the neck, and have carried the marks of that youthful folly ever since.

We were rather given to rowdiness in the Peckwater district, a large supper more than once culminating in a bonfire, when coal-boxes and any mortal thing were used as fuel.

The unlucky episode of the marble statues being brought out of the college library occurred very soon after. They were put to warm at the fire - unluckily, too near for their safety, for no destruction was ever intended.

Of the three victims to college justice on that occasion, one was killed shooting in Africa by a wounded beast; another became a Cabinet Minister; and the third died, regretted by everyone, partner in a well-known brewery - all three useful and popular members of society.

Reflections on the educational system of Oxford are out of place here. It has been greatly changed since those days, and Latin and Greek, not to speak of Logic - the hopeless pitfall of so many - have not the glorious pre-eminence they then held. Even the amount learnt of them was very limited, and Max Müller relates his astonishment when he went to Oxford at the very little even the best-read undergraduate knew, and I must make the same remark as I made of school teaching - that anyone who had had the same long years of learning any modern language - even Arabic - and knew so little of it, would be considered a congenital idiot.

So much for construing, parsing, verse-writing, and such-like waste of time.

What master, and how few tutors, in beginning a new book, prose or verse, ever took the trouble to explain to his pupils what it was about, or tried really to interest them in it! It was dryasdust, word for word, hammer and tongs, grammatical driving in, regardless of sense or story. No wonder Byron exclaimed: "And good-bye, Horace! Who I hated so!"

Then, why were we educated for only six months in the year, which cost some £200 a year at least? The origin of that was when many boys came up who had to go home and help their fathers with the harvest and other work; but that was ages ago, only now the Dons don't at all fancy cutting short their holiday, and leave only too many undergraduates idle for half the year.

In due course there arose the family question of what I was to do to make a living in life.

My father would have liked me to follow his profession, and take Orders, but I had no inclination that way; so it was decided that I should stop short of my degree and go into the Civil Service, and Sir John Pakington gave me a nomination to the Admiralty.

At the risk of boring some of my readers, I am including the popular song of "The Thoroughbred Christ Church Man", which I and others sung at supper-parties with much success. The original, "The Thoroughbred Oxford Man", was, I believe, written by George Blackstone, who got the Newdigate, and died very young. This was our version of it:

"You may argue for weeks of your Romans and your Greeks,
    And all such company,
But I'll venture to say there's a fellow here to-day
    Who will rival antiquity.
To its uttermost bound search the wide world around,
    And try wherever you can,
Be he sober, be he mellow, you'll ne'er find me such a fellow
    As the thoroughbred Christ Church man, man, man!

"In the morning, if you wait at the Canterbury Gate,
    You'll see him turn out in his Pink.
Hedge, fence, and stone wall, he'll overtop them all,

While the green ones go out with a stink.
And when Reynard's nearly done with a forty-minutes run,
    Still leading the red-coated clan,
When the field is getting thinnish, who is in at the finish,
    But the thoroughbred Christ Church man, man, man!

"In literature, too, he can play his part a few,
    When the midnight oil burns bright,
Till the first streaks of dawn usher in the welcome morn
    On the footsteps of the waning night.
And with pleasure he'll look back on the well-beaten track,
    When first in the race he ran,
When the honours of a double crowned all the toil and trouble
    Of the thoroughbred Christ Church man, man, man!

"And when the sun's bright rays lengthen out the summer days,
    On the Bullingdon and Christ Church ground,
The champions of cricket encircling the wicket,
    Flannel-clad, bat in hand, stand around.
And the name of Monkey Long must not be without a song,
    We shall ne'er see his like again,
And to make the list yet fuller there's his cousin Charley Buller,
    Such a thoroughbred Christ Church man, man, man!

"And Cambridge at last must confess herself surpassed,
    As Henley-on-Thames can tell,
Where the gallant Oxford crew, in spite of all that she could do,
    Have proudly borne off the bell.
And on that same Henley water, not long ago, we taught her
    A lesson she won't like to learn again,
When victorious past the shores we rowed in with seven oars,
    Like thoroughbred Oxford men, men, men!

"And Bloxham* full well and Bickerton† can tell
    The fifties in their time they have scored,
When the ball's ivory rattle proclaimed the nightly battle
    On the surface of the smooth green board.
And when Tom's‡ nightly calls re-peopled the old walls,
    And the cards were dealt round for Van,§

Oh! you'd laugh to see the tin swept so cheerily in
 By the thoroughbred Christ Church man, man, man!

"And through all the strife and the turmoil of life,
 Be he parson, lord, or squire,
He's as well known to all in the cottage and the hall
 As the vane on the old church spire.
Oh! you'll ne'er find his match, tho' you search the whole batch,
 That have been since the world began,
For all people must declare that there's no one can compare
 With the thoroughbred Christ Church man, man, man!"

We used to play cards a little, but high play was very rare. Van and Lansquenet were the round games in fashion. Whist, of course, we played, the ideas of most undergraduates on which were, to say the least of it, elementary.

Fifth of November town-and-gown fights were, of course, in fashion, and we could then put in practice the lessons we had learnt from Aaron Jones, the celebrated pugilist, who instructed us in the noble art.

I remember being hauled up before the Proctor after one such evening, and when he saw the row in front of him, and their battered appearance, he let us down easy, and said: "Well, young gentlemen, you seem to have had a lesson, so I will say no more" - probably mindful of his undergrad days.

Christ Church was rather divided into small sets, which made the first start of a Freshman not very easy, and the sort of life he led depended very much on the lot he got among at first start.

In those days there were Noblemen - "Tufts", from their gold cap-tassels - Gentlemen Commoners, and the ordinary undergrad. This helped a little to keep up exclusiveness. There were also the Students, who rather kept together, and the Servitors, called "Scrivs", who were poorer, and also held together.

Also, something depended on where you had rooms. It was a long way from Peckwater to the Old Library, and that rather divided us

* Keeper of billiard-tables.
† Keeper of billiard-tables.
‡ Big Tom, the bell in the tower over the gateaway into Tom Quad, which rang at nine in the evening.
§ Vingt-et-un.

up. I am afraid that we of Peckwater were the rowdy lot. Tom Quad was inhabited by Dons, Students, and Tufts, also Canons - Dr. Pusey being one. Also, the Dean lived there.

After my 5th of November trouble, some of my "pals" thought I had been rather victimized, so a large bundle of crackers and fireworks was hung on the Dean's door-knocker and set light to by a man who in later life was a most quiet and respected country parson.

The snow was a great snare in winter, and led to severe contests in and out of college, and innocent passengers through the college had a rough time. I saw the Member for Oxford pelted, and he - a very pompous M.P. - stood on the steps of the library to lecture the pelters, until a snowball took him in the mouth, and he fled without any dignity left.

One dark night I saw one of the Censors coming. He was also junior Proctor, and not much loved. I lay in wait for him, and put a large ball into the nape of his neck, and then fled for my life, but in the cloisters and dark places I outpaced him and escaped. I remember in after-years sitting by him at wine in the Common Room!

In those days we were allowed to keep dogs, and Peckwater was full of them. I had two terriers - Dandy and Gripe - in my rooms.

There was a very doggy set known 'as the Ratcatchers, who were mostly friends of mine, though I was not of them. They were afterwards respected parsons, bankers, etc. The dog-dealers were Freeman and Luker - naturally known as "filthy" Luker. A friend of mine bought a dog of him one day, and he said, to conclude the bargain, he would give him a rat "graciously" (gratuitously) to try the dog on. Badger-baiting still went on occasionally, on the sly.

To bathe we often rowed down to Sandford, and sometimes jumped off the monument put up to Gaisford and Phillimore, who were drowned in the big Lasher, into which we went when not in flood. It was a splendid feeling as it rolled you over and over, and you came up about forty yards below. The bathing-place of Radley is just below.

At Christ Church it was too much the fashion to dine out of hall, the early hour of dinner - five o'clock - and its indifference having something to do with it. Sometimes we had small parties in our rooms, sometimes in the "Christ Church" coffee-room at the Mitre.

That strange mortal, Carlo Hamilton, brother of the Duke, came up for a visit, and after a severe dinner there, scrambled upstairs, and proceeded to try the wrong door. A waiter came racing up. "Oh, pray don't go in there, my lord! It's a newly-married couple!" "Oh, is it!" said my lord, and put his big shoulder to the door. "I'll have a look at them!" The poor bridegroom, very indignant, jumped out of bed to protect his bride. Carlo, a very powerful fellow, turned him over his knee and spanked him!

He was advised to leave Oxford early next day, which he did.

The ordinary festivities of college were wine-parties (wines) and suppers. Wines were frequent, and very little was drunk at them, though a large one often ended in a bear-fight, oranges and apples, etc., being used. Suppers were rare, and rum punch was powerful for young heads, some big row often ending up the evening, perhaps a bonfire.

Some absentee was punished by being "drawn", his oak smashed with coal-picks, and his room "made hay of". I remember once two or three of us climbed along the stone carving to the window of a deserting friend, who defended himself with that awful weapon, a hot poker! This was risky, as Oxford stone is very rotten. An unfortunate young fellow was afterwards killed by the stone breaking, and his falling on to the pavement below in Peckwater.

Christ Church was also divided up by two small and exclusive clubs, the Loders and the Rousers (Carousers). I was later on made a member of the latter. They were very pleasant little sets, but no guests were allowed.

I must not forget the water and fountain in the middle of Tom Quad, familiarly called "Mercury", from the statue of that God of Elegance and Theft which once stood in the centre.

"Mercury" was the subject of so many midnight tricks by undergraduates that he at last retired - I think not into the museum.

In the ancient days of Dean Gaisford he was seen one morning in a cap and flowing gown, which the early morning tidiers of the quadrangle had not removed.

Gaisford sent hurriedly for the porter, on his way to chapel, and ordered the robes off instantly. "But really, sir—" said the man. "Don't talk to me! Off with them at once!" The water was bridged by a ladder, and "Mercury" was disclosed with one part of his body blue, another red, and another gilded.

I have known obnoxious youths well ducked after midnight in "Mercury", and baths taken in his waters on a warm night.

Chapel at Christ Church, held in the Cathedral, was in those days at seven o'clock in the summer, and the service was still in Latin. It is now in English - I don't know why the change.

The prayers were read by what I once heard a lady call "the lower orders of the clergy", "the chaplains" - much despised by the lordly Canons, etc. A story was told of a very pompous old Canon relating with horror how once a chaplain, who very much wanted to be absent, had presumptuously asked him to read the prayers for him. "What did you say?" said the other man. And the Canon replied: "I gave the young man to understand that the distance between a Canon of Christ Church and a chaplain was immeasurable!"

Gaisford ended a sermon about the benefits of a knowledge of Greek thus: "It not only elevates above the vulgar herd, but leads not infrequently to positions of considerable emolument".

Chapter III

ADMIRALTY

*H*aving left my cap and gown with my scout in Peckwater, I proceeded to London to prepare for examination before the Civil Service Commissioners, the heads being then my relative Sir John Lefevre and Sir Edward Ryan.

One of the chief objects seemed to be to examine the wretched candidate in subjects of which he knew nothing before, no matter where he had been educated, and the knowledge of which would not be of the slightest use to him in his work for the Government.

Godfrey Webb, a cousin of both Sir John and myself, wrote some amusing lines on the subject, beginning with:

> "I am an English Gentleman,
> My age is twenty-two,
> Yet I cannot tell what wares best sell
> In the mart at Timbuctoo.
> I do not know how far Pegoo
> Is from the Irawaddy,
> Nor, to my belief, what Highland chief
> Invented whisky toddy".

I was placed under Mr. Dusayer, the famous crammer of the moment, and he certainly stuffed me with a variety of facts which were turned out hot and fresh at the examination, and were mostly forgotten directly after. He was much amused that one of his pupils who had to take up drawing found, among the requirements of the examiner, that he should draw with proper measurements, machinery, and fittings the plan of a "lavatory"!

Having struggled through that competition, I was introduced to a seat in the office of the Surveyor of the Navy, Sir Baldwyn Walker, in Whitehall. The same official is now called the Controller.

I stayed there a few months before being transferred to the office of the Secretary of the Admiralty. I made in that office the friendship of Coghlan McHardy, who has since been so well known as one of the energetic founders of the Navy League.

My change across the Admiralty courtyard entailed another examination, and another sojourn at Dusayer's, where I had for a most amusing companion Edward Stracey, and with him afterwards made the acquaintance of the old-fashioned haunts of pugilists and dog-fanciers, old Jimmy Shaw's, the Jane Shore of Shoreditch, being the best known of them. There and at Nat Langham's I picked up something more of the noble art than I had learnt at Oxford, and came away one day with such a pair of black eyes that I had to take a short leave to the country, not being fit to appear in the service of my Queen.

My duties lay in the Commission Branch of the office, the head of which was that clever, agreeable man John Heneage Jesse, who wrote the "Memoirs of the Stuart Family", and other things. It was his father, a splendid old gentleman, who wrote the book about dogs, and, when far over seventy, was brought up for assault on a much younger man, to our amusement and admiration.

Our room was once the dining-room of the house of the First Lord, and it was said that in that room Collingwood expounded his famous plan for breaking the enemy's line of battle, and illustrated it with walnut-shells on the table.

What an amount of port that room must have seen consumed by great sailors, for the Portuguese vintage was more in their line than that of Bordeaux!

One is reminded of the lines about the two wines, contrasting that drunk by the English with that by the Scotch:

> "Firm as a rock the Caledonian stood;
>   Old was his mutton, and his claret good.
> "Let him drink Port! the envious Saxon cried:

He drank poison, and his spirit died!"

I passed a pleasant enough life in that bright, sunny room, which looked over the Horse Guards Parade and the Admiralty garden.

Overworked we were not, and we looked with respect, and I may say admiration, at the person and character of our chief, the Duke of Somerset, whose wife, once the queen of beauty, we now and then saw in the garden.

Our hours were easy enough, though we were a little too much disciplined to be able to have said, as one of the Harbords in another office is reported to have answered when rebuked by his chief for coming so late to the office in the morning: "Yes, sir; but you forget how early I go away in the afternoon!"

Among the characters who used to drop in for a talk with old Jesse was Tommy Garth, the subject of much discussion as to his royal parentage in the Creevy papers. He was very amusing, and very free-spoken, and always knew the latest scandal about town, whether about cards or fair ladies. Now and then he brought his pretty daughter and her little white poodle. Someone called him "that demmed amusing blayguard!"

Harry Keppel also came in now and again to ask Jesse some question about some youngster in whose career he was interested. He always was ready with a jovial, amusing yarn on the subject in hand.

I cannot say that I was always quite as careful in my duties as I might have been, as this incident shows.

My business, among other things, was to keep an eye on the list of mates (now called sub-lieutenants), and to note the incidents of their careers. This, I must confess, I did rather casually, till one fine day a ship turned up from the China station with a mate on board who had been court-martialled, and turned out of the service nearly two years back, and who was still in active service, and on full pay.

What was best to do ? Jesse advised me to go to my uncle, Sir Michael Seymour, who had just returned from the command of that station, and consult him. He referred me to his secretary, who told me that the boy was not a bad sort of boy, and that they were sorry for him; and as no orders came to send him home, they kept him on.

Jesse and I made a due report to my lords, who were pleased, under the circumstances, to "condone" his offence, and I was enjoined to be more careful.

I have, unluckily, forgotten the boy's name, but he may be now a distinguished Admiral on the retired list. Such are the chances in life.

We were a very festive lot of youngsters in the office, and generally made up for dull office hours by following Tommy Moore's advice:

"And the best of all ways to lengthen our days
Is to steal a few hours from the night, my Love!"

And this we certainly did, for in those days there were no closing hours. I remember going to the closing night of old Vauxhall, and Cremorne was in full swing. I fear I must have got what is called "known to the police", for one Derby night, when I was particularly trying to keep out of a row, I heard the voice of the tall, well-known Inspector Silverton: "I see you, Mr. Seymour; now I've got my eye upon you". However, I got off with nothing worse than the iron-shod heel of a policeman's boot on my patent-leather-shod foot, from which I went lame for many a day.

On the night of the Licensed - or, as they were called, Licentious - Victuallers Fête someone heard the despairing cry of the Père de famille publican: "Here's a pretty go! Both the girls off in the dark with young men, the missis drunk, and the last bus gone!"

It was only just before that that the well-known Augustus Bernal was "took" for debt in the garden. He told his captors that as he could not escape, they might as well make a night of it while they were about it, to which they agreed. They were watching a balloon go up, and just as it was off, he jumped over the ropes, and said: "Here's a fiver to take me!" In he jumped, and did the "bums" that time.

"Society", jealous of the accounts of cheery times at Cremorne, thought it would try what it was like, but female society had some rude surprises in the company in which it met its nearest and dearest, and after some disagreeable scenes on the spot, and stormy interviews at home, the experiment was given up.

This reminds me, anent awkward situations, of an evening at Southampton, where I had gone to see off to a distant colony two friends, who were starting as Governor and Colonial Secretary.

After dining at the hotel, we found the evening hang fire, so we asked the waiter what amusement the town afforded. He strongly recommended the music-hall, to which we at once went.

We took the best box, and had not been long in it when the door opened, and in walked two rather painted ladies, who proceeded to make themselves at home.

One of our party was brother to the Colonial Governor, and was a most eminently respectable man, in a high position at Court. His horror may be imagined, and he withdrew to the back of the box. Then the stouter of the two fair dames plumped herself down on his knee, patted his cheek, and said: "Well, my little man, and what makes you so shy to-night?" It was highly diverting to us because of his overweening sense of his own importance and dignity. It can be imagined how he fled as soon as he could shake off his charmer.

As dancing "dogs" were as necessary to balls as the band and the waiters, we boys got a great many invitations - more from our usefulness than our personal popularity, though we made many most charming friends, both old and young, and danced our way into general society.

Out of the season there were in those days many dancing-places, balls of various kinds, fancy and masked, and we took full advantage of the opportunities for nightly amusement. At one of these dances Harry Herbert let out a bag of rats he had brought with him, to the awful horror and consternation of the ladies. At one large dance, where I was fortunate enough not to be present, some man threw a paper of cayenne pepper on the floor - a very poor practical joke.

At another dance, during supper, some silly joker filled the trombone up with beer. All that is now changed, but I don't feel sure that grandmotherly legislation has so much improved the present condition of boys, or their prospect of future usefulness. Anyhow, they don't have nearly so varied and amusing a life as we used to have, and everything now is much more costly, the theatres being about double what they were then. These were not quite the "Tom and Jerry days", but the transition state.

To keep up some sort of activity, I became a member of the London Fencing Club in Cleveland Row. There we cultivated the aristocratic foil with French professors, single-stick with corporals of Life Guards, and boxing with Ned Adams, and then Johnny Walker, who was so tough it seemed no use whatever to hit him. They said he might have been champion if he did not sell his fights.

Single-stick is a fine game to try one's endurance. Twice I had a contest which was to end only by one of us, as Mr. Jorrocks said of the foxes, crying "Capivy!"

On one occasion I selected my friend's leg to operate on, while he distributed his cuts anywhere. I worked on the outside of his knee, till down he came, and could not stand up. I remember I went to a ball that night, not much the worse, but I looked like a man tattooed in stripes for some days, when I was, as the Indian says, "all face". On the other occasions I went for my friend's upper arm, till he could hit no longer. I was sorry for his arm when I saw it next day. Of course, our heads were protected.

I strongly recommend a trial to boys who want hardening, and to see what they can stand.

Ned was a good teacher, but had a weakness. So one day I found him very unsteady, and nearer my own capacity. Next day one of his eyes was decidedly discoloured, and he said: "Ah, Mr. Seymour, you took an advantage of me. It was hardly fair". But he was not revengeful, luckily for me.

Little Creagh taught us gymnastics. He was a pocket Hercules, and could easily use the same dumb-bells as Fred Burnaby, who was a regular attendant.

I look upon my membership of the club as most useful in every way, morally and physically, and it counteracted the late hours and the office life. The members were a most pleasant set, largely Guards and Life Guardsmen.

I tried little Creagh's temper one day by climbing a rope up to the top of the place, and hanging by my toes from the beam. He called out from below: "Now I have protested, gentlemen! I call you all to witness that I have protested!"

Leotard just then set the fashion of the flying trapeze, at which he was so active and graceful. So we started one with thick mats below. I tried, but one day I missed the other bar, and landed far away on my back clear of mats, and felt my ardour rather cooled by the shock.

Of course, we had not much spare time for cricket, but I used to go to Lord's to practise, and now and then played in some match of the Civil Service, against Free Foresters, Harlequins, etc. I also belonged to a small club called the Dingley Dell, mostly composed of young barristers, and we had many very pleasant one-day matches round London.

Just as I came up to London the St. James's Club was started, and the originators of it were kind enough to make me an original member of it. It was a charming club for a young man. All the young members of the Diplomatic Service and the Foreign Office belonged to it, and a great many of the boys of my own age beginning life in London. I still belong to it, but there are hardly a dozen of my friends of that day left in it. Nearly all are gone to "join the majority".

I also belonged to a very sociable and amusing society called the Eclectic Club, which used to meet in Charles Street, Berkeley Square, every Saturday evening, in a very large room, once the studio of Watts, the great artist. The whole of one side was decorated with a picture which he painted in Italy. The subject was from Boccaccio's "Decameron" - the picnic-party given by a young gentleman to some friends, among whom was the young lady he wanted to marry, but could not quite get her consent. He knew that on certain occasions a girl who had kept her lover off and on till he died was seen, as her punishment, to run across the forest glade, in the dress of the "Wasser Maid", pursued by the ghost of her lover, and phantom hounds; and there was the chase admirably done as large as life.

Sometimes we had excellent music, also singing, amateur and professional, and we kept very good company with whisky and sandwiches well into Sunday morning.

As we wished to be exclusive, one black ball excluded; but one evening a very popular man was put up for election, and the Secretary - now a very well-known squire in the southern counties, and, I am glad to say, still alive - found a black ball put in. With great presence of mind he called out, "Hullo! someone has made a mistake", and popped it into the other box, and, amid a roar of laughter, our friend was elected.

Among the curious sights of London, I went with a party to see the execution of Catherine Wilson, the celebrated poisoner.

We had supper at the Raleigh Club, to which I belonged for a short time, and then went to the room we had taken in the house just opposite the Debtors' Door, where the scaffold was placed. It answered to the description of the Magpie and Stump in the well-known Ingoldsby Legend. The crowd was a very curious sight, both to look at and, in one's oldest clothes, to go among and talk to, where in the dark one passed as a pickpocket or burglar on holiday.

People asked me if it were not very dreadful, but the impression it made on me was more like a scene in a play than real life. Since then

I have witnessed many curious scenes.

Of our little company, King Harman, whose burly, handsome figure was so well known; the good-looking Vere Fane Benett, of Pythouse; Wiley Willats, the clever amateur caricaturist; and Alfred Tichborne, have all departed. I and Harry Fane alone remain.

Curiosity took much the same party to see the five pirates of the Flowery Land hanged. The crowd was tremendous, and very rough. I saw a young Guardsman whom I knew, whose party had a room close to ours, and who had been unwise enough to come in evening clothes, beset by roughs, and held against the wall while his pockets were turned inside out. It was not possible in that crowd to offer any help, and they did not do him any bodily harm, but roared with laughter over the job. One of them patted me on the back, and said: "Well, old bloke, this beats anything I ever see before!"

My impression was certainly not that a public execution had any useful effect on the spectators, and as long as the public feel sure that a man is really hanged, it may be as well that it should be done in private. The days have passed when parties were made for ladies to go and see great criminals tortured.

Those curious in such subjects will be much edified by reading the account of the execution of Damiens in that amusing work, "The Confessions of Jacques Casanova".

Speaking of the Raleigh Club reminds me of a curious incident among the members of it.

One young gentleman had dined exceedingly well, and then sat down to play cards. I am not sure of the game - I think it was écarté. He, however, proved so exceedingly far gone that the two others who were playing with him thought it wiser to transfer the contest to a bedroom upstairs in the club, where some of them had their temporary domicile. It naturally ended in his losing a considerable sum. Next day the others suggested a settlement, to which he demurred, as he had no recollection of the transaction. Most unwisely they said it came under the club rules for the settlement of card debts, and referred to the committee. The committee did not think a bedroom was the same as the card-room of the club, but decided that, under the circumstances, they had better all retire from the club.

A curious trick was played on a tipsy friend about the same time.

There had been some play, and in the morning one of the party called on the inebriated member of the party, and said he had come to pay him the money he had lost to him. The victim said that he had no remembrance of it, and would much rather not take it. "Oh no!" said the sharp one. "Tom can tell you it was all right, and I shall certainly pay you" - a hundred or some such sum.

Soon after in comes Tom, who hoped he was not the worse for a wet evening, and also reminded him of the few hundreds which he had lost to him. The victim saw the joke, but having accepted money, however intoxicated he may have been when playing, he had no way out of paying what he was said to have lost. He could pay, and did; but a coolness grew up among the friends afterwards.

I remember some years later meeting a very nice boy at a dinner-party, and happening to walk away with him; and as I had then seen a good deal of the world, he said he wished to ask my advice. He had lately come from the States, and on the boat had made the acquaintance of some regular card-sharpers.

They had asked him to come and dine at the Metropole Hotel, and had taken him up afterwards to their sitting-room.

Cards were proposed, but he said he played very little at any game. However, cards were produced: he was almost forced to play at cutting through the pack. Naturally he lost a fair sum, but not very large, and had not got it in his pocket. He hesitated about paying, but they talked of making a scandal. His father was a very well-known man who had business with New York, and to him a card scandal about his son would have been most unpleasant, however his son may have been swindled, as there are always two ways of telling a story.

The sum was not enormous, so I advised him to pay it pleasantly, and take the lesson, and also to tell the story to young friends beginning life. And so it ended.

Though caring little for racing, I had many friends who were constant at race-meetings, and I used now and then to go with them.

One day - I think it was at the Egham Races - a friend came up to me, and said: "I have here a foreign friend, who has been done by card-sharpers in the train coming down. "It seemed that he had happened on a carriage packed for the purpose.

The three-card trick, of course, and they all pretended to play, and invited him to have a turn. I, like many boys, had been caught in the past, and knew the ways of them. He had lost his ready-money to them, then his watch, and then he gave them I.O.U.'s. He had promised to meet them, and go back with them in the train, and settle up for a good sum of money at his hotel in Jermyn Street. This, not knowing the country, he thought he should be obliged to do.

I said I would go back with them, and see him through, but that just then I wanted to make an honest penny on the races. I told him not to recognize me at the station, and to do just what I told him. I got into the next carriage, and at Vauxhall tried to get the station officials to help, but they utterly refused.

At Waterloo I joined him and his two men, and as the station policeman would not listen to me, I followed them out of the station down into the street. There I spoke to a policeman, but they were getting suspicious of me, and prepared to make off. The bobby said, "Do you give him in charge?" I said, "Yes". So he collared one of them; the other bolted, with me after him and my foreign acquaintance in the rear, down a narrow street, down a passage, and into a large room, where there were some twenty men, and I thought I was in for a warm reception. I was much relieved to be followed directly by the bobby and the other man.

I insisted on the watch being given up; the money I thought the young diplomat deserved to lose, as a lesson.

One of them said: "I suppose I am to call to-morrow with the I.O.U.'s?" So I said: "Certainly; you will find everything ready for you!" So we retired; but being suspicious, I kept my eyes open, which was lucky, for as soon as the policeman's back was turned, one of them let drive at my head with a big stick. However, I was ready, and got out none the worse.

Just outside we met an inspector, to whom the policeman reported. I then told him the story, and he took me back into the room to point out my men; but they had had warning, and bolted. He told me that it was the headquarters of the racing thieves and cardsharpers. He pointed out to me the head man, and I saw more than one whose face I knew at race-meetings. Their "get-ups" amused me. There was the young country farmer, the quiet tradesman, the simple clerk, etc.

Curiously, I met my foreign youngster, who was much pleased to have got off so cheap, dining at the St. James's Club that night.

One year we made a most pleasant party for the Good-wood, Brighton, and Lewes racing fortnight. Some seven or eight of us took rooms in a sort of small hotel, then well known and very well managed, which we about filled.

Full of spirits (natural), and sometimes champagne, we kept things going day and night.

There was then a man named Atkinson, who was known as "Atkino", and he ran a gambling-place, having, as was his custom, taken a large house and "squared" the police.

There was a roulette table, but hazard was the attraction; and I made my first acquaintance with the dice-box, "and called the rattling main".

I had not the least idea of the intricate game, but when my turn came I put up ten pounds, and called, "Seven's the main, the player casting in". On it went, and innocence had a good time; and when my run was over I picked up over £150.

I don't think chicken-hazard is now played anywhere. It is years since I have heard of it.

Fred Granville, that clever, amusing, unlucky man of ups and downs, was one of our party, and coming back on a coach one day from the races, we found the door beset by bum-bailiffs on his track. As soon as the trap was seen, everyone slid down, and bolted in every direction, upsetting one or two of them; and that time Master Fred got off. He was very much the right-hand man of the Marquis of Hastings, who was down there in the middle of his glorious career. Fred also engineered the sudden marriage of the Marquis, which so amused and startled London. He procured the parson necessary - dear old Knipe from Warwickshire, most genial, kind-hearted, popular of men - who was greatly astonished at what he had done when the wedding was over.

Fred married happily, and led a most happy domestic country life while his charming wife lived, and he ended by keeping a hotel in the island of Cyprus.

I nearly ended my days by the shore of the quiet little village of Shanklin, where I happened to stay for a night while doing a walk round the Isle of Wight with my friend Hubert Dormer of the Admiralty.

It was a rough morning, and a spring-tide at its full height. I wanted a swim, but the man of machines declined to run one down, but said I might undress in one if I was fool enough to go in, as I probably should not come back to dress.

It was easy enough to get out by diving through the breakers; but when I wanted to return, I found I had been carried up to the end of the sea-wall, and the heavy seas were breaking on the cliffs all the way up to Sandown, towards which the current set very strongly. I had to decide whether to make for Sandown or take my chance against the sea-wall.

I made for the wall, and the fisherman threw me a rope, which I caught and held on to, as the undertow was so strong. Then I got to the wall, and lay at the bottom of it when the next sea broke, and then was pulled up; and I looked a poor object as I trotted all along the parade to the machine, "all face", as the Indians say. I reached home to breakfast rather the worse for wear!

Among the public offices there was a curious gradation of social prestige among the members, rather recognized by society as far as they knew anything about us.

The Foreign Office was the smartest; the Treasury stood high, and had so many good berths into which its members were transferred in due time. The Admiralty at Whitehall and the Colonial Office ranked about the same; but there were appointments going in the Colonial Office, while the Admiralty had none. The offices of the Lords and Commons stood rather apart, as of a different nature.

We looked upon the members of Somerset House and its various offices as of a lower rank in social condition, and though we had many intimate friends there, we loftily felt sorry for their hard lot.

Anthony Trollope describes it well in "The three Clerks"; the infernal navies were evidently at Somerset House.

For one thing we did pity them - that their office hours began at ten instead of eleven, the hour of all the Whitehall offices.

There was one young fellow in the Admiralty at Somerset House who was a great friend of ours - he was a most jovial, harum-scarum boy. One night he had joined some of us in a late supper, and had gone home in rather a mixed state. It seems that he had early in the evening decided on taking a pill that night, which ceremony he duly performed; but one of us going into his room in the morning to see how he was, saw on the table a stud-box with two studs and a pill in it.

The same young gentleman lived with a widowed mother and a pretty cousin. One morning the young lady did not appear at breakfast, and the old lady asked the maid where Miss —— was. "Please, my lady, Miss —— had a baby in the night!" Tableau! It then appeared that Master Dick and his cousin had been quietly married some time before, so it was "all right". In after years he married secondly into a well-known family, and was most popular in a prominent position in the Isle of Wight.

In my days at the Admiralty I had a very pleasant trip to Spain. There was going to be a total eclipse of the sun, visible in great perfection in the North of Spain.

The Government had put at the disposal of the Astronomer Royal and other astronomers the old troop-ship Himalaya, and Captain Seccombe, who commanded her, kindly offered to take two or three of us youngsters out and back for the trip. My companions were Herbert Carroll, who has left us now many years, and Hubert Dormer.

However much at home in the heavens, many of the scientific men were not the same on the ocean, and the Bay of Biscay was not very kind to us on our way to Bilbao.

We boys were not very keen on eclipses, and thought we would have a run to Madrid, so we took places in the banquet of the lumbering old diligence - a place with a hood just behind the driver, very cramped, full of fleas, and with a fine odour of bakalao - dried stockfish - which was loaded up just behind us.

We enjoyed ourselves as best we could for sixty-eight hours, now and then getting a run up hills to stretch our legs. It was midsummer, and pretty warm, and the dust was truly Spanish.

We had a long string of animals, mostly mules, but a postboy rode a horse always in the leading pair. There were from ten to thirteen animals in the team, according to the road. The driver had reins to the wheelers; the rest ran loose.

We had only one change in postboys in all that long journey, and they appeared to live on cigarettes almost entirely. At times the "boy" would join the coachman on the box, and the whole team was guided by their shouts, and by a free use of a long whip to all it would reach.

I have in after years known Spain almost too well, and know that the shouts to the beasts must have been insulting remarks on the extremely lax morals of the parents of the unfortunate animals.

The old diligence has disappeared, but though railways have changed travelling, the Spanish people, as conservative as Easterns, change very little.

Madrid has been built on to a little since those days at the Prado end, but otherwise is exactly the same, except the new grand bull-ring.

We arrived rather dusty at the Fonda Peninsulares, then the great hotel, but now not much considered; and we tried to wash off the dust and the traces of fleas and their larger cousins. I remember once from a diligence arriving from the Portuguese side a passenger got down, and the master of the hotel brushed off one of the larger insects from his collar with the remark: "Se vé que el Señor llega de Portugal" - "One sees that the gentleman comes from Portugal" - ignoring the existence of similar insects in the great domain of Spain.

In those days the Court remained in Madrid in the summer, and we went to see Isabella driving in the Prado late at night in evening dress, a plump and well-jewelled figure.

Of course, the great thing to see was a bull-fight, and it made a greater impression on me than any of the many I have seen since.

I saw then a man do what I have never seen since - wait for the bull to charge, put his foot between his horns, and jump over him.

On this occasion, in the Plaza de Toros, a royal baby was held up for the people to see at its first introduction to the national sport.

Our journey back to join the Himalaya at Santander was not quite straightforward, and as our knowledge of Spanish was nothing, we had some trouble - first diligence, then a sort of carriage, and the last few miles a baggage-mule and on foot.

We had a most facetious driver to our strange trap, who drove three horses "unicorn". We slept one night at a fonda, where we found our room with two beds. A third was made up on a table, on which Dormer had turned in. When our coachman came in for his orders in the morning, he was so amused at the sight that he proceeded to tickle him in the ribs, with shouts of laughter, much to the destruction of the dignity of our companion.

At one place Carroll wanted some bacon, so he took a knife, made signs of taking a slice out of the upper part of his leg, grunted like a pig, and held the knife to the fire. It was successful.

From Madrid we visited the Escorial, that vast pile built by the gloomy Philip II., which combines palace, monastery, and church of grey granite, built in the form of a gridiron, in honour of Saint Lorenzo.

We found the eclipse had been a great success, and after seeing another bull-fight there, we made a good passage back to Portsmouth.

This was about the time of the Volunteer movement, and I was enlisted in the Six-foot Regiment. The foot-guards sent us a six-foot-six-inch sergeant to drill us, and I picked up some ideas of goose-step and right-about–face. We were a long lot, but some were rather weedy. The uniform was red, and didn't look bad; but somehow the corps fell to pieces, and that was an end of my soldiering.

It is curious to remember what a mixture there was in it of serious enthusiasm, and chaff, and ridicule. "Who shot the dog?" was the common cry after a man in uniform.

The Government was, of course, as cold as possible towards it, as it always is to any sort of patriotic movement among Britishers at home or abroad.

The Briton, however, is hard to repress, and even Haldane's confused scheme of Terriers and half-trained artillery finds it hard to prevent Englishmen being ready to defend their country.

Poor man! He has to try - or pretend to try - to provide a force ready and sufficient to defend England against 100,000 well-drilled troops once landed in the country.

This he, as well as everyone else in England, knows is impossible with his present scheme of Terriers.

He has three troubles: First, he must please the economists by not spending money, and the stinginess of his details is almost beyond belief. Second, to hide expenditure he must get people locally to spend money, so that it shall not appear in taxes, though it comes out of the same pocket. What a fraud! Third, he has to try and please the quaintly religious, who say it is a sin to teach boys to shoot; and the Socialists, who know that they cannot exist in a strong military country, by pointing out to them that his army is, after all, like the housemaid's baby - "such a little one!"

CHAPTER IV

HOUSE OF COMMONS

*A*fter I had been some time in the Admiralty, my uncle, Sir Dennis Le Marchant, who was the Clerk of the House of Commons, kindly offered me a place in his office as junior accountant of the House of Commons. This I joyfully accepted, as the work was pleasant, and we had hardly ever to be there, except when Parliament was sitting.

There were two of us in the office, and all accounts passed through our hands, including the fees on all private Bills in Committee of the House.

I had to pass yet another examination, one subject being book-keeping by double entry, and I don't think that any Government accounts were ever anywhere kept by that system. However, what did the Civil Service Commissioners care? Examined you must be in different subjects for every office, no matter what its duties might be.

I therefore, as we said, "mugged up" book-keeping by double entry - a fine system of checking vast transactions in a great grocery or drapery, but totally useless for our accounts.

My senior partner was getting elderly, and had been a professional accountant in his young days. He was of a very humdrum, middle-class nature, and looked on me as a smart young man-about-town, not of much account for work.

I soon found that between our office and the other clerks, especially of the Private Bill Office, there existed a sort of feud. However, as I had two cousins among them, and several friends, this very soon ceased, and we helped each other to keep things straight. Also I was good friends with the parliamentary agents, who paid us many thousand pounds, and I have gone to the bank at the end of a week with ten thousand pounds or more in my pocket.

I found some useless complications in the accounts between us and the committee clerks, and much simplified the system, till one day my chief said to me: "Look here, young man, if you simplify this much more, they will be doing away with one of us".

That most amusing creature Reginald Wilberforce became a committee clerk, and made everyone laugh when he first began work by his coolness. A most serious and important member happened to be chairman of his committee, and said to him: "Your father is a great friend of mine, and I shall be happy to give you any assistance which I can". "Would you, then, kindly swear the witnesses while I go to luncheon?" was Master Reginald's cool answer.

One of the committee clerks told me that one day a Jew witness came to be sworn. He had no Old Testament handy, so he promptly swore him on an Italian grammar, which was on his table, and looked black and serious.

One year the head librarian was in very bad health, and was therefore able to attend very little, and not at all at night, and the nights there went on often till two and three o'clock. I was therefore kindly offered temporary work as junior in the library for the session, and I found no difficulty in doing the two jobs, as between eleven in the morning and two or three next morning there were many spare hours. Of course, these long hours were only for four days a week, and for six months in the year.

I found the library a very pleasant place, and it brought me into contact with many pleasant members.

Mr. Gladstone one day got impatient because I was a long time in routing out a pamphlet among the vast collection of such things, but as a rule he and all were most courteous and pleasant. There was a charming air of quiet and decorum in that long suite of rooms looking over the river, and I got through a great deal of reading on dull nights.

As we had the run of the house in the gallery for members, or in any inconspicuous corner, I saw and heard a great deal that was most interesting in the years I was about the House.

I used often to take the divisions for any of the division clerks who wanted to take a holiday for the evening, and it much amused me.

I remember taking that when the Government were beaten in 1866. There had been a very urgent whip, and the Whips had to keep an eye on more than one who had dined very well, and might be missing when the bell rang. One was lost for very long, having wandered up into the dark corridors above, where were the committee-rooms, and one or two others slept very soundly till shaken and pushed through the division-pen. One elderly member I did not know, and when I asked, "What name, sir?" he said, "Hee, hee, hee!" A friend told me his name. He was queer in the head, and had not been in the House for ages. It wanted close attention to mark off accurately in a big division, and there was an anxious moment to see if one's numbers agreed with those of the Tellers.

In those days there were often classic quotations in great speeches, and I always looked them out, and in the morning I marked the books ready on my table, as our unlearned members were sure to ask for them.

Quotations from, and references to, the Bible I always had ready, and when Bright made his famous speech about David and the cave of Adullam, there was a great run on the reference, few knowing where to find it. The well-known Mr. Whalley, who was by way of being very religious, asked me if it was not somewhere in the Book of David!

I have always been glad that I heard all the great speakers of that time. I thought Bright the greatest. Palmerston could put the House in good humour when he wound up a debate, however wearied and cross it had got, and that was in the days of the rhymes–

> "What is it makes the House so late?
> 'Tis Spooner and dull Newdigate!
> Why does the house not rise up sooner?
> Because of Newdigate and Spooner!"

Dizzy was always attractive, but at times dramatic, especially so when he followed Gladstone in the lament for the death of dear old Pam.

Lord Palmerston had been from his earliest days a pet of society and "the ladies". In his youth, from his fresh, pretty complexion and curly hair, he was called "Cupid".

He was reputed, as years went on, to be rather "enterprising" and free in his ways with young ladies, and some mammas said he must be spoken to, so an old friend of his was deputed. She pointed out to him, as in duty bound, the impropriety of his conduct, and added: "But really, Lord Palmerston, in addition to that, do you really think it is the best way to make them like you?"

"As to the propriety or impropriety, I will not argue with your ladyship; but as to the policy of my conduct, you must leave me, after many years' experience, to be the best judge of that".

Among stories of Lord Palmerston, a friend asked him how he could remember so many people he met in the street. He said: "But I don't very often know who they are". His friend said, "But you always find something to say to them"; and Pam said, "Well, if they are getting on in years, I say, 'How are you, my dear fellow, and how is the old complaint?' They are sure to have an old complaint, and are gratified to think I remember it".

I can see him now, leaning back in his seat on the Treasury Bench, his hat over his eyes, half hiding his clever, pleasant face. When everyone had had enough, his neighbour would tell him in a few words what had passed since he went to sleep, and he wound up the debate, and sent everyone home, happy and contented to think the affairs of the greatest nation were in the hands of such a man, trusted and respected by the whole world.

We could generally tell when Disraeli meant a really big speech by the extra-gorgeous waistcoat he came down in.

In those days a low-crowned or a soft hat was all but unknown, and a jacket scarcely ever seen.

In my youth I admired the florid rhetoric of Whiteside, and that brilliant man Horseman was a fine speaker. What an end! Roebuck spoke very interestingly and convincingly. Bob Lowe was the fastest, always to the point. That great man John Stuart Mill was a great disappointment. Bernal Osborne tried to be a buffoon very often, and succeeded. Gerard Sturt made them laugh on the subject of horse-breeding and "haras". He described one Government experiment which failed, and he said: "I give you my word, sir, the mares were no more in foal at the end than I am" - placing his hand on his lean tum-tum.

The Ladies' Gallery on a dull night was not a bad place for a whispered talk with a fair lady. At one time I often saw there a most charming friend, interested in politics, who was afterwards the wife of a Cabinet Minister, and for whom I had the greatest admiration.

I came round one evening, and said to the pleasant and popular guardian, "I came to see if there is anyone in the Ladies' Gallery"; and he promptly answered, "She's not here to-night, sir!"

She died long ago, but how pretty and charming she was!

A curious ceremony was the rush of members when summoned to the House of Lords on the opening of Parliament. It was more like a football scrimmage than an Imperial Parliament. I once saw Gladstone jump up on one of the stone benches to avoid being knocked down in the rush.

"Who goes home?" was the welcome cry of the doorkeepers when the House was up, the origin being, "How many armed members will guard the Speaker to his house?"

The search of the cellars and vaults was another curious old ceremony; it was to hunt for a successor to Guy Fawkes. I dare say it still goes on.

The ancient one of a country house where Lord Palmerston and the Bishop of Oxford were staying, and one drove to church on a wet Sunday, while the other walked, is often told. Mr. Woodgate, in his amusing book, locates it at one place, while the biographer of Canon Flemming locates it in his more serious book at another.

I don't think that this story of Bishop Wilberforce is well known.

He went to stay at a small parsonage, and was to be called in the morning by the boy.

The boy had been instructed to knock at his door, and when the Bishop said, "Who's there?" to answer, "The boy, my lord!" All went right till the boy had to make his reply, and then, full of zeal, he called out: "The Lord, my boy!"

His expression for a dreadful fate is, of course, known, when he said: "It is as bad as being preached to death by wild curates".

An eyewitness told me he saw him, when seated in a very conspicuous place in church on a hot summer's afternoon during a very dull sermon, pricking his leg with a penknife, to prevent falling asleep.

This is too good to be forgotten.

Travelling with a friend one day, he saw at a railway-station a country parson who evidently knew him well. The genial Bishop went up to him, asked how he was, and added: "And how is the old grey?" Then the country parson: "Oh, how good of you, my lord, to remember the old horse! He's quite well, I am glad to say". His friend afterwards said: "Who was that?" And the Bishop: "I have not the least idea, but he seemed to know me well". But how did you remember the old grey horse?" "Oh, well, I didn't, but didn't you see the white hairs on the legs of his trousers?"

Before I was occupied in the evening by the library of the House of Commons, in order to get more exercise and fresh air, I joined the Kingston Rowing Club, and lived in lodgings at Surbiton.

Walter Woodgate, the celebrated oar and sculler, whose book of an Old Sportsman is so amusing, lived down there, and had taken it in hand, managing everything, and training and coaching the boats.

He was an old school-fellow at Radley, and we had always kept up our friendship. He had done much to make his college boat, Brazennose, so successful, and rowed several times in the Oxford Eight.

I had never really taken to rowing, though two of my brothers had rowed in the University College boat, and helped greatly to head its place on the river, and one of them rowed in the Oxford Eight.

I set to work hard, and improved under Woodgate's knowledge and powerful command of old Saxon expressions. Someone asked him as to my usefulness, and he said: "Oh, he's as strong as a horse, and as rough as a donkey!"

It was a very pleasant and healthy life, and there were some very good fellows among the boating men and older residents. One got up early, went out in a skiff and had a swim before breakfast. It was a very pleasant let-up from life in London, fashionable or otherwise, and very wholesome.

We had trial eights, and then Woodgate got up a crew to row at Henley. Cardale, an Oxford man, was stroke (he had been at Charterhouse with me), and Griffiths, once captain of the boats at Eton, and in the Cambridge Eight, was in the boat; also Charlie Talbot, of the 14th Hussars. He was afterwards with me in Argentina.

In due course we went to Henley, quartered at the Old Lion. Nothing can be pleasanter than that last week of work on the charming Henley reach. One was so full of animal health and spirits, and so desperately interested in it all.

Those were the days when only local people and those interested in racing went to Henley. To people like me, who knew it in its quiet days, the great London crowd who come down for a picnic rather spoil the thing.

People forget that the first race between Oxford and Cambridge was rowed over the Henley course, and I was interested to hear from my father, who had rowed in the Christ Church boat, that, happening to be present on horseback, he was asked to be umpire of the race.

People often talk of the seven-oar race at Henley between Oxford and Cambridge, which occurred in this way: The names of the crews were sent in, and it was not held lawful to change a man after that. One of the Oxford men was too unwell to row, so it was not within the rules to put a substitute in his place. Whether or not the side asked to be allowed to do so I cannot say, and I don't think anyone alive can answer the question. But, however it was, Cambridge, if they refused, were quite within their right, though, of course, when the Oxford crew won, they swaggered accordingly.

The supper after the races was apt to be a bit noisy, but no real mischief was ever done to the town, and nothing can exceed the interest and help given by the townspeople and neighbours to the regatta.

We won the Grand Challenge Cup after a fairly severe race, which, as Pepys would say, "mightily pleased us".

The row back to Kingston, sleeping on the way, was delightful.

Of course, we had to contest four-oar races at various regattas afterwards, there then being no eights anywhere but at Henley, and some very hard races when half-trained were the result.

The following year we had to try again, and our crew, with that delightful companion and splendid oar, Bob Risley, as stroke, did the Henley course in the fastest time before sliding-seats. Billy Willan and Woodgate were also in the boat.

As far as I can make out, sliding-seats would just beat fixed seats, but they came in after my time, and I could not help to coach such a boat; the style was so different, and to me so ugly.

We won all the four-oar races up and down the river afterwards, but more than two months' training was enough for me, particularly as I got "cut over" at cricket, and had to drive down to the boat for some days. After that I made my bow to the river for racing, content with two Grand Challenge medals. Afterwards I mostly took to punting, which is splendid exercise, but can be taken easily, as you give the time yourself, and have no stroke to take it from, or coxswain and coach to cuss you!

Nothing is more comfortable for a lady than a well-cushioned punt, and nothing pleasanter for the punter than to take his well-earned repose on his share of the cushion under a shady tree, on a hot day, in a quiet backwater. As a well-known, charming hostess at Maidenhead said, "The ideal of a party is chacun avec sa chacune, and meet at lunch, tea, and dinner".

I spent a good deal of one recess at Bordeaux, where I went to pick up some French. My home was with two nice old ladies, Madame Godoy and Madame Seignac, the widows of sea-captains - wine and ships making the life of Bordeaux. Madame Seignac was gloriously talkative, which helped greatly.

I worked hard at the fencing-school, one of the teachers having the splendid name of Katzamfors, and being a remarkable left-handed fencer. I got on very well, after going twice a day, and I remember at last feeling quite pugnacious, and fully understanding the eagerness of many youngsters to have an affaire, to see how the real thing worked out.

I tried singing-lessons, too, but my master had a contempt for the closed-up voices of the British, and for their want of mouth action. He said I had la langue paresseuse, and suggested exercises to make it wag properly!

Bordeaux is one of the most hospitable towns in the world, and no society can boast of better cooks and cellars.

I dined both Christmas Day and New Year's Day with that king of wine-merchants, Nathaniel Johnston, the head of the house which stood first in Bordeaux. The tradition of the house had been to send the sons to England to be educated, as they wished to remain Scotch as well as French; and most useful French citizens, and members of the Assembly, some of them were.

I remember Mr. Johnston giving us at both dinners some Imperial Tokay, a present from the Emperor of Austria - the only occasion on which I have tasted the real wine, though it and the grand vins de Bordeaux were rather wasted on my uneducated palate.

I made friends with Baron Clossmann and his family, he having a large business, and at that time being owner or lessee of the Château Margaux vineyard. He was most interesting to talk to, and, among other experiences, he had been prisoner in England in the days of

Napoleon - an experience he did not look back to with much pleasure, though he had a good opinion of the English nation.

His son had married a very pretty Miss Considine, who, I need not say, was Irish, and who also was most kind to me, I having a letter to her from her brother, who was then working in the Foreign Office.

She had two pretty daughters, with the elder of whom I was soon engaged in a youthful and earnest flirtation. We used to sing duets, and wander about in the pine-woods. Happy days!

She married a man in the army, who was a very distinguished officer, and was killed at the Siege of Thionville. Secondly, she married a general officer - not the writer of these lines.

CHAPTER V

ITALY AND PALESTINE

Another winter I started off with Wily Willats and Butler Johnstone, who had both been at Christ Church with me, and Edwyn
Arkwright, to the Continent.

At Paris, where we lingered for a little, I renewed my acquaintance with that most charming of doctors and friends, Alan Herbert,
who was then beginning his very successful career there.

We had settled to go to Egypt, and took our passages from Marseilles; but there was such a delay in getting our luggage out of the
Louvre Hotel to start that we missed our train, and so our boat.

What were we to do? We sat on our luggage till a train started to
which we took a fancy, and we got as far as Lyons. We visited Avi-
gnon, and then went on to Marseilles.

We next - that is, Willats, Arkwright, and I: Butler Johnstone had
left us - made for Genoa. The railway was not then made, so we
drove, and saw the beautiful scenery and the great work of Napoleon
far better than even motorists do now in their absurd hurry, as we
slept several times on the way.

At Genoa we took ship for Malta in a miserable little boat, and
got on pretty well as far as Naples. There it came on to blow, and our
boat with a cargo of salt fish, when battened down, was not violets! I
saw even the man at the wheel seasick. I was a victim, and the heartless Willats, who was not, amused himself with a sketch of me:
"Again he urges on his wild career" - to the ship side.

We put back twice into Naples, and the second night arrived in the dark; and I determined to go ashore, if possible, and, to everyone's amusement, shouted for a boat in curious Italian. However, at last a voice answered in the dark, and I got them to explain to the boatman to tell me when to jump, which I did with my bag into utter darkness, for the captain said it was impossible to lower the ladder. I fell in a heap, and broke my shins across one of the seats; and as soon as I could get my wind I told Willats it was very easy, and he also came down in a lump, I trying to break his fall.

So off to the shore, and Hôtel Vittoria, Arkwright refusing to jump. A wash, a good feed, and off to the opera - we were young in those days.

The gale went on, so we got what things we could out of the boat, and let it struggle away two days later to Malta.

We did Naples thoroughly, Pompeii and everything, and then took a bigger boat to Messina. We did a bit of Sicily, and then on to Malta. Poor Messina! how lovely it looked then! At Malta my relative, Sir Gaspard Le Marchant, was Governor, and he was most hospitable, and we went to a ball in the splendid palace of the old Knights of Malta, which he had so well restored.

We were made free of the club, and enjoyed a few days at Malta very much. Then in the old P. & O. Ellora to Alexandria. There I went out shooting with the ship's doctor, who twice missed shooting me or my donkey by his gun going off by accident.

Cairo was then really old Cairo. Shepherd's Hotel was of wood, and stood by itself, and where the Esbekizeh Gardens now are was a hollow, the haunt of stray Arabs, donkeys, and their boys, and there were two wooden French sort of café chantants at which singing, dancing, etc., went on.

I forgot that one evening at Alexandria, when we went to a gambling-house, one gentleman, I think American, had lost, and swore that the table did not run fair. He produced a six-shooter, and insisted on the roulette board being examined. However, nothing was detected, as it was in my experience many years later, of which in due time, and of how I helped to find it out, I will tell the story.

I won some money, and was sitting by an old Frenchman, who asked me if I were alone, for he said: "I know Alexandria well; and there are some of these men watching you, and if you go alone, you will never get to your hotel". However, I said we were a party, and he said: "Mind you keep close together".

Alexandria was then the refuge of the scum of both East and West. It was told me later that the Khedive, wishing to clean it, ordered a sweep-up of the worst characters, and had them put on board an old steamer.

This was commanded by a confidential captain of his. Holes were bored and plugged, and when well out at sea, the crew took to the boats at night, after having pulled out the plugs. The Khedive's purge with a vengeance!

It was most amusing, the life at Shepherd's, the constant coming and going of the overland passengers to and from India. Only a little of the line was built, so camels, horses, asses, and bullocks went in the caravan.

Some of us went out at night with our donkey-boys and their paper lanterns in search of adventures, and I always wonder that we turned up safe again.

Of course we did the Pyramids, going one beautiful moonlight night, across by ferry with our donkeys. There was no bridge, and we were at the top of the Pyramid to see the sun rise.

At Cairo we met our friends Keane and Bob Fitzgerald. Bob was the well-known cricketer, who was afterwards secretary, etc., of the Marylebone Club, and raised the money to buy Lord's Cricket Ground. He then offered me the place of assistant-secretary, with the prospect of succeeding him when he had arranged things. However, I did not close with him.

Edmund Pepys was of the party - he and Keane Fitzgerald had been in the same regiment, and in the charge of the Heavy Brigade at Balaclava; Jack Arnaud, Victor Drummond, Frank Grant of the 9th, then of the 5th Lancers, just back from India, and one or two others. Most of them were going up the *Nile* to the Second Cataract in diabiahs; but I had not time to join them, as I had to be back by the meeting of Parliament.

I joined Frank Grant, who was invalided home after the Mutiny and the China business, and had a bad cut on his head and the remains of fever, but was nearly well. We engaged a dragoman, Mahomed Massoud, a curious character, and started off in an Austrian Lloyd little boat from Alexandria en route for Jerusalem.

We had on board a cargo of Russian pilgrims who wanted to get to Jerusalem. They had passed Jaffa once, but it was too rough to land, so they were hoping to do so on the return journey. It was pretty rough when we got to Jaffa, and there was some doubt if the boats would come through the reefs, as there is no harbour.

However, at last they came, and as it was too rough to lower the ladder, every time the boats rose as the ship rolled a lot were pushed in head over heels, till all were off the ship. We had a Russian passenger who was bound for Jerusalem, an old officer, but he got nervous over his disembarkation. I saw him sitting on the bottom of the boat with one arm round the seat and a revolver in his other hand, but for what purpose we could not say.

He afterwards rode to Jerusalem with us, and related how he remembered, as a child, the taking of Moscow by Napoleon - how he was hidden in a cellar, and how the city was set on fire. I came across him in much trouble afterwards, as he wanted to go into a mosque without putting on the ceremonial slippers over his boots.

On first going to the East, Jaffa strikes one as so thoroughly an Eastern town. Its white and yellow flat-roofed houses lying along the shore under the hills behind make a very attractive picture, and one can in imagination pick out the house of one Simon a tanner, though the line of ships in one of which Jonah took his passage is now replaced by the Austrian Lloyds.

The celebrated groves of oranges and lemons extend for a long way under the hills, and some of the trees are very fine and tall, beyond any I ever saw in Europe.

Our dragoman collected some animals, and I got a very pleasant dark grey of about fourteen hands, which I rode through Palestine to Damascus and on to Beyrout, and he was never sick or sorry.

Frank Grant, standing six feet four, with his fine, commanding figure, was not a light weight, and he rode a good-sized nearly white steed. They were all stallions, of course - Arab breed of a sort, generally known as Syrians.

We slept one night at the Convent of Ramleh, and got to Jerusalem next day. Now there is a railway. Jerusalem is now so well known that there is no need to say much about it.

When we went over the Mosque of Omar, on the site of the Temple, old Mahomed Massoud amused himself by telling the big, enthusiastic Mussulman who took us round that Major Grant had performed the Hadj - been to Mecca - and, as he himself wore the green turban of the Hadjie, he addressed him as Hadjie Major.

We saw the Holy Places: the guard of Turkish soldiers sitting smoking in the porch of the Church of the Holy Sepulchre, to keep order among the pilgrims, was curious.

But now and then there have been riots between the different sects of Christians.

The violent emotions of some of the pilgrims were curious to watch. One was very glad of the powerful smell of incense in those stuffy, airless shrines, for pure and unadulterated pilgrim would have been rather overpowering.

I went into some of the old tombs, sometimes crawling on all-fours with a candle. I could not help an uncomfortable feeling about meeting an asp.

We made friends with the Spanish Consul, who told us that the Jews in Jerusalem, who all spoke some Spanish, used to come to him in any difficulty. They were descendants of the exiles of Ferdinand and Isabella, whose children to this day preserve the custom of talking Spanish in many parts of the world.

One curious sight is the Jews' wailing-place, where once a week many go to lament in front of some huge stones, the foundation of the old Temple. I saw a little Moslem urchin tie together behind the flowing robes of two elders, and run off shrieking with delight to his mischievous comrades, and pursued by an angry Jewess.

I rode out one morning to look at "cool Siloam's shady rill", and found it was the place for killing sheep for the market. Rough, blood-stained men and dogs did not make it look sacred or romantic.

One Friday, forgetting it was the holy day of the East, I rode out early, and was locked out for some hours, and, unable to speak Arabic, was much puzzled to know what was up.

We rode down to Hebron, and peeped through a hole at the reputed sarcophagus of Abraham, and, returning, arrived at Bethlehem on Christmas Eve. We put up at the Latin Monastery, and attended the service, which began before ten o'clock and went on till two. Soon after twelve I was handed a large candle, and followed the Bishop, who was carrying the Bambino, down into the stable, where he laid it in the manger.

It is lucky that there is a difference in the dates of the ceremonies of the Greek and Latin Churches, as they both use the same Holy Places, or there would be ructions between the processions.

We returned to Jerusalem and went down to the Jordan. It is, as near as I remember, some twelve to fourteen miles down. One had then to pay a small backsheesh to the Bedouin tribe, who in a way held Jericho, and a man went with us to see that we were not waylaid like the man in the Scriptures.

Just before we came an American would not pay, and defied the Arabs. Some hours later he returned on foot with nothing on but his gloves, his band of thieves not using such coverings.

The whole valley of the Jordan, from its source in Mount Hermon, is below the level of the sea. We left a little snow in Jerusalem, and found a soft summer evening at Jericho.

I have often thought what a resort for climate and health it would make. In the days of the Herods there was an establishment for such complaints as rheumatism, invalids using the briny water of the Dead Sea. In these days a roulette-table might be added! I have no doubt the Sublime Porte would grant permission.

I had a bathe in the Jordan, where the pilgrims get their only wash on their long pilgrimage. Then we went down to the Dead Sea, and I also had a dip in that. The water is so salt and buoyant that you cannot get all your body under at once. There were small waves, on one of which I literally sat and came along.

We had with us by chance a pleasant young German, who was not by nature a horseman, and who had not had the foresight which we had to provide European saddles.

The native one rather galled him like John Gilpin, and he howled during his pickling in the water.

It was two or three days before I got rid of all the salt clinging to me.

We went then to the curious old convent of Mar Saba, near Engeddi, so well known from the account of it in "The Talisman". It is in a most inaccessible spot on the wild, rough shore of the Dead Sea. Nothing female is allowed in it, but we spent a comfortable night on the great divans all round the rooms. It is most curious to see how the great cliffs are honeycombed with the cells of the hermits of years ago.

It was on the shore of the Dead Sea that the curious sect of the Essenes lived. Some have thought that Jesus Christ lived with them for a time. Josephus was a member of the sect for a short period.

From Jerusalem we struck north to Nablous, Nazareth, and put up with Jacob Shellabeh, who had been in London, and was head of a curious sect, the tenets of which I did not quite make out.

He took us to see their place and mode of worship, which was quaint enough. They put on garments like much-used and crumpled night-shirts, and most of the time seemed to be in the position of all-fours. I saw a well-bearded elder severely box a small boy for playing the monkey.

We rode on over the Plain of Esdraelon, and saw the scene of the Transfiguration, and at last arrived at the small village of Gennesaret, on the shore of the Sea of Tiberius. Here we were delayed by Frank Grant getting a touch of old malaria, so I rode about with our Bedouin guides, and had a race with one. Fish we did not get, and boats on the water I saw none.

As soon as he was better we pushed on over the Bridge of the Sisters of Jacob into the Hauran, the wild district across Jordan.

We joined some Bedouins who had got with them some freshly raided cattle, and who rather expected an attack in the night, which did not come, rather to my disappointment, though we heard a shot or two. But there was a row in the night, as their mares upset the decorum of our horses, and Grant's horse next day had one eye bunged up, and the marks of many teeth on his white hide.

A not unpleasant ride of I forget how many days brought us in sight of Damascus, somewhere about the reputed locality of the vision of St. Paul.

It was from here that Mahomet was said to have seen Damascus, and to have refused to enter it, saying that it was "too beautiful". Certainly the distant view of the oldest city in the world, with its domes and minarets over the sea of dark olives, is most striking - the huge Mount Hermon away on the left, the wild rocks of the vast desert on the right, and the Lebanon in the far distance.

We found Damascus rather disturbed, as it was not long after the Druse incursion, and the massacre of Christians which roused Europe till the Sultan sent Fuad Pasha to put it all down with a high hand. This, I believe, he did by trying his predecessor by court - martial, and shooting him out of hand!

The streets of Damascus, like all in the East, have blank walls, and very small barred windows in them. One can form no idea of the beautiful houses sometimes inside them. I remember going into one with two large courts, with gardens, fountains, and orange-trees, and into fine, richly-furnished rooms.

This secluded, hidden - away life has always added so much to the charm and romantic mystery of the East, and forms such a great part of the fascination of the stories in the "Thousand and One Nights", "Tales of the Genii", etc.

The house of Mr. Rogers, the Consul, contained a charming garden-flowers, trees, and fountains.

We obtained the permission of the celebrated, beautiful Lady Ellenborough to call on her, and she was most pleasant and hospitable. I was presented to her husband Miguel, a handsome man, the Sheik of the Anazeh tribe, with whom she used to go to the desert. In Damascus her house was more like a European one.

We considered the possibility of visiting Palmira, in which case they would have given us a guard, but time did not allow, and we next went to Balbec. Few sights in the world are more interesting than this. The great ruins standing out on the plain look magnificent. The foundations are formed of the ancient buildings, the famous three great stones forming one side. The stones are placed two of them end to end, and one of equal size on them. They are, I think, about sixty feet long and fifteen feet each way, and weigh over a thousand tons.

The quarry where they were hewn is about a mile away, and near it is another stone that has been moved a short distance.

The mystery of how they were moved, and at whose command, has never been cleared up. The ruins above are of the Temple of Jupiter and that of the Sun, some very fine columns having survived the destructive earthquakes. There are two smaller temples.

The Lebanon was too deep in snow for us to attempt to cross it, so we took the newly-made French road to Beyrout, where we had to wait a day or two for a steamer. I found the ship of my cousin, now Admiral Sir Michael Culme Seymour, lying there, and was very glad to meet him, and hear news of everything.

We took ship to Alexandria, where we met some friends from England - Sir William Throckmorton; Marmaduke Maxwell, just dead, alas! as Lord Herries; and his brother Bill, gone too, I am sorry to say. We took a messagerie boat for Marseilles, and I dropped my companion at Naples, and after a very rough passage came via Marseilles to London.

Our boat to Alexandria was full of pilgrims who had made the Hadj to Mecca, and their cleanness in contrast to the Russian pilgrims, our old shipmates, was very remarkable. Those Christians, like some of the old hermits and saints, did not agree that "cleanliness is next to godliness".

CHAPTER VI

CHANNEL ISLANDS

*A*nother very pleasant expedition which I had was from Portsmouth to the Channel Islands.

My uncle, Sir Michael Seymour, was Port Admiral at Portsmouth; and my brother, now Admiral of the Fleet, Sir Edward Seymour, was his Flag-Lieutenant.

Curiously, as to Portsmouth, my grandfather, Sir Michael Seymour, was at Portsmouth; then his son, Sir Michael; then his grandson, the present Sir Michael. My brother, Sir Edward, did not finish his professional service at Portsmouth, but at Plymouth.

The Port Admiral at Portsmouth used every year to visit certain places, among them the Channel Islands. He had a steam-yacht, the Fire Queen, and he most kindly asked me one summer to come along, which I joyfully did.

The Fire Queen was not exactly meant for the "luxurious slave", whose soul, as Byron said, would sicken on the heaving wave; and my soul, or, as we should now call it, "little Mary", was of that order. But I draw a veil.

We arrived at Alderney, where we inspected that disastrous waste of money, the breakwater to the phantom harbour. My active sailor brother led me over some horrible places in the temporary works, and I returned alive, so we went on to Jersey.

There inspections were made, and I saw what I could of the island, and the old castle where the window was shown of the room in which Charles the First was imprisoned, and out of which, thin as he was, he is said to have been too stout to escape.

That immortal sailor, Jack Saumarez, was living in comfortable retirement in the house of his ancestors, and entertained us grandly. His house was furnished with beautiful things from China. He observed the Admiral's eye going round, and said: "Those are the few poor things I was able to pick up in China, and then they accused me of looting!" The story ran that he and Roderick Dew used to slip off on independent little expeditions, and when they saw a likely-looking Chinese country-house, made a boat attack and a clean sweep.

It was said of Roderick Dew that, when about to sail for China, he was boarded by importunate creditors. So he "liquored them up" well, and then put the case before them. "If you stop me, you get nothing; if I am successful, you will be paid". They let him go; of the sequel I know nothing.

Jack Saumarez was an out-and-out supporter of the Admiral, and when Laurence Oliphant, the secretary of Lord Elgin in China, was thought to have complained unfairly on behalf of his chief against the Admiral, Saumarez challenged him to mortal combat, which, however, did not come off.

We visited Guernsey, and were most kindly treated, and at a ball I met a charming native lady, who explained to me all about the social difference between the two sets, the forties and the sixties. The state of society has now grown peaceful, but once there was a strong taste for duelling, much as in Dublin after an excited debate in the House, or in South Carolina.

Sark we went to, and had lunch with the owner, who lived in a very pleasant house protected from sea-breezes by high hedges of fuchsias, for they grow almost into trees in that climate.

It was blowing very hard when we left the island, and my cousin, young Mike, being very unwell, was left behind with his mother and the Fire Queen, while we went on in the old Enchantress, a much steadier boat, commanded by a great character, Staff Commander Allen, who related to us his experiences of royal passengers in bad weather, and how he had to act nurse to a fair creature he named "the Princess Gogorina", who was in the last misery of sea-sickness, but still felt a little shy at being carried about in the lightest of garments. "Oh, never mind me, ma'am; I'm a married man!" I, who have never been promoted to that dignity, have never quite understood why married men are supposed to be so much more trustworthy or sexless than bachelors. My observation has led me to think that the contrary is the rule, and that the trust placed in the père de famille is only too often misplaced. He cannot be obliged to "make an honest woman of her".

We had a good "dusting" going to Cherbourg, and I, having recovered a little was amused to find, after a good go of old Allen's excellent brandy, which had not paid duty, the Flag-Captain secreted in a corner, very unwell; and I saw the Admiral, with slow dignity, blot and fold up a letter, and retire defeated by the movements of Neptune's element.

I suppose I was troubled with perpetual restlessness and a wish to try every sensation, for I took a fancy to put my name down as a student of the Inner Temple, and for a time left the old Rabbit Warren in Clarges Street, and took chambers in Essex Court, the windows of which gave on the fountain in the Court of that name.

They were five rambling rooms, one of which I later on let to some serious law students, one a cousin of mine.

When I took possession I found the water cut off. My predecessor had declined to pay water rates, so the water-man declined to let me have water till I paid his debt. There seemed no help for it, so I paid it.

It was on the fourth floor, and if I wanted seclusion I might have it just as well as if I had been at the North Pole.

There was a window which gave on the stairs, and commanded a view of my oak, so that I could see the nature of a visitor before allowing that I was in. Once when I wanted privacy, I put on the oak, "Mr. Seymour on the Continent", and the end was gained.

I ate my dinners, generally going to the theatre after the early dinner and regulation port wine, and was by way of reading law, but I did not get very deep in Chitty. I, of course, kept on my work at the House of Commons, and dined out in London, and danced a little - not quite as much as before. The Temple is rather out of the way of the West End.

My nearest neighbour was that most diverting of friends and brilliant speaker, Teddy Leeson, soon after Lord Milltown. He stood six feet five, forty-eight inches round, and very powerful. We often dined together in the old Bohemian places round the Temple, or at the St. James's Club. He introduced me to the Law Courts when I had time, and to the well-known Young Lawyers' Debating Club, where he was most amusing, and we often returned to the quiet Temple by early daylight. No early closing then!

He amused me one day when we were hearing a garrotter tried at the Old Bailey by saying, "Look out for your head! I think he's going to throw his boot at the judge!"

Later on in the Lords he was a useful debater and committee man. When the Criminal Amendment Act was passing, he said he got rather vexed with the Bishops, and thought he would have a shy at them, and said: "And now, my Lords, in another Bill that's just been before us we've had a great many quotations from Scripture now I'll give you one after all the moral talk we have heard"; and, turning to the Bench of Bishops: "Let him that is without sin among ye cast the first stone!" I think he had them there! The other Bill was the Deceased Wife's Sister.

I don't know what life in the Temple may be like now, but it was very, so to speak, Bohemian then - ways of living not unlike the Quartier Latin in Paris.

That life, however, ended when I went off to the River Plate.

One Temple story amused me, that of the celebrated Fox Maule, who returned home after supper and burnt down the "Paper Buildings". It was said that he put the candle under the bed, and blew out something else which he placed on the table!

Chapter VII

ARGENTINE

I

*A*t the end of one session I felt a very strong longing to wander.

I settled to go and pay a visit to my brother Dick, who, with Frank Goodricke, our old neighbour in Warwickshire, was running a sheep and cattle *estancia* in the province of Cordova in the Argentine Republic.

I persuaded Hume Kelly, son of an Irish squire, who had rowed in the same boat against Cambridge with my brother Albert, to come with me, and we both took ship on board the *Humbolt*, of the Landport and Holt line from Liverpool to Buenos Ayres, which boats are all named after astronomers.

There were several young fellows on board who were going out to try their fortunes in the Argentine, and we had a pleasant enough party, though the living was not luxurious.

I learnt to go aloft, and could go hand over hand up a rope into the top, and scramble up the pole to the truck. We played various games, some rather violent, and kept in fine health.

After a delay by a breakdown, we got into the magnificent harbour of Rio Janeiro, which I always think has the finest scenery in the world.

We were at first stuck in quarantine, and I have learned to hate that horrible yellow flag which keeps you prisoner to the ship.

When free, we had a good run ashore, and I visited the grave of my grandfather, Sir Michael Seymour, who died Admiral of the station.

A run up to the beautiful Tejuca, and then off to Monte Video.

We had to make the entrance of the Rio de la Plata, or River Plate, in very thick weather, and I noticed that the captain seemed very uneasy.

I mentioned it to my friend the first officer, who said: "No wonder; he has already lost one ship near here, and by his reckoning we are now two miles on shore!"

The coast is very flat and shallow, and very badly lighted. There had been a light on Lobos or Seal Island, but the owner complained that it frightened away the seals, and got it removed.

We had a run ashore at Monte Video, and I saw for the first time one of the great saladeros, where they used at times to kill and salt down a thousand head of cattle in a day.

I went to the opera, and was struck by the remarkable beauty of the women.

We made our way with a very careful pilot up the difficult shoal water to Buenos Ayres.

The ships at that time had to lie a long way out - some large ones, when there was not much water, as much as twelve miles.

Then, before the days of steam-launches, one got into a whale-boat, which might take two or three hours to beat in, and lastly, into a high-wheeled cart, and so to shore.

Then the new-comer was beset by Custom-house officers and harpy porters, *changadores*.

Everything was opened in the open air, and boxes nailed down and cased in tin were burst open to demand payment for saddlery, etc., and you were left to shut them up as best you could.

Buenos Ayres was then far from being the fine, luxurious city it now is. However, we did not mind.

After a short delay, I and Kelly got up to the little port in the river called the Tigre, and in a boat of small draft went up to Rosario de Santa Fé, a town of which I was to see a great deal in the next few years.

We went from there to the little *poblacion* (village) of Frayle

Muerto, on the River Tercero.

I made out that the name was derived from the tragic death of an unfortunate friar, who shocked a local family by being caught, as the nigger said, "paying some attention" to a member of it. The male portion of them sat him on the edge of one of these great hard-wood chests, with some of his flesh pinched by the closed lid, and while in that inconvenient position slowly put him to death. Other days, other morals!

The Central Argentine Railway, which now goes on for hundreds of miles, was only finished so far then.

We found that things were rather upset by one of the periodical incursions of the Indians from the south, who drove off horses and cattle, and left a few dead outlying dwellers as warnings to settlers.

We therefore avoided the direct road to Monte Molino, where my brother and Frank Goodricke were located, and rode to the estancia of Trotter and Watt, about thirty-five or forty miles from Frayle Muerto, and some seven or eight from Monte Molino, being the nearest neighbours.

We found two or three men there, rather apprehensive of an Indian attack, against which there was little means of defence. However, it did not come off, and we lingered there a couple of days, and got on to Monte Molino in very wet, cheerless weather.

Monte means either a mountain or a forest. The Pampas do not deal in mountains, and two or three trees constitute a forest for the name of it. But why "mill"? As no one had ever lived there since the Creation, it was hard to say.

This was in the middle of the vast Pampas, across which, if you go in a slanting direction from south-east to northwest, you can ride for over fifteen hundred miles without ever going up a hill or seeing a stone.

It lies in the zone of thorn-trees, and, except on the banks of the rivers, every tree is a stunted, hard-wood, knotty thing, useless except to burn, and very hard to cut, and with tremendous thorns. The rivers have a few soft-wood trees, willows, etc., on their banks.

A corrugated iron hut, with a *rancho* (hovel) by its side, built of *adobes* (sun-dried bricks), thatched with grass and mud, in the middle of an endless waste plain, does not look much like home, but one soon got to regard it as such.

We had to cross the River Saladillo, which at times was very low, and always very muddy, but when full, a great width across, with a certain distance to swim in the middle.

We had as warm a welcome as might be, and settled down to see the ways of life, and help as far as we could.

There was plenty to do: up at daylight, the of horses to be driven into the corral, and those wanted lassooed and tied up; sheep to let out and attend to, cattle to be rounded up; some animal slain for food and also cooked, for on the Indian frontier it was hard to get even a native woman cook to risk her skin, so we took it turn and turn about, and I got a name as a fancy chef, but the materials were rather of a sameness.

Quite our nearest neighbours were Charley and Gerald Talbot, the one late 14th Hussars, who rowed in the Kingston boat with me at Henley; the other had been in the Rifles.

They, however, were leaving their place, and had bought land in the province of Santa Fé away to the north, outside the range of Indian incursions.

They lived on with us a long while at Monte Molino while arranging for the change, so we were a very pleasant party.

I took such a fancy to the life and country that I decided to leave the Civil Service, and try my luck as estanciero (squatter) - Spanish sounds best in the Pampas.

The Indian raid seemed over, and we were left in peace for some time, but several very good horses had been driven off, which it took a good while to replace.

As we were sheep-farmers, we lived mostly on beef; but these two animals were the alternatives. The one was mostly very tough, the other generally had a woolly or goaty taste, but hunger did much for us.

In hot weather the beef was often "jerked" - made - into what the natives call charkee. Cut into long thin slices, hung over a lassoo or cord to dry in the sun, and often rubbed with salt, it keeps better, but acquires the firmness of a Life Guardsman's jack-boots, and a flavour of wherever it happens to have been packed.

I remember once when "the Indians were in", and supplies cut off, putting some charkee through a mincing-machine with salt, pepper, and onions, and frying it with a tallow candle - all the grease there was. The company swore that the "rissoles" were first-rate. I did not mention the tallow. As Sam Weller said of the cat pies: "It's the seasoning as does it".

But we constantly got ducks and geese from the river, and the ducks which had never seen salt water were A I. The *Pato Reale* (Buenos Ayrean duck), as big as an Aylesbury, is the perfection of food.

Horse we now and then ate (not by choice); it is stringy, and the fat does not set firm, and it is yellow and oily. Donkey once - very poor diet! I shot a jaguar one day, and we tried him, but I don't recommend him.

The delicacy of the Pampas is the armadillo. There are several sorts, of different sizes and shells. They taste like a mixture of fowl and sucking-pig - too rich hot, but delicious cold.

Indian corn – maize - in all sorts of states and ways of cooking, pumpkins and melons - any quantity of these - and cucumbers. At their season, near the sheep-folds, mushrooms by the acre.

The rule of life was: Up at daylight, take tea or coffee, or yerba (*maté*), the Paraguayan tea, but seldom with milk, tame cows being almost unknown on a new estancia. Some ate some bread or biscuit - bread is a luxury; many copied the natives, and ate nothing till midday. Then a good square meal, and in summer a bit of a rest and siesta. Work again till sundown, and then supper.

This went all well on an old, well-going place, but was very scrambling on a new one. At times everyone was too busy, or too something, to cook, and I have known what it was to ride in at dusk, find nothing to cook, take a rifle and shoot a sheep, lug him home, and dress and cook him before there was any supper.

We drank tea and water at meals, but the white rum from Brazil (caña) was always on tap, and a shocking snare to many. It was fiery, strong, full of fusel oil, and cost less than three shillings a gallon, so you could get very drunk for threepence - *and such a head!* It is the curse of the country.

There were serious councils when I and Kelly got there as to whether we should "clear out" from the Indian frontier or "see it out".

The alternative was the province of Santa Fé, which was too far north for their raids; or possibly to go right up to Cordoba, about one hundred and fifty miles further west.

We decided to see it out, with the result which I will describe.

The great mistake we all made was not to go, before (starting "on our own", to some old *estancia*, and learn the trade, and save our small capitals; to have studied the pros and cons of sheep and cattle, and of the various "locations". However, we did not; but let any young "shaver" who reads these lines take counsel from an "old buffer", and learn his trade in any line before he strikes out on his "own hook".

Wanting some horses, Charley Talbot and I took our saddles into Frayle Muerto, and there picked up the *diligencia* going via Cordoba to Jujuy and Tucuman.

A few years before I had travelled by the conveyance of that name for three days and nights in Spain. I don't think even Jonah can have had a much more uncomfortable vehicle for that period than that was; but this was a very different affair. Imagine an old post-chaise made to hold six. There is no driver, but a pole, to which are fastened traces of twisted raw hide, and these again attached to the *sinch*, or girth, of a horse on which a man is mounted.

From six to ten horses are used, according to the state of the ground, and each horse is mounted. Made roads do not exist; only a track, cut to pieces by traffic in wet weather, for the ground is soft, and there is no stone for hundreds of miles. The so-called road may be quite three hundred yards wide. The springs and wheels of this cage of torture are bound with raw hide, to strengthen them, and the small quantity of luggage possible is bound on the top, till it is part of the affair.

Then with shouts away you go! Full gallop, over ruts and stumps, the thing bounds along. I leave the passengers to imagination. *And* at night!

All things have an end, and if you don't find that a revolution - another name for a change of government with a little shooting - has broken out, you get out leaner and more tender than you got in. I remember once thinking that my neighbour's elbows must be steel-shod!

After the dreary Pampas, Cordoba is charming - a range of hills of many miles, with rocks, woods, and streams. I often regretted that we did not elect to settle there, and take to raising fewer horses and sheep, to fatting beasts, and to agriculture and gardens. However, it was not to be. If we had, I should very likely be there now, and not have led a wandering life. We found some very pleasant people there, one or two English, and the young ladies of the place welcomed us strangers. They were pretty and cheery, and we danced and enjoyed ourselves as one can at that age.

We got together a *tropilla* of some sixteen horses, and with regret said good-bye to our friends and the "China" girls, as native girls are called.

One rapid stream was rather a job to cross, for fear the horses might be swept off their legs, in which case it was certain death against the rocks.

Also, the Rio Segundo was a nasty one in flood. Rather rashly, we took no natives with us to help, and in the thorny forest, which ran for miles, we had great trouble with these animals, who did not know each other. However, we got through with the loss of only one. I nearly lost my saddle, for, as I was leading one very obstreperous beast, he got the leading-cord wound up in my gee's tail and hind-legs, so we came to grief, and my mount "cleared out". I had to hunt him for two hours on another, with no saddle, and only a cord in his mouth, and caught him at last; but my animal had a backbone, and I was rather too close to it!

We had to cross a district where the water was very bad, and I wound up with dysentery, and my companion with gastric fever. The horse with the food on his back rolled in some mud, and we camped out one night in a thunder-storm, which lasted nearly all night. I dozed off at last, and woke up in three inches of water.

We got our horses down, but it was a rough job, though very good training. I was soon well, but Talbot took long to get strong.

As I had decided to give up Civil Service work in London, and join my brother and Frank Goodricke, I settled down to steady work. Hume Kelly also joined us, but Charley and Gerald Talbot left us to go to the place which they had started in Santa Fé. They said that they had had enough of the Indian frontier, and, in truth, they were right.

We set about building a good-sized house and ploughing some land; also fencing a certain amount. With the varied work, time passed quickly and pleasantly; but we were too far away, and too much exposed to Indians, to succeed there.

Drinking-water was a trouble. You might sink half a dozen wells in an area of ten acres, and find nearly all brackish water. The soil is fine and deep loam, which changes into a sort of marl, called *tosca*. It is very hard, but easy to break with a pick, and goes to some very considerable depth. I have no idea what is below it. Water is found at from thirty to sixty feet. I got pretty good at well-sinking, and if anyone wants back-muscle exercise, I strongly recommend it, and then shin up a rope when your spell of work is over.

Breaking in bullocks to plough is trying to the patience, and their persistent obstinacy is calculated to increase one's vocabulary in Spanish, in which language they are always spoken to. The expressions of reproach and abuse in Spain and its colonies, whether to man or beast, are a mixture of, so to speak, scriptural words and accusations of ancestral shortcomings and personal family defects, often absurd, but not admitting of rendering into English.

I have heard a China woman (pronounced "Cheena") teaching her infant to speak beginning with words that would make a schoolteacher's blood run cold.

The Gaucho of the Pampas is a strange production. He may be of pure Spanish blood, or have a touch of Negro or Indian tar in him. The product of two hundred years' wildness, living in huts (ranchos) or in the open, on horse-back, from an infant, subsisting by horse and cattle dealing and stealing; light-hearted and convivial when he can be fairly brave - not very; reckless of the lives of others, but not so very ready to risk his own; fighting with the knife when obliged, or full of caña, but rather preferring the safer course of sticking a knife into his friend's back; with no hesitation about taking life, and as ready to cut the throat of a man as of a sheep.

I remember, in the sequel to a revolutionary fight, while feeling was still hot, a party catching a poor devil of the other side. The leader called out "Which of you boys would like to cut the throat of this...?" Half a dozen jumped off their horses, and shouted: "I, padron! I, padron!"

The way they did it was to seat the victim on the ground with his back between their knees, pull his chin up by his beard, if he had one, and put their long, sharp-pointed knife into his throat, just as they would to a sheep.

In the time of Rosas, the Dictator in Buenos Ayres, he had two enclosures (corrales) as for animals, and here wholesale throat-cutting went on. It was jocosely called "playing the violin!" In later days a famous throat-cutter rose in the world, and one evening at a party a man pointed him out to me, and set a stranger on to ask him to favour us with his violin - to his intense fury, and the surprise of the stranger, who could not make out the joke!

The Gaucho is not given to washing, and his hair is guiltless of the comb. I remember a local official, having to punish one one day, said: "Let him be combed!" And he was operated on with a strong horse-mane comb, and his yells were piercing.

But they were good swimmers, and very clever in crossing animals over the rivers in flood.

The Rio Tercero was very violent in a flood, and after a heavy storm, would rise from a stream you could walk across to a torrent nearly thirty feet deep. I nearly came to grief the first time I tried my hand at swimming horses across. I had two with me, and, having first crossed with my clothes and saddle in a dry hide tied up at the corners, I started with both horses together, as I had seen the natives do, swimming below stream of them, and splashing in their eyes if they turned down-stream - they never turn up. But I got the cord of the further horse twisted round my legs, and I had to turn on my back to untwist it, and then we had missed the pass - the place to get up the bank. I dared not let one go, for I should never have seen him again, and it was a long job to get both out, and a good lesson.

Sometimes horses were very hard to get into the water if the bank was not shelving, and they would not plunge in. I have had to back them to the bank, and pull them over backwards, diving away at once, and then getting at their head. It is curious what a good grip you can get on a horse when he is bare-back and you have nothing on.

When crossing riding with a saddle, never keep your feet in the stirrups - many have been drowned by that and never pull the reins - they turn over backwards at once guide them by the neck or by splashing.

A good swimmer will carry you well across; but it is best to have one hand in the mane and swim yourself, or often to hold the tail, if a long swim, and the horse is sure to go straight.

I often swam the flooded Saladillo late at night, and at times nearly freezing, clothes, saddle, and all.

II

We were troubled over and over again by Indians, and once had to drive them off the new house with repeating-rifles; but they were too numerous to attack in the open, and we lost horses and cattle.

Once, after they had been in, some of us rode over to see some neighbours, and found the place burnt, and their bodies lying near the house.

Again, being short of animals for food, my brother and I rode out to see if we could pick up any stray ones not driven off. After much search, we saw a couple of young beasts, and I, on the freshest horse, rode round them with a stock-whip.

We were about fifteen miles from home, and I had just joined my brother when we made out with field-glasses a few Indians rounding up some horses.

We started for home, but kept the beasts in front of us, as they could go as fast as our horses.

Then, looking round, we saw about forty more Indians, who got sight of us, and came in chase. We had a good two miles start, and it was getting dark.

We had set fire to a long patch of high grass to guide us in re-turning, and we got to that, and rode about a couple of miles in the thick smoke. Then it got dark, and we got clear off; but it was not pleasant, and if one's horse came down - and the ground was full of holes - there would have been an end of us, for one could not have left the other, and at that time we shot the Indians "on sight", as the Yan-kees say.

All this was very discouraging, and that colony really did no good till the Government sent out sweeping expeditions away south.

A friend of mine in the Argentine army gave me an account of an expedition that he was with. They were picked men, with many horses, and, to travel fast, they carried some flour and biscuits, and for meat killed and ate the spare horses they drove with them.

They did a little fighting, and then arranged with one or two of the chief tribes what was to be the limit of their territory.

Before they got back, a man overtook them, to say that the Indians were in again, and had robbed and murdered.

My friend told me that they rode straight back, and there was a wholesale massacre of most of the two tribes.

Since then they are dying out, or have become half tame, and are no longer any terror.

If one reads Sir Francis Head's cleverly written journey across the Pampas of years ago, one finds the chronic terror of the Indians everywhere. He makes in his book a great deal of the ground covered by him in twenty-four hours, but there was nothing remarkable for the Pampas in anything he tells.

A good horse, *not pressed* - that is, left to go at a *troticito*, about six miles an hour - would cover a great distance in a day. On the great roads there were post-houses, with relays of horses, and one could ride post if in a hurry, and do quite twelve miles an hour, for ten, twelve, or more hours. It must be remembered that we all lived on horseback or at hard work.

One day I had gone to buy cattle, and started from Frayle Muerto the first thing in the morning. I went to a place some six miles away, and helped gather the cattle, and cut out the ones I wanted, which entailed some galloping. Then, leaving two Gauchos to bring the cattle back, I rode to Frayle Muerto. It was afternoon, and my horse had had little to eat, so I tied him up to fill himself with *alfalfa* (lucerne).

I there came across a friend - a Scotchman from down-country - whose brother had been murdered by Gauchos, and they thought they were on the track of one or more of the men who did it, and he asked me to join. I said I would if I could find a horse, but I could not. However, mine looked pretty fresh, so I gave him a feed of Indian corn, and at last we started westward.

We had with us the Commandante of the place, and a few ragamuffins called soldiers. We rode slowly all night, meaning to reach the place where it was suspected the man or men would shelter just before dawn.

My friend was tired and worn out, and once fell asleep and tumbled off his horse. It was bitterly cold, and we halted about an hour before light, but it was much too cold to try to sleep.

There were three or four small houses, and some trees and bushes, and the Commandante asked me to creep up to one door and promiscuously shoot anyone who ran out.

Presently they whistled and called me. As I left my post, I saw in the dim light one of our party - a Scotchman - whose head was completely turned by fatigue, kneeling down and covering me with his revolver. I used some strong expressions, and he started and said, "Oh, it's you!" So I was just in time to save my skin.

The Commandante had also lost his head, and he shot the wrong man, and we did not catch the murderer this journey.

We got back to Frayle Muerto in the course of the day, and as my horse was all right, I rode him thirty-six miles home the next. He was a very staying animal, sometimes very nasty to ride and hard to tie up. The only safe way was to hobble his forelegs, or one of them, tie the cord of his headstall to his foot, with it running round a bar or post. I have never understood why our cavalry never do that. There could never be a stampede, as a horse cannot possibly break away: he is only pulling against himself. But our army are as slow to try anything new as system and rule of thumb can make them.

Some fifty miles north of us was the estancia of Las Rosas, the well-known horse-breeding place of Kemmis, Cookson and Wheatly. The two former are, alas,! dead. They had all been in the same regiment together, and came out together.

Kemmis was a very good steeplechase rider, and he turned his attention to breeding with thoroughbred stallions, and "Worldwind" was the sire of a now very numerous stock of half-bred horses.

His place was most well-conducted, and increased to such importance that in the booming days he was offered £100.000 for it and the horses.

I much enjoyed a run over there. It seemed like civilization after our lonely frontier.

While I was there once, Wilfrid Blunt, a relation of mine, in the Legation at Buenos Ayres, turned up with his sister, a Norwegian Carriole, and a black imp whom he had purchased at St. Vincent, and who answered to the name of Pompey. It was delightful to see a refined, pretty Englishwoman in the wilds, and she roughed it splendidly, and rode easily sideways on a man's saddle.

Later on I went down to Buenos Ayres, and had a very pleasant little time of civilization there. Sir William Stuart was Minister, with his very pretty wife, and both were most hospitable to the rough cowboy, and for the only time in four years I put on evening clothes. With Wilfrid Blunt and Hildyard in the Legation, I thoroughly enjoyed a return to another life.

The Café de Paris was *the* place, and was, in fact, nearly as good as anything in Paris, and nearly twice as dear.

Necessities of life, meat and bread, etc., cost next to nothing; luxuries enormously dear.

There were three standards of money: the hard (metal) dollar, worth four shillings and twopence; the Bolivian, also metal, worth three shillings and fourpence; and the Buenos Ayrean "paper dollar", once worth its nominal value, now reduced to currency at twopence-halfpenny! - a small bit of very, very dirty paper.

Gold was now and then seen, the English sovereign generally, but there also existed the onza (ounce of gold), a fine coin worth four pounds.

The Provincial Governors, now and then in collusion with some local bank, used to issue paper money, and some made a fortune at it. As few Gauchos could read, the value of the notes was known by the picture of the animals on the notes - a horse, a cow, a sheep, a goat - and the engraving, done in New York, was often a work of art.

I met in Buenos Ayres, and travelled back up-country with them, two very well-known and different individuals - one Sir Richard Burton, the other the Tichborne Claimant - and saw much of both.

I had the pleasure of several days with Burton, who was on his way across to Chile. I never met a man who so deeply impressed me. His manly charm of manner and great personal - I can only call it fascination, for it was a kind of magnetic power over everyone which he carried with him - were extraordinary. Of great physical strength, his fine figure was remarkable, with his enormous moustache and extraordinary eyes. If you looked into them, you never seemed to get to the back of them. I never wondered at his domination over men and women, savage or civilized, or at his strong mesmeric powers.

I had a great deal of most interesting talk with him, and have always felt that he first induced me to strike out an independent line of thought on every subject for myself.

One evening at the railway-station at Frayle Muerto, where the temporary feeding-place was kept by a very go-ahead Frenchman, he said: "Voilà, Monsieur le Capitaine, du jambon, du saucisson, du pain, une bouteille de caña: je vous laisse avec Monsieur Seymour pour la nuit". And I certainly learnt more of curious information in that night than in many, many others in my life put together.

He said: "If you have any individual force of intellect, any power of thought and reflection, why submit yourself things out to the opinions and dictums of anyone ? Think for yourself, come to your own conclusions, be a law to yourself. Satisfy yourself as to the correctness of your views, and if you have really satisfied yourself, then, as far as you are concerned, what you think is right is right".

The Claimant was fat then - not quite as big as at the trial. Burton used to draw him out most amusingly. He was much puzzled because Lady Burton was an Arundel, closely related to the Tichbornes, and the Lady Tichborne he claimed as mother was a Seymour, so he had to be careful not to give himself away.

I can hear old Dick Burton's genial voice now: "Yes, *Sir Roger,* and what happened then?"

He told me about the wreck of the *Bella*, and how some six of them escaped in a boat, were picked up, and got to Australia. I said: "Why don't you produce some of the survivors?" And he: "Oh, I shall produce them all right when the time comes!" And so he did - the well-known Jean Louis, who had two years in choky for perjury!.

Sir Roger was by way of going across the Continent to Chile, but he thought better of it, and returned to Buenos Ayres and England. He later on told a cock-and-bull story of how lucky it was he turned back, as the *diligencia* he would have gone by was stopped, and the people robbed and murdered, and he darkly insinuated that the whole thing was a Catholic Tichborne plot to get him out of the way!

My acquaintance with him continued in London, when I amused myself by going to see him, and my Tichborne friends had me subpoenaed to testify as to what he told me in South America on the great trial.

Another witness amused us by relating how he went to call on him, and found "Lady" Tichborne with a black eye. He was sympathetic about her accident", but the stout Sir Roger said: "No accident! She gave me some of her sauce, so I blacked her eye for her!"

I went a little way across with Burton, and then tried a little expedition on my account.

Things were jogging along quietly at the *estancia*, and they could do well enough without me for a few weeks, so I agreed to have a run up the River Parana, and see if we could not do a stroke of business in bringing down in a raft some (so-called) cedar. It is a white wood - a sort of cross in appearance and consistency between pine and deal and real cedar, nearly white. There is a good deal of it higher up the Parana, and it sells very well indeed.

I don't think now that we found out enough about it in any way for business purposes, but we satisfied ourselves enough for the venture, and we wanted a change.

We were a curious party of six, who bought a small cutter and fitted her out.

Our skipper was Jerdein, who had been in the P. & O. service and the Royal Mail. He was a well-practised sailor, and the best company in the world. He could turn his hand to anything, and sing a good song most amazingly. Some of his friends called him "Ding dang doo", from the chorus of a very quaint song.

He told how he had run away from home at twelve to go to sea, was caught at Liverpool, whipped, and sent to school, and in revenge, as he said, shipped off at fifteen to sea; how he had been an expensive officer, as, when junior of the watch, each of the lines had lost a good boat.

He was the practical sailor in that curious book, "The Voyage of the *Falcon*", a ten or twelve tonner from England to the Plate! when the cat committed suicide as it was so monotonous on board.

Another was Tim Doolan from Tipperary, an old Californian gold-miner. He was trying a sheep-farm near Rosario. He was rather free with his six-shooter, and had had some difficulties with the *serenos* (policemen) in Rosario, was a mine of capital songs of all sorts, and had a liking for a cheerful glass. Poor fellow! he died later on of cholera up the river.

Penrose, who I remembered as a very smart officer in a very smart regiment in England, had had "words" with his father about money matters, and had come to Buenos Ayres for change of air!

Seaton Symonds, who had been a midshipman, had, I always fancy, retired from the service without beat of drum. I have seldom met a better built and more active and athletic young fellow - good shot, excellent reckless rider, could draw and paint well, and was A I with the gloves. But he was, as one might expect, little to be trusted.

The other, Morris, was a curious animal - had been a sailor once in a whaler, and half a dozen other things, among them a second-class light-weight pugilist. But we didn't value him highly, as both Symonds and I could knock him out with the gloves. His yarns of strange kinds much amused us, and Symonds used to draw him out and chaff his head off. He had a touch of malaria one night, and Symonds asked him what made his teeth rattle like playing the bones, and he said it was "mud fever!"

We bought a thirty-six-gallon cask of caña from a Jew, who sent it on board at the last minute, and poor stuff it was. I should not have envied him much if he had been up with us some cold night when it was our only comfort. I think he would have been "keel-hauled"!

A good-natured Irish Fenian who ran a *saladero* gave us two barrels of mares' tongues salted. They were excellent, and helped out many a meal of various sorts.

We got on well enough for nearly a week, except one night when it blew very hard, and we had a rough time. The river at Rosario, from which we started, is thick with islands and swamps, and is thirty miles wide, so it is no trifle. Then one unlucky evening we came too near inshore. It was blowing, we missed stays, and drifted on to a half-sunken tree, and got "snagged"! There was a muddy island with a waste of twenty miles of islands and swamps on one side, and three miles of open river on the other.

We got what we could to eat, and slept how we could. The boat was full of water, and the shore too muddy to lie on. I and Penrose hugged each other for the night on two planks placed in two tubs - not much of a four-poster!

We had a tent, such as it was, and we rigged it up, cut boughs and things, and made a sort of floor, and agreed to stand by the wreck and stores and see if we could not go on.

Some were to return and see about another boat, or help to repair ours. Jerdein, Penrose, and Morris got lifts down to Rosario in native boats of sorts; I and Symonds and Doolan stayed a good while. I was there three months in all. We lived largely on *carpinchos* - a sort of amphibious river-hog - and fish. Birds there were none worth shooting to eat.

The *carpincho* was not bad eating, and salted down very well. We found he was hard to stalk, and had to be killed, or he plunged into the deep water and was lost. His skin was also useful in many ways.

The best fish was the *dorado*; it ran up to seventy pounds, but I never saw one over forty. It was like a second-class salmon. I don't know anything about its nature or habits. Our tackle was very infirm, so it was very hard to catch them. I believe with good tackle we might have had fine sport. Catfish were excellent eating, rich and fat. I was out one day in the canoe with gun, rifle, fish-spear and lines, far away from camp, and caught one of about thirty-five pounds. He was so lively it was a question which of us stayed in the canoe, so I up with the spear and let drive at his head. The first hit only went through the bottom of the canoe; the second transfixed him. But I had to tear off the tail of my shirt to stop the leak, or I should never have written this, and shirts were very scarce! Fresh and salt, he did for some days.

At last I got a cast down to Rosario, and, finding nothing could be done, and our pals had given it up, I got a lift up with Captain Hawksworth Fawkes in the gunboat he was taking up to Paraguay, and we gave him a barrel of salt *carpincho* hams for his kindness.

Then Doolan got down, and I was left with Symonds, but we had to give it up, and he said he would stay a bit and join some of the jaguar and *carpincho* hunters in the islands, so we parted. The last night was miserably wet and cold, and the grog was all gone. We had the remains of a bottle of chlorodyne, so we warmed some water, and had a chlorodyne grog and a good sleep!

A man and a boy turned up in a sailing-boat, so I agreed with them to take me down. We thought, with the flood and a strong wind, to do it in thirty-six hours, and had no food, but it did not matter to us for that time. However, it blew harder, and the man was afraid the mast would carry away, and ran inshore for shelter, and we had to pass another night out. We dared not go close, for there was a tiger a few yards off roaring like a bull, and he was sure to have a mate near. It froze hard, and we only had a bit of sail and an empty stomach to try to sleep on. However, we got in next night all right, and after three months of open air and that life a little fasting did not matter. So ended our river excursion. My companions did various things, and I returned to Monte Molino.

We now and then saw something of the so-called revolutions in the country, and looked on at a little fighting, but nothing of any importance. I remember a scrimmage in the Rosario streets when a few men were killed, but, as old Kaspar said, "what they killed each other for I could not well make out". A silly coward of a boy lay down on a flat roof and fired his revolver over the parapet into the crowd, and the paper seriously extolled his remarkable courage!

Once a very good fellow was killed, and we wanted to give him a good send-off, and paraded in force unarmed for his funeral. We got some way, when the "enemy" - the other party - opened fire on the procession from a thicket. We dropped the body and fled, but returned next day in armed forces and buried him royally.

A funny thing occurred one day. There was a regulation that anyone passing the barracks must not walk on the side-pavement, such as it was, but in the muddy street, unpaved! One horribly muddy day I was passing the barracks, the streets being nearly a foot deep in mud, and kept the pavement. The dirty little sentry challenged me, and I told him to go to anywhere but heaven. He put his bayonet at the charge, and the next sight was a long-legged Britisher in long brown boots legging it hard with a short sentry's bayonet just behind him, amid the shouts of the populace.

It reminded one of the story of the escaping Yankee: "Go it, shirt-tails! Bowie-knife's gainin' on yer! And he were!" Well, I got off, and it was luck for me his musket was not loaded!

I seemed now and then to take the lead a little, and was once asked to head an expedition against the Indians; but there was not enough go in the frontier men to make anything really of it, and it was given up.

However, once when I was at Rosario, laid up with a touch of fever, a man came to ask me to come and head a party to lynch a man who had murdered a friend of ours, and whom the native authorities would not execute, and wanted to allow to escape. I showed him that I could not sit on a horse, but made out the plan of action, which they were by way of carrying out. They surrounded the *carcel*, thought they had got their man in the dark, shot the wrong one, and galloped off to finish the night with *caña* and poker! Such a life! And death! the man would have said, if he could. And no one even cared one rap!

There was a curious character among us, a Captain ——I won't mention his name. He had been a rather distinguished soldier in the English army, and had seen service in it and in a foreign army; but the bottle was his real enemy. He was very good company, till, late in the evening, he would lay his revolver on the table and begin to talk of it; then we cleared out to bed. One night in Rosario I met him in the street in a very mixed condition, and spoke to him. All he said was, "I've killed the skunk!" I said, "What?" "I've killed the skunk!" Presently I heard that he had had words with a very good fellow in a drinking-bar, and had shot him dead. The authorities caught him later, and he was pressed into the army as a punishment.

But life did not count for much in a not large town, where the police said that there was an average of over one dead body found somewhere every morning. I have no doubt it is now as peaceful as Piccadilly.

When there was nothing else to shoot at, some would let off their revolvers at the *serenos* (night-watchmen). They at times would hang their cloak on their pike by a post, and put their lantern by it, stand in a doorway, and look on at the revolver practice.

There had been once a serious feud between some of the men making the railway and the night police. They had killed some railway-man, and I am afraid to say at this distance of time how many *serenos* they had laid out dead one night at a corner of a street.

Rosario was rough enough in those days: there was the Gaucho element, the river shipping men, the paid-off railway-men, Italians, etc., and the general loafers.

It was wise at times to walk home at night in the middle of the street with your revolver in your hand.

During the cholera time my brother was nursing an old German sailor who had been shepherd with us, and who was living in the outskirts, and was taken with cholera. He was riding into the town to fetch some remedies, when he was stopped by some men, and, being unarmed, was robbed of all he had on him.

He himself had a bad touch of cholera up at Las Rosas, and was pulled through by great care, and rubbing and hot things to his feet and stomach, but it was only touch and go.

At one time in Rosario the only traffic in the streets was the dead-cart, mostly bodies without coffins. I knew a man, a carpenter, who actually got out of his coffin! But he really died a day or two afterwards.

My friend Tim Doolan gave us some trouble one day in Rosario. There was there another wanderer from the Emerald Isle, by name McCraith, come of a law-abiding and peaceably-living family. He had elected to stay in the town and deal in horses, which he let or sold, and so on.

He and Tim had fallen out, and their friends wanted to bring them together, when I had by chance run down to Rosario. The reconciliation was being sealed in potations of *caña* at the stable-yard, and in the middle of it in walked a man who Master Tim could not abide.

He bolted into the house, and we at once knew that he had gone for his six-shooter, for he had just arrived at the shooting stage. We sang out to the man to make tracks as quick as he could, and he bolted down the street. Two of us put our backs in the doorway, and this delayed the impetuous Tipperary boy; but he was through the window like a cat, and the next minute racing down the street, emptying his piece at the retreating enemy.

We said: "He's off straight to the *policia* (police-office). You jump on a horse and clear out for the camp". The open country was called *el campo*. He was just in time, for at the first corner he met the headman, and two or three followers, took off his hat politely, and then galloped away. He was absent a week or two, till it blew over.

One night he had got into a difficulty, and only had a broken-down revolver but he beat a successful retreat by holding the hammer with one hand, and so letting it off enough to keep his pursuers at bay.

One night at Frayle Muerto I was sleeping close by another man, with our beds' heads to a window. I was woke up by a shot close to my ear, and found that a man was trying through the window to pull away the coat from under the head of my neighbour; but he woke up, let drive, and missed him. We both jumped through the window and pursued the thief, but he got a good start, and in the bad light we could not catch or hit him.

Rosario was a casual place then. Two of my most intimate friends left us one morning at the hotel to walk to the station and catch the morning train. Near the station was a large piece of waste ground, covered with hemlock as high as a man's head. Out of this suddenly emerged some Gauchos, who bade them stand and deliver. They were unarmed, unluckily, and had to do both, and looked very crest-fallen when they joined us again soon after.

III

Where everyone carried a revolver, and many knew little of the use of it, I often wondered that more men were not killed, both by accident and on purpose, by their reckless use.

I had a shave one night. There had been some horse robberies by men galloping up and stampeding the horses when it was dark, but starlight. There was a noise and a confusion near the house before we had gone to bed, and I ran out first, others following. I may say that the *caña* had circulated rather freely.

I was a few hundred yards from the house when I heard a shot behind me, and a bullet just passed my head. I at once turned, and said: "Who fired that?" An Irishman, Dan Mulligan, with whom I had had words, and who was leaving next day, said: "I did; I saw a man running, and fired at him".

They told me that he knelt down, put his revolver on his left arm, and took aim at something. Well, anyhow, he nearly hit me. I felt much inclined to shoot straight back, but they said my language was strong, at any rate!

Now and then there happened some sort of duel, but rarely. I was asked by a goose of a man to be his second one day, over some silly squabble, so I said, "Yes, if you like". I never thought a man could be in such a mortal funk. He said to me, mentioning a neighbour who had picked up a most elementary idea of surgery on a campaign, "D-don't you th-think we might ask him to be p-present? He might be useful to extract the b-bullet!"

However, no harm came of it, and no bullet had to be extracted.

I had a difficulty with an American Colonel, whose name I have quite forgotten, but I suggested that he could not speak the truth, which was a fact. I rode into Frayle Muerto to meet him, but he had gone to keep Independence Day with some pals on the railway, and they expected some fun when he returned. I had to wait a couple of days for him, but the life we led was against nervousness, and, as Byron said,

"But after being shot at once or twice,
The ear becomes a little Irish and less nice".

My friend returned in a most peaceful frame of mind, said the whole thing was a mistake, and asked me to have a drink, which I did, and was pleased, for he was one of the best revolver shots I ever saw. He got royally drunk, and fell off his horse as he rode away.

I came down to Rosario one evening, and fell in with some friends, who said: "Oh, do come to-morrow morning! Hynde is to fight a duel".

Now, Hynde was as like a duellist as Bob Acres or Mr. Winkle, and it had only been by several cocktails and much flattery that his courage had arrived at the point of agreeing to stand up to be shot at.

Time, place, seconds - weapons everyone carried - were all fixed, and a party arranged, after coffee and cocktail, to go and see the "fun".

I, luckily for once, was rather late, and I met a sad procession of principals, seconds, and onlookers returning in the hands of a crowd of policemen.

The gallant warrior had groaned so in the night - he was a married man - that his wife became anxious. She really thought him a silly ass, but did not want him killed, and so pressed him hard to know why these heart-rending groans. He gladly enough divulged the truth, that he was to contend in mortal combat in the morning. So, at the first peep of day, she went off to the head of the police, whose business it was to spoil sport, and the caption of the whole party was the result.

She was a pretty little woman, and had repented her marriage once, and that was always, and didn't respect *him* much more after this.

He was not like the Irishman, whose coolness I much liked. The two were stood up, and the commanding second said: "Are you ready?" "No, stop!" shouts one combatant. "What's the matter?" "Sure, he covered me dead. Now go on".

Speaking of recklessness of life there, I heard, and had reason to believe it was true, that there was a murder club in the province of Buenos Ayres among the young "bloods", in much higher position than Gauchos. They used to go out at night, and practise stabbing unwary passengers in the back in dark places on the outskirts of the town. One of the most notorious, a man of good Spanish family, was killed in a duel by a Russian, and well deserved his fate. I know that this sounds rather like a Louis Stevenson story!

We came across a very curious character, Machell, brother of the well-known racing man here. He had left his ship on the coast when a midshipman, and joined some Gauchos. A few years later he happened to see an advertisement in a paper saying that he had been left a good sum of money, which he could have if he was alive.

He went home, had a good time, spent it, and returned to his old life. My brother saw a good deal of him, and liked him. He was very handy with his knife, and a good fighter, but he said he thought nothing of getting rid of an enemy anyhow, knowing the other felt the same towards him.

He was killed a little later by being stabbed from behind when playing cards.

I have seen knife fights, but they were gory affairs, and rather disgusting.

Racing is naturally a constant sport among people who live on horseback, but the Gauchos liked very short races of never more than two horses, and a distance of only five hundred or six hundred yards. The whole, or nearly the whole, of the skill was jockeying for a start, but it was not a real start till both the riders said, "Vamos!" They would have any number of false starts, and to a stranger it was most tiresome to watch a race.

They always rode races barebacked, and often with a whip in each hand, and flogged the whole way.

We started races near Rosario on English lines, Kemmis taking the leading part, and they were of a mile to a mile and a half. Also hurdle races were instituted, to the great astonishment of the natives, who had never seen a horse jump, as the country presented nothing whatever to jump over.

They were very pleasant gatherings, and men came from a great many miles round, and probably many only met there once in the year.

I came down once the day before the races, and in very hot weather went to the barber. He said, "How much off?" I said, "Make a clean sweep", as I had then a very bushy beard. I went out of the shop, and soon met my brother walking with Wheatley, and went up to speak to them. They stared at me, and one of them said: "Oh, don't take any notice of him; he's some 'new-chum' - he's drunk!"

I was amused one evening on the race-course at a fist fight between two men, one a Yank. He had got his man down, and was proceeding to "boot him". We said: "Oh no; fair fight! Let him up again!" " What! let him up again! If you knew the trouble I've had to get him down, you would not want me to let him up again. Not I!"

My brother was unlucky enough to get a bad touch of a sort of low fever, which began with rheumatism, and he had to get down to Buenos Ayres. Eventually he had to go home for a complete change.

Agriculture was then in its infancy, and that now great wheat-growing country had then still to import flour.

We had an enterprising Scotch neighbour named Melrose, who began by dealing in sheep, and then turned his hand to ploughing.

He got some land about forty miles from us, and then went back to Glasgow, raised some money, married a wife, and brought out two steam-ploughs, and started on a large scale.

As was usual, his first year's crop was Indian corn, which came up splendidly; but one of the plagues of Egypt was too much for him, for the locusts came in their millions and ruined the crop. A plant bitten by locusts is poisoned and done for. This was a great blow. However, readers of the "Ingoldsby Legends" may remember the writer's reminding his readers of what he heard at a prize-fight -

> "The advice that's contained in these short words ten,
> Take a suck at the lemon, and at him again!"

Melrose went at him again, but the cart was again upset, this time in Rosario. There a man met him, and looked hard at him, and asked if that was "Steam-plough Melrose". Melrose recognized him, and returned at once to his place. We saw him in Frayle Muerto, and he said he was off to Buenos Ayres on business. "Good-bye, you fellows!" he called out as he got into the train. "It will be a precious long time before you see me again".

We soon found out the meaning of this. The man who saw him said that Melrose's name was Wright, and that he was a forger who had bolted from Scotland a very few years back, leaving a wife and family. Certainly he had pluck, enterprise, and perseverance, but - a past! I heard of him by chance later on in California, but know no more about him.

The locusts were a horrible scourge. We lost all our Indian corn and potatoes one year.

They come in a flight which looks like a silver snowstorm in the sun. They settle somewhere that looks green, and at once proceed to breeding and egg-laying. These flying ones do very little mischief. They never rise again - dig holes, lay their eggs, and die.

Then out come the little black grubs. They crawl and eat everything, grow very fast, and march slowly in an army in line, climb over everything, and eat everything they can, even get into the house, and try to bite anything.

Trenches are dug in their way; they march on, fill the trenches with bodies, and march steadily on. It is despairing work fighting them.

Once, near Frayle Muerto, they crossed the line in such a swarm that the engine's wheels would not bite, and the train was stopped for some time. Gradually their wings grow, and they fly away and begin again. Every now and then the wind takes them to sea, and there is an end of them.

I tried one wheat "spec" with a neighbour named Calder. About fifty miles from us some men had settled, and cultivated some ground. The Indians had come in and killed them all, but there stood a very good crop of wheat.

We agreed with the surviving relation, and were to pay him a small sum, as he would not risk his skin to harvest it, and go and harvest it ourselves.

I started with some horses, but rather late, and got into the dark, and could not find the house I made for. The night was very hot, and the mosquitoes were awful. I had great trouble with the horses, and thought I should die of thirst, as I had mowed an acre of wheat the day before with a scythe, and half an acre that day.

I picked up Calder, and we borrowed a reaping-machine in Frayle Muerto, and got to the place. It looked desolate enough, partly burnt, with the holes in the roof through which the Indians had lanced the inhabitants.

Calder left me with the horses to go and get some natives to help in the job. The courtyard was sound, and I shut the horses in that at night, lit a fire, and cooked my food.

I had two repeating-rifles to welcome the Indians with if they visited the place again.

There was some good *alfalfa* for the horses, and I made a hammock of sacks and slung it in the only room with a sound roof. I shut the half-door, and made a fire covered with green *alfalfa* for the mosquitoes, and the horses fought all night which could put their heads in the smoke; the insects were maddening. Fleas, of course, swarmed.

I may here mention, in connection with mosquitoes and fleas, the *binchuca* - a gigantic "B" flat, nearly the size of a shilling. He frequents the thatch of the roof, and will playfully drop down on the sleeper, and play Old Harry before the victim awakes.

There came one of those tremendous thunderstorms lasting for hours and hours.

I had a lively three days there, with food running short, and nothing to do but mind the horses, cook my food, look out for Calder and Indians, and read a copy of Carlyle's "French Revolution", which I brought with me.

At last he came, and after great trouble we harvested the blessed crop, and got safe back to Frayle Muerto.

We sold the corn, and balanced up the account, and found that we were either three or four dollars to the good! So much for labour, discomfort, and risk of life. The best spoil was a very nice pussy-cat, which Calder took home with him, which had escaped the Indians. It was very active: I saw it catch a swallow one evening.

What with locusts and Indians, things went on very slowly, and life was very uphill work, and one year succeeded another with poor prospects.

So it went till I was unlucky enough to drink some bad water, and got a touch of enteric fever.

I got into Frayle Muerto in a cart, and was laid on some sacks in a goods-truck going to Rosario. I could stand just enough to get into a conveyance, and drove to a friend's house, who kept me most kindly and hospitably. I shall never forget Duguid's kindness.

My treatment and nursing were rather primitive, but I did not die. I was given fifty grains of quinine one day, as the giver said, "If I don't kill the fever, it will kill you".

Some friends came to say good-bye to me, but I made up my mind not to die out there.

Some had very long faces, some were jovial - "Cheer up, old man!" - and so on, and they would sit on the bed!

One had fortified himself with cocktails, and swayed about over me a good deal, hiccoughing freely: "Never mind, old chap! There's a better place above. You remember what the Bible says". But there he was beat, and could remember nothing. When someone came in I was in giggling hysterics.

I was fed up as soon as I could cat, and did not die of it, as so many do; only I had chronic indigestion for a year or two.

My kind friends at Las Rosas put me up for a bit, and I used to take the racers for walking exercise; but I could not pick up, and made up my mind to get to Buenos Ayres and England.

I found on board that most pleasant and enterprising traveller, George Musters, late Lieutenant, R.N., just returned from his strange long visit to the Patagonian giants.

We got news of the outbreak of the Franco-German War as we started, and at each port we touched heard of the French disasters, which seemed to come even quicker than they really did, as we met the news on the way.

The exultation of some Germans who had to return to the army was rather blatant, and greatly distressed a sweet little French actress on board, whom Musters took under his wing.

I got very much better on the voyage, but careless feeding on recovery left its mark for a very long time on my digestion.

On leaving Vigo, and off the Bay of Biscay, we saw and heard men-of-war firing, and hoped we had come in for the excitement of a French and German engagement, but soon saw that it was the Channel Squadron at gun-practice.

It was the day after the loss of the *Captain*, and there had been no bad weather, which showed how very little wind upset a ship that never ought to have hoisted a sail.

And so we ran once more into Southampton.

Chapter VIII

THE FLYING SQUADRON

As I have said, I arrived at Southampton in the early days of the Franco-German War.

The hotels at Southampton were full of French families, who had fled across via Havre or St. Malo, and I was struck by the number of pretty girls there were among them, and so well-bred-looking.

I went back to Warwickshire, but I was a long time picking up after my bad fever, and at one time I almost gave up any idea of ever being strong again.

By way of sea air and a change, my cousin, Mike Seymour, who commanded the *Volage* in the Flying Squadron, kindly asked me to come for a cruise.

I joined at Portland, and we sailed for the Baltic, the plan being to go to Kronstadt.

Sir Beauchamp Seymour was the Admiral, in the splendid old Frigate *Narcissus*.

We rounded the Scaw in rough weather, and the *Volage*, which was one of the new "composite" vessels - a sort of compromise between a steamer and a sailing-ship - was very uneasy, and her guns made her roll most uncomfortably.

We landed at Copenhagen in a gale, and we carried away one of our masts, snapped short off, in going ashore in the boat, and were pretty wet as well.

It soon cleared up, and we spent a few very pleasant days in that bright, clean little capital. I think it is the cleanest town I ever was in.

Of course, the Admiral, etc., were entertained by the King, and I, with some of the junior officers, did the place thoroughly, enjoying the charming gardens, which had a "switchback" long before there was one in London. It seemed a most orderly and sociable town, and the King and his family walked about in the gardens like any other citizens of Copenhagen.

The Thorwaldsen Museum, in the middle of which he is buried, is most interesting. There are many of his original works, and very good copies of many others. His ghost might say: "Si monumentum quæris, circumspice!"

There is a very curious old tower, to the top of which, legend says, Peter the Great rode. The question of its height was asked, which no one knew. He had with him a new English watch, giving the seconds, so he ordered one of his suite to jump off, that he might count the time it took him to reach the ground.

From Copenhagen we cruised up into the Baltic, but our orders had been changed, and we only went as far as Carlscrona, a naval arsenal of Sweden.

There we were fully feasted, and a Swedish banquet was no child's play. Toasts with everyone - cry "Skoll!" and turn your glass upside down. Then Swedish punch, a strong and seductive compound. It is all preceded by the "Smergoost" sideboard, with every sort of thing like smoked lax (salmon), anchovies, etc., the mixture being washed down with glasses of Swedish vodka. A very pleasant ball introduced us to many fair ladies, among whom was a plentiful display of good looks, without any striking beauty; but they were most hospitable, and very many spoke English.

Our voyage to Stockholm and Kronstadt had been given up.

Then to Christiania, and we had a glorious day to go up the bay and lovely fiord.

Norway seems to me to be a larger and wilder Scotland, much the same, only "more so".

I saw one day at the hotel on the menu, "Cock of the woods", and, thinking it meant woodcock, I at once ordered it, and was rewarded by the toughest old caper-cailzie, tasting of turpentine!

The view of the Froner Saater (as pronounced), the highest point near the town, is magnificent - over distant sea, lakes, mountains, fiords, and pine forests, with the pretty town below.

The Squadron was to go from Christiania to Christiansund and

Trondhjem, so, having a longing to see Norway, I arranged to go by cariole across country to that place, and my cousin very kindly gave leave to Malcolm Drummond, a mate on board, to go with me, and the best of companions he turned out.

Of course, we knew not a word of the language, or the road, but that did not matter, and we got safely over the Dovrefeld in snowy weather, and I only upset twice in snowdrifts.

When we got to Trondhjem, we got a wire to say that the Squadron was only going as far as Bergen, and we were to join there.

Curiosity took us to the cathedral to see a fashionable wedding, and the gravity of my comrade was quite upset when the patriarch, a most dignified man, with a long white beard, at the end of the service, before giving the exhortation, took a quid of tobacco out of his mouth, and placed it on a little shelf by the side of the altar. But it appeared that everybody in Norway chewed.

We took boat, and arrived at Bergen, where we found the ships, after our very pleasant trip.

What a beautiful spot Bergen is! And the view from above it is glorious. I went once or twice to shoot reeper (Norwegian grouse) with my cousin, who is still a very keen all-round sportsman.

A sad event disturbed the pleasure of our time.

On board one of the ships was the brother of my old companion, George Musters. He had gone out shooting with a party, who missed him, and had to return without him in the dark.

Next day a large body of men was landed, and, guided by many natives, a line was formed to beat the whole ground; and we found the body where he had fallen from a great height.

His funeral was very striking, being partly naval and partly Norwegian, and, according to their custom, the procession was headed by a band. Altogether their idea is to make it a much less gloomy ceremony than we do.

I found the hospitality of the Squadron most noble. Sir Beauchamp, so well known as the "Swell of the Ocean", was the best of dinner-givers and hosts, and his wine was exceptionally good. His Flag-Lieutenant was Lynedoch Moncrieff, who was afterwards one of my greatest friends, and my partner in business.

"Ned Sullivan", later Sir Edward, was a fine specimen of the British skipper - a remarkably fine-looking, powerful man, and most popular in the service. He, too, gave excellent dinners, and was a charming host. His memory carried him back to the days when a captain on a distant station was omnipotent, and he had experienced the wrath of one who, when he was a midshipman, disrated him - that is, put him before the mast as a seaman, and sent him to berth and mess in the forecastle - a startling and unpleasant experience.

My cousin's First - Lieutenant was Jack Fullerton, so much appreciated and liked by the Queen later on as Sir John Fullerton, Captain of the Royal Yacht, the best of officers and good fellows.

It was very interesting to have really seen what life is like on a man-of-war on service out of England - the daily routine, the drill, and the exercise of the Squadron in manoeuvring. It was about the last of the old masts, yards, and sails, though the ships had auxiliary screws, which could be raised up into a sort of well when the ship was under sail.

This was a part of regular drill, and a tremendous job it always was to disconnect the shaft and haul the great affair up.

Lowering the topmasts was a most dangerous-looking business. I always admired the nerves of the man who had to stand on the cross-trees, I think they are cared, hold on to nothing, and let this great spar down with a run almost between his legs.

When we left Bergen we went straight across to Leith, and fell in with a gale when under sail. The *Narcissus* and *Immortalité* weathered it well enough, but our "wallsided" ship was not at all easy, and we took many seas over us. One jerk snapped the fastenings of the large table in the Captain's saloon, and it was a long job to screw bolts into the deck, and make it fast as it pitched from side to side of the cabin with our rolling.

My pleasant cruise had quite restored my health and strength, and I was quite fit for more wanderings.

Chapter IX

RETURN TO OXFORD

*M*y long trip in the Flying Squadron having completely set me up in health after the touch of enteric fever I had in South America, the question was, What was to be my next trade or profession?

I should myself have liked something practical and active, and I thought of working for mining engineering, which was then not the overdone trade which it has since become.

I did not want to re-enter any branch of the Civil Service, and I had no business training or connection.

I suggested to my father that a year or two at Owens College would give me a practical training, and be a step to a useful or active career; but he did not like the idea, and, still hoping that I might change my mind about the Church as a profession, kindly offered me to go back to Christ Church and take my degree, saying that I could there give some of my time to chemistry and natural science.

It was therefore decided upon, and Dr. Liddell was good enough to say he would take me back into the arms of Alma Mater, and the childish memories of the fifth of November were things of the past.

I once more, therefore, found myself back at the House.

I had rooms in college, first floor in N° 6 Peckwater, looking into Bear Lane, and I found old King still there, who was my scout when in garrets on the same staircase.

What account he gave of my former career I don't know, but there was much curiosity to see me.

On the same staircase were Algernon and Frank Parker, Herbert

Hope, Lord Harris, and Willie Higgins, and I was soon an intimate friend of that very pleasant set.

Among others who I saw every day were Lancelot (now Colonel) Rolleston, Lord Londonderry, the present Lord Pembroke, Gerald Duncombe, Lord Antrim, Sir Frederick Milner; and I saw a great deal of Lord Randolph Churchill, who belonged to Merton, and was a great deal with the men I have just mentioned. A very amusing companion also was Walter Campbell, of the Blytheswood Campbells, who was a capital hand on the banjo, and sang very well to it.

One night at a party at the Deanery he sang:

> "It's no matter what you do if your heart be true -
> And his heart was true to Poll!"

The Dean remarked that the moral was not of the highest elevation!

Life at Christ Church in such pleasant society was charming after the few years of cowboy life on the Pampas, and although I attended chemistry and other physical science lectures, I found that most of my time was taken up by reviving my knowledge of Latin and Greek, the latter particularly, for the necessary examinations, so that I was not likely to gain any great practical good from my time at Oxford.

I found it very easy to seem young again, and to enjoy the companionship of the young men round me, and the club to which I belonged, the "Rousers", which I mentioned before as one of the two small clubs of Christ Church men, was a very agreeable place to meet at.

I also saw more of the younger Dons than I should have done if I had come up fresh from school.

I played cricket a little, and rowed a little, and now and then had a ride. The Christ Church Harriers were hunted by Rolleston and Seaham, afterwards Lord Londonderry, both very keen sportsmen.

There was a drag now and then, and I managed to break my collar-bone with that one afternoon.

Undergraduates seemed to me to be a little more orderly and to have fewer bonfires than in my previous time, and the little society who used formerly to meet most evenings at the Buttery had come to an end.

Tufts and Gentlemen Commoners were extinct; the levelling ideas of the day had swept away the privileges of wealth and rank.

I found a change in one thing since my former residence, which was that there was more freedom of talk and less diffidence in discussing the questions of religion and science. Darwin, Huxley, and Herbert Spencer had had an effect already on the restraint which the atmosphere of Oxford had so long held on any freedom of thought.

The tradition of the superiority of Christ Church over other colleges still existed, but the contemptuous term of "Squill" for out-college men seemed to have died.

It was while I was at Oxford that Temple and Stanley happened to preach their first sermons in the University pulpit at St. Mary's since the commotion caused by the book "Essays and Reviews".

This was looked forward to with very considerable interest, as it was expected that they would say something about their opinions, and how far they supported the general tone of the book.

Temple preached a good enough sermon, but utterly commonplace, and with no sort of reference to doctrines or opinions.

Stanley preached one of the most interesting sermons I ever heard.

He began by saying that he remembered years before going into the rooms at Oriel College of one of the most remarkable among the many great men of Oxford, meaning Newman.

Over the mantelpiece was a view of Oxford from Headington Hill, and under it Newman had written, "Can these dry bones live?"

Stanley then went on to speak of the narrowness of views which had done so much harm to Christianity and to learning through centuries, and by the enforcement of which the Church of Rome had so retarded every sort of progress for ages; how the great colleges and Universities of Italy, Spain, and Portugal, of all Romish Church countries, had gradually decayed and died, with their life dried out of them by the pinching fetters of the dogmas and decrees of the Pope and his councils.

Then he came to speak of England, and said that the time had come when liberality of opinion must advance as science and knowledge advanced, and that if the Universities, hampered by old religious limits, refused to advance with the time, the day of their decay and death was not far distant.

I also heard that fine scholar and charming personality, Dr.

Jowett, preach his first sermon in the University pulpit. He had never been selected to preach, as many of the authorities disliked his theological views, but as he had become the Head of Balliol, he took his natural turn.

It was a good sermon, but there was nothing very remarkable in it, and nothing whatever controversial. We observed Dr. Pusey and Dr. Liddon sitting below him looking very stern and critical, and as I walked away with that very clever and agreeable man, our College Professor of Chemistry, I remarked it to him, and he said: "I really believe that they would go and see him burnt as a heretic, and think it their solemn duty to do so".

I said something to him about how little such a great scholar and clever writer as Pusey had written that was interesting to a layman, how limited in view it all seemed, and he observed: "It is very hard for a man to dance gracefully in irons!"

A strange variety of doctrines gets preached in course of time in the pulpit of St. Mary's.

Some old Oxonian on a visit recognized the man who leads the procession on Sunday, carrying what we used to call the "holy poker".

He said, "Hullo, Thomas! are you still here?" Yes, sir, and I've heered all them sermons, and in spite of it, thank God, I am still a Christian!"

The bearer of the "holy poker" reminds me of the reply of the guardian of a country church when some visitor asked him his position. "Well, sir, some calls me the beetle, some the sextant, but the rector calls me the virgin!"

A story is told of Dr. Jowett staying in a country-house where there was a large party of all ages.

As the evening wore on, the host said: "Dr. Jowett, we are going to adjourn to the smoking-room; I don't know if you will like to come?"

"Yes, I'll come; I'll come".

Soon some young gentleman, who had dined well or who did it for an ill-judged joke, fired off rather a broad story. Some of the party were wondering how Jowett would take it, but all he said was: "Hum, hum! More dirt than wit, more dirt than wit!"

The story was told that on the occasion of his arriving at a new position of dignity at Oxford, one of the men officiating in the ceremony said: "Dr. Jowett, will you sign the Thirty-nine Articles?"

"Yes, yes. Bring me a pen; bring me a pen!"

An Oxford story is told that the heads of three colleges were known to society there as "the World, the Flesh, and the Devil".

The daughter of the latter, not knowing the soubriquet of her father, exclaimed one day, to the amusement of her hearers:

"Oh, look! There are the World, the Flesh, and papa all walking together!"

CHAPTER X

FACTORY INSPECTOR

*F*ound after some time of residence, and a very pleasant life at Christ Church, that the time spent in violent efforts to pick up Latin and Greek again was not likely to do much for me in the way of making my living a bit later on. Also, that it was not easy to learn as much as I hoped to of chemistry and practical science, and that therefore I was rather wasting time and money. There was also the fact that my father would still have liked me to take Orders, a kind of life which my way of thinking did not fit me to undertake.

Just then I got the offer of an inspectorship of factories, which, all things considered, I accepted.

I again had to face the Civil Service Commissioners, but the old certificate from them carried me through several subjects, and political economy was the subject of which I was most ignorant.

I placed myself as a pupil of that very clever and amusing man, Thorold Rogers. He had been professor of that subject, but the Oxford Dons did not approve of his orthodoxy, or his want of it, though this was not a subject his professorship had anything to do with, so they ejected him, and elected a more orthodox teacher, Bonamy Price.

Under his guidance I took a canter through Adam Smith, Mill, Ricardo, and Fawcett, and at the end really knew something of that large and intricate science. With Rogers as tutor, it was most interesting and often amusing.

Many subjects came up, and I remember asking him one day: "Mr. Rogers, what do you consider the origin of the idea of the Devil? " "Cheapest policeman they could find".

This doubt as to the objective individuality of the Evil One reminds me of what happened some years back at Clifton, near Bristol.

A worthy clergyman there, who on other matters appeared to be an orthodox minister of the Church of England, could not bring himself to believe in, or to teach the existence and active individuality of the Devil, as held in the past by most, and still by some.

The disciplinary question arose as to whether, as holding such opinions, he was still qualified to have a cure of souls.

The matter was carried into the courts, and at last to the House of Lords, when Lord Westbury was in power there. Under the guidance of that humorous and versatile jurist, it was decided that a strict belief in the Devil was not required of a clergyman of the Church of England.

When in due course Lord Westbury "slept with his fathers", a facetious barrister wrote his epitaph, part of which was this: "He dismissed hell with costs, and deprived the earnest Christian of the sure and certain hope of eternal damnation".

I left my friends at Christ Church with many regrets, and took up my residence in Birmingham.

Birmingham was divided into three districts, and mine had in it seven hundred factories and two thousand workshops, so that to inspect them with any care was no sinecure. I may say that a factory is where a certain number of hands are employed, while a workshop is where under that number work.

It has so pleased the Lords and Commons that the regulations for factories are more stringent than those for workshops, whereas we inspectors knew that the abuses in workshops were far greater than in factories, and I amused my spare time in writing an article or two in the papers on the subject.

One of our frequent jobs was to do policeman's work, and see that small boys under age went to school instead of to work, or, if employed, were "half-timers" - half day-school and half work. This system gave little satisfaction to either school or work master.

If employers persisted in breaking rules, we had to prosecute them in the police-court, an anything but amusing job. While waiting one's turn, one heard some curious specimens of lower life in Birmingham.

The proletariat were fond of bringing each other up for abusive language, and, considering the natural force of their daily talk, it was not easy to see where they drew the line at what was actionable. I saw a very stout, red-faced lady of Dutch build bring up a smallish man for making remarks about her person and character in fine strong Saxon. I myself, being used to colonial talk, could only think he accurately described her. He only used the expressions of Squire Weston about his cousin, my Lady Bellaston. I can hear now that genial man and excellent experienced magistrate, Mr. Kindersley: "Well, well! Get on! get on!"

One funny case I had one day was when I went to see a workshop where the occupier didn't know me. I told him my business, and he said, "Well, sir, if you will wait a minute, I will go with you", and off he went to the back. Now there was in the back wall what I had often noticed in such places - a peep-hole. This could be looked through both ways, so I applied my eye, and saw a small boy shut into a cupboard.

Back the man came, and I went round and found things in order. Then I said: "Don't you employ a small boy? and placed my back against the door. He argued a bit, and then said, "Oh, there is a lad about sometimes", and shouted for Bill. No Bill came, so I said: "Don't you think he would come out if you opened that door?" Out he came. So I told him what a fool he was, and that I must "run him in". So he was fined.

Once I found a small boy employed who was the sole support of his mother. I inquired into the case, and found that he attended a night-school, and did his very best, and considering that he was sure to make a good citizen, I left him alone.

I confess myself defeated once. We were often getting information, always spiteful, and one notice I got was that a dressmaker's business went on in the forbidden Saturday afternoon hours.

I raided the house, and found several mature dames sitting round at work. I expounded the paternal, or grand-maternal, orders of the Government, and said it must not be, and that they must take a half-holiday. Up rose a dame (not ninety years, like Tennyson's nurse, but getting on), who said: "And what do you want us to do? If we like to sit round and have our tea here and work, why shouldn't we? Do you want us to play with our hoops instead of sitting by the fire?" etc. I fled defeated, and said no more.

The "brickies" were not so pleasant, and it was wisest to go in couples to inspect them. I never quite got my head broken, though nearly.

Life was not lively in Birmingham; the club was not exciting, and the evenings hung horribly; but among the dwellers in Edgbaston there were some very kind and hospitable folks, as I gradually found, and enjoyed some very good and pleasant dinners.

Mr. Chamberlain was spoken of as the young rising man, but I never had the luck to meet him.

I had a cousin who was curate to the well-known Rev. Baines of the great church at Coventry, the largest - not cathedral - ecclesiastical edifice in England. With him I went to spend a Sunday, and was honoured by a request to read the lessons, which, being fond of the sound of my own voice, I readily did.

I was told I was very well heard, as I had done what a great speaker told me to do, to address myself to a man by the door at the bottom of the church, and feel that my voice carried to him.

I always hoped to come across a manufactory of relics or antiques, but could not hear of one, though I found where the great bits and curious stirrups and spurs of the Pampas were made. The Birmingham Mint was interesting, but was kept absolutely private, as foreign potentates who gave orders to that very well-managed house of business were not anxious that it should be known where some of their money was turned out.

One had sometimes to take a meal where one could get it, and England is behind almost every country in the way of places of eating, decent or indecent, whereas you can get drunk at every other corner. Talking to one of my colleagues, we were discussing the awful want in that way in England, and he said one day after luncheon he asked the young lady who attended him for a toothpick, but she said: "We don't keep them now. Father found that the gentlemen took them away with them".

I had a most pleasant outing to Meridan, where is the establishment of the Ancient Order of the Foresters of Arden - a cheery and very hospitable club.

Besides ordinary archery, they still had clout-shooting. A carpet spread on the ground has to be transfixed at some fabulous distance by an arrow shot up into the air, and the spot is marked by a man in an ancient uniform. He shows by strange antics where the arrow, which he has dodged, has fallen, and I was told that he had to stand on his head if the clout was struck; but I believe the memory of man did not go back to his having to perform that feat.

A good feed and a most lively ball finished it up.

I met a charming young lady, whose first ball it was. Being a lovely summer evening, I said: "Let us have a turn in the open". She said: "All right, as long as we don't pass the windows where my father and mother are". She has lived to make an excellent marriage, and be a pattern mother, and I have no doubt that her daughters now take moonlight walks; while she is a charming widow, and one of the great Warwickshire ladies.

Inspecting factories was not suited to my restless nature, so I was off again to the wilds, as told in the next chapter.

I must make one remark about Birmingham, and that was the singular want of beauty among the female workers there, and I had the chance of viewing a very large number of them.

CHAPTER XI

PARAGUAY

I

My soul wearied to death of inspecting factories in Birmingham. Little half-timers did not interest me, and the monotony of the occupation was very trying to a wandering nature.

Without doubt, some men, also animals, are by heredity disposed to a sedentary life, while others have the roving instincts born in their blood.

What my line of life might have been if my father had early thought this, and so had despatched me on some active course, I cannot, of course, say, but the clerical-ecclesiastical line which he designed for me was always a restraining force.

I concluded that I would cut the factory inspecting as soon as I could, one very good reason being that the pay was much too small to keep body and soul together in the way expected of what is socially called a gentleman.

One day I got a letter from my old companion, Charlie Talbot, to say that he had been asked if he would go to Paraguay. He went on to say that a certain firm, who asked him, wanted someone with some experience in out-of-the-way life and a knowledge of Spanish, so perhaps it might suit me to think of it.

I saw the heads of the firm, and asked what there was to do - as well as to get - and they said that I was wanted to be a sort of general agent - "to see with our eyes, to hear with our ears".

As most people have only the vaguest idea of where Paraguay is, I will give them one in as few words as possible.

Paraguay is in the interior of South America, with Brazil on the east and north, the Argentine on the south-east and south, and the Gran Chaco on the west. This is a magnificent tract of country some five hundred miles across, and more from north to south, but is still a sort of No-man's-land. The Salado River is to the south, and forms a sort of division between it and the provinces of the Argentine; the Vermejo and the Pilcomayo run through the Gran Chaco.

It is very little explored, and is given up to Indian tribes, who have disagreeable poisoned arrows, which deter visitors. It appears to be very well watered, and not very thickly timbered, and in the future will be a splendid place for cattle and agriculture. Being just out of the tropics, the climate will suit many men and productions, but it is too hot for sheep.

Paraguay is a little south of the latitude of Rio de Janeiro, and the north is just out of the tropics. It lies in the fork made by the Rivers Alto Parana and Paraguay. The point where they join and form the Parana is the southern point of Paraguay, and near the town of Corrientes, in the Argentine.

The Alto Parana River is to the east and the Paraguay to the west of the state of Paraguay.

The Paraguay is navigable for a great distance north into Brazil, but the Parana is interrupted by one of the greatest waterfalls known, and by rapids. The Parana runs into the Rio de la Plata above Buenos Ayres, about six hundred miles south.

Paraguay is about three hundred miles from north to south, its northern boundary being about latitude 23. Its greatest width is about two hundred miles.

Its climate for six months is delightful, and much resembles a fine English June. The other six months are hot, but rarely oppressive.

The scenery is charming, not grand, but a succession of beautifully wooded hills and valleys, with good-sized open grass plains between the ranges, where cattle do well. The trees are magnificent, some sixty varieties of splendid hardwood giants often towering sixty to one hundred feet without a branch. The soil is very deep and rich, and produces dye-woods, gums, drugs, perfumes, vegetable oils, and an endless variety of fruits and vegetables. Tobacco grows luxuriantly; in fact, it may truthfully be stated that Paraguay can produce all that grows in both tropical and temperate climates. Gardenias grow in profusion - great bushes covered with blooms. They call it there "Jasmin Paraguayo".

It dates as a Spanish colony from about 1535, and the Jesuits became the supreme power in about 1608, which lasted till overthrown by Spaniards and Brazilians in 1758. Having become free from Spain soon after that time, the supreme power was taken by Dr. Francia, who was Consul in 1811, and Dictator in 1814. He ruled the country with the iron rod of a despot till his death in 1840, at the age of eighty-four. Such was the terror of his name that I was often told that for many years no one dared speak of the *Carai Guassu* (Great Man) out of a whisper, in case he might not be really dead!

His prisons were always well stocked, and horrible holes they were, as I was to know later on; and it was said that he never moved anywhere without celebrating his journey by one or more executions. The tree was still standing by the river at Asuncion under the shade of which his many despotic murders in that town were committed.

He completely isolated Paraguay from the entire world, and the unlucky French naturalist, Bonplon, was kept in the country for many years, free to move, but from the isolated position of Paraguay it was practically impossible for a foreigner to escape without permission. Francia was succeeded in 1844 by Carlos Antonio Lopes as President for ten years.

He threw open the country, and it became very prosperous, though hampered for a time by a war with Buenos Ayres. Carlos died in 1862, when his son Francisco Solano Lopes succeeded him.

His reign began very well, and, having been educated in Europe, he made treaties with England, France, etc. Vanity and love of ostentatious power were, however, his ruin.

He created an army, and had a bodyguard dressed in the uniform of the Life Guards. A friend of mine told me that he one day went to see the President, and found the dark brown sentinel pacing up and down with bare legs, having placed his painful jack-boots by his sentry-box!

He began to build a really splendid palace, beautifully situated, and its unfinished remains are there as a monument of his folly, and a not bad specimen of Italian architecture.

He, unfortunately, became involved in disputes with Brazil, which resulted in the disastrous five years' war which ruined Paraguay, left the country almost without grown-up men, and only ended with the death of Carlos Lopes.

The courage and tenacity with which the Paraguayans fought was extraordinary. The Brazilian troops were composed very largely of coloured men, and for these macacos (monkeys) the Guarani warriors had the greatest contempt.

The Brazilians had some ironclad gunboats up there, and one of these was boarded and taken by men in canoes, led by my friend Goiburu, and they were only driven out of it again by another gunboat pounding it with grape. I saw the destruction caused by the volleys of her consort.

He had a charmed life, my friend Goiburu. I saw him in a street-fight ride his horse up to a barricade, spur it till it put its fore-legs against the obstruction, empty his revolver among the soldiers, and ride away untouched by the volley aimed at him.

Peace was made, and in 1872 Jovellanos was President. Just at this time it became the fashion in London to make loans of a few millions to needy South American republics, and the firm which I represented brought out a loan to Paraguay.

To make the prospectus acceptable there had to be a picturesque background to it, and for Paraguay there stood a bank, and an influx of colonists, who were to show the benighted natives how the Britisher colonists could work and start independently. It almost seemed as if the financial promoters were disinterested philanthropists. The natives were glad enough to get the dollars, but took the rest as a nasty pill to be swallowed along with them. They were right in thinking that it wasted money to no purpose.

Among other things, the loan was to extend the benefits of education to the juvenile Paraguayan, and I saw some of the school - books sent out. Among the rubbish sent were pamphlets, and advertisements of quacks about disagreeable diseases, etc.! This is a fact. These were in Spanish, and only the rather educated in Paraguay spoke anything but the Guarani language.

I may observe that South America is, generally speaking, divided as to speech between Guarani, the language of the east of the Cordillera, and Keechwar, that of the west. There are many dialects, but these are the roots. Patagonians and Fuegians are apart as to language.

I cannot say what happens in regard to banking and education now; I have lost touch with Paraguay.

I forgot to say that there was a suggestion of helping the railway, of which I will speak later.

Before leaving I went to the Foreign Office, and saw the Under - Secretary, and told him where I was going, and asked if he could in any way help me. He said that he could not in any way whatever; that England had no representative of any sort there, and did not contemplate having any; that I went at my own risk, and he should much advise me not to go!

I took ship in a Royal Mail boat for this land of promise at Southampton. My financier friends had provided me as a companion with a strange little man of uncertain age who was blessed with the name of Archangelo, which he told me was caused by his family being Greek, which language perhaps he knew. He did speak English of a sort, but his knowledge of Spanish, a useful thing in a Spanish colony, was all but absent. What he was to do I could never at all make out. He certainly could not instruct that very cleanly race in washing, for when we arrived in Buenos Ayres after our three weeks' voyage, and I told him I had a chance of getting some things washed before we started up the river, he was quite offended at the idea.

One voyage is much like another, and the Royal Mail line, in many of whose boats I have sailed, keep up a very good average of comfort.

We took a river boat at the Tigre, then - perhaps still - the little port near Buenos Ayres from which the up-river boats start, and I found myself once more in familiar scenes. We passed Rosario and Santa Fé, and I viewed the spot where, years before, we lost our boat and I spent three damp and chilly months.

It took about seven days to get up to Asuncion and five to come down to Buenos Ayres - rather monotonous, as the scenery on the bank was almost exactly the same all the way, and the company was generally very uninteresting.

The sort of delta of the river runs a very long way up - quite one hundred and fifty miles - the main channel being along the western bank, and opposite Rosario the islands and series of swamps extend for thirty miles wide, the main channel being about two.

The shore is either low, and often swampy, with a fringe of willows and a few other uninteresting trees of no size, or it is a low cliff of marl tosca, for rock or stone is not seen till well up into Paraguay.

The great water-weeds and flowers (camelotas) in time of flood break away in enormous masses, and boats have to take care not to get entangled in one of these floating islands. I was told that one was passed once with a tiger sitting in the middle of it.

When Corrientes is passed there is the enormous plain of the Gran Chaco on the left bank, extending across the continent to Bolivia.

A few natives have crossed it. My invaluable Bolivian servant, Manuel, had come across, impelled, as far as I could gather, by a desire to get away from the consequence of some error against the laws. He spoke Keechwar and Guarani and very good Spanish, was a first-rate rider and horse-keeper, good cook and mender of clothes, and very honest.

I and my curious companion landed in Asuncion, naturally knowing no one, and with some doubt in my mind as to our reception by the Government when we presented our letters.

Asuncion is prettily situated on ground gradually rising from the river, and from the hill which overlooks it there is a magnificent view of river and hills inland, and a stretch of mile after mile of water and trees in the Gran Chaco across the river.

The town is a jumble of a few good houses, built with the Spanish courtyard (*patio*), and generally with flat roofs (*azoteas*). The houses in between are often thatched hovels.

The street has now and then the remains of an attempt at pavement, but it is mostly sand quite a foot deep.

There was a sort of hotel kept by an Italian, but an Englishman was nearly as rare as a dodo.

I was soon "spotted" by a very cheery, burly fellow in the person of James Horrocks, who was making and managing the new tramway line for a company in Buenos Ayres. He was kindness itself, and I found with his help a home in the ground-floor of a well-built house, with a large *patio* for horses.

The owner was a widow whose husband had been killed in the

war, and she and her family lived in the upper story. Her eldest girl, by name Felipa Davaloz, managed things, and what a pretty girl she was! - of the best Spanish type, very pale, with plenty of black hair, large dark eyes, and the longest of eyelashes, and the figure which is the great beauty of Paraguayan women.

A few of the Paraguayans are of pure or almost pure Spanish blood, but they vary by mixture with the old Guarani natives, who were a very fine type, with tall, well-set-up figures and regular features. A plain woman was quite the exception among them, and they are the brightest and gayest race of women on the face of the earth - strong, active, and useful in every sort of employment.

When I got there I do not believe that there was one surviving grown-up man to ten women!

I went to visit the President Jovellanos, and was referred by him to Benigno Ferreira, the Minister who looked after my sort of job, and really ran the whole show. He was a severe, reserved man, who eyed me with suspicion and dislike, which I fully returned before many weeks were passed.

He said plainly that I and my bank, etc., and particularly the immigrants, were most unwelcome, but that they were forced upon them with the money. He regarded the newcomers much as Sir Anthony Absolute regarded the heiress - if you took money, you must take the live stock with it!

He said he had nothing to do with it; that there was plenty of vacant land, and I might plant the people where the – something - I liked. He passed me on to the sort of Government Surveyor, Colonel Wisner, a queer old Austrian, who had been in the country since the days of old Dr. Francia and who growled at me and told me to do what the ———— I pleased. He had a pretty young wife who was a friend of Felipa's, and poured out to her her woes with the surly old fossil. Felipa told her that he was so old, he must die soon, but she said: "Oh no! He would live long; his nails still were so hard!"

I found in Asuncion an Englishman who had been up-country helping survey, with the engineer of my friend (later on) Charles Waring, for the continuation of the railway from Paraguayri to Villa Rica.

He had begun life as a midshipman, and had wandered about since, and knew something of surveying, so I at once engaged him to help me locate my valuable colonists.

Before I left England I had plainly expressed the opinion that the colony scheme was certain to be a failure, and I would not be responsible for it, and that all I would do was to find some spot for these unfortunate people to do their best upon.

They were coming out under the guidance of an Australian named Billiatt, who had distinguished himself in one of the great exploring expeditions across Australia.

With my surveyor, Congreve, and my faithful Manuel, whom I had picked up, I started off to look at places which Congreve had seen near the existing line of rail to Paraguayri, and on beyond it.

We went through the most lovely country in glorious weather, and it seemed difficult to imagine a more perfect country to live in. But unluckily man requires something more than sky and scenery to keep life together.

We lingered a day or two by a lovely lake with most kind and hospitable people, passed Paraguayri, and on beyond the River Tebecuary-mi, a fine stream running into the Paraguay, and at times hard to ford.

Later on I hired a little steamer, and proved it to be navigable up to the spot where the road to Villa Rica crossed it, and now the railroad spans it.

A mile or two beyond the river were the hills of Itapé, a gentle slope not too much wooded, and a perfect site for large or small farms. This I fixed on to plant out Mr. Billiatt and his flock of black and white lambs.

I left Congreve to mark it out, and returned to Asuncion, and informed the powers of what I had done, and they again intimated that I might do what I —— pleased!

Then I had to sit down and wait for the arrival of Billiatt and Co., and not bother about bank or School-board.

With letters once every ten or twelve days, and no telegraph, it was impossible even to guess when the boatful would come.

With the help of my energetic friend Horrocks, I made what little preparation I could to receive them, and to feed them, and hoped they would bring tents, as no shelter could be found, though luckily that did not matter so much in that climate.

I also made arrangements with Colonel Thompson, who was manager of the railway, to give me a train up to Paraguayri when they came. He had been in the army of Lopes, and, a civil engineer by profession, he was turned into a military one during the war, and had been invaluable.

He was a charming individual, of whom I saw a great deal, and also of his most pleasing Paraguayan wife.

At last I heard that the boat was in sight, and went down to the jetty to meet it. She was pretty full of a most miscellaneous collection of what the Yankees call "hard-ups and dead-beats" that can be imagined, to the number of three hundred and fifty - few country-folk, mostly collected by advertisement in the streets of London at so much a head. They were about as unfit to form a new colony as can be imagined, and there were very few that an old colony would give a "Thank you" for.

I suggested that they should sleep on board, but they had no idea of anything of the sort, and flocked on shore.

I had a feed prepared in the big shed of the tramway with Horrocks's help, and somehow – anyhow - they camped for the night.

The next thing was to get them up-country. A more helpless, shiftless lot of men, women, and children - and lots of the last two - were never put together. It was maddening work to deal with them in such a place. Billiatt meant well, but, of course, he knew not a word of Spanish, and nothing of a new colony, his only experience being the long settled provinces of Australia.

We got most of them into the train and up to Paraguayri, but with long delay, and not till near morning, for the engine broke down, and it poured with rain. One child died in the train, to make things more cheerful.

The scramble at Paraguayri must be imagined; I need not dwell upon it. A few creatures had been left in Asuncion, and women and children and the most helpless had to wait at Paraguayri till some sort of shelter was made for them at Itapé, the journey to which had to be made on foot or in country carts, which were few and rickety.

The disappointment of the people was great. It had been represented to them that there were a number of farms - one can imagine their picture of house and stable, etc. - empty from war's desolation, and going begging till they turned up and stepped in. They said to me: "We was to be taken from our 'omes in England and put down in our 'omes in Paraguay, and this is what we finds!"

They were all to be provided with cows. Now, a tame cow was a very rare bird anywhere in South America where they did not then run to dairy-farming.

I made an effort to carry out the contract made with them, and offered contracts to supply cows. One man who was anxious to contract offered me a commission, and the prettiest girl in the district into the bargain! It was his niece, I found, and a very pretty girl she was. But the bargain was never completed, and he accused me of trying to carry off the girl without buying the cows. But I was much too busy for any such frivolity.

We did what we could, but it was hopeless work. Then "Phansey my phelinx!" as James Yellowplush said, when another boat with another four hundred dead-beats arrived. The same wretched story over again, and the work to feed them all!

These were done something with, and yet a third small lot arrived.

These I located nearer Paraguayri at Ita, under the care of a first-rate young fellow, Maurice, who turned up. Such a fine, strong, energetic man he was!

There also turned up my old friend in the Pampas, Alexander Baillie - a most practical, useful man, who knew the country and Spanish, and who was invaluable.

Billiatt did his best, but the whole thing was quite hopeless from the start.

A sad incident occurred near Itapé. A very nice couple, man and wife, among the best who had come, were beginning to shake down in a small house, when one morning they were found murdered - a most unexpected occurrence, for the Paraguayans, unlike the Gauchos, are most peaceable, and good neighbours. I got a line to tell me, also, that the man was caught. I got on my very good horse, and soon did the eighty miles to Itapé, determined that, as the Government would not help us, the man should be hung out of hand.

I had left Alexander Baillie there in charge, but he was so dead against hanging him that I had to give it up. He argued that he was in charge, and that it was not fair to force him against his judgement to help to hang the man. Of course, the authorities let him escape.

The woman's sister had gone into the household of Colonel Thompson, and I had to break the news to her.

A complication turned up - one of those natural epidemics in South America, a revolution.

The "Out" party thought that Jovellanos, Ferreira and Co. had been in long enough, and that it was time they had a turn. Their head man was Bareiro, a fine-looking, intelligent man, who prided himself that he had nothing but Guarani blood in him. I was amused to find that he had, when representing Paraguay in London, belonged to the St. James's Club.

The militant member was General Caballero, who had commanded the Paraguayan army in the great two days' battle of Las Lomas Valentinas, where they killed more Brazilians than there were soldiers in all the Paraguayan army. He was a great friend of mine, and, I am glad to say, lived to be later on President. His henchman was old Colonel Serano, a rough, jovial soldier, but with rather a poor record for cruelty in the late war.

The Church Militant was represented by a very clever, energetic man. I went to visit him, and found him living with two charming ladies, one the sister of Bareiro. But these were trifles in Paraguay!

They all promised to help me if I would be of service to them, and if they had succeeded I think I could have pulled things round a bit.

Among the agricultural implements there had been packed a considerable number of rifles and ammunition, and these I handed over to my friends, as they were of no use to us.

I got a letter from the old Colonel, who was rash enough to write and thank me, and my curious Greek friend got hold of it, and nearly passed it on to the powers, as he had a grudge against me about some nonsense, in which case I should never have written all this.

The beginning of the revolution was planned in the town of Asuncion, where the Government had no more suspicion of the Outs than it always has in South America.

There were in Asuncion two useful men in such matters. One, an Argentine, quite a professional revolutionary promoter - an active, busybody little man, who dressed in a uniform of his own, and when on active service looked like a monkey on a horse instead of on an organ. He joined the Government. The other was a Spaniard, Angulo. He was one of the band who murdered General Prim in Madrid, the bullet-marks of whose volley on the opposite wall I remembered so well. He was a scowling, sinister-looking ruffian, with a deep growly voice, and ever very fond of holding forth in it. I took a dislike to him as soon as I met him, before I knew his occupation in life. He had a very attractive Spanish lady with him, who seemed devoted to him.

He and the revolutionaries proposed a dinner to celebrate the new republic in Spain, to which all the Ministers were to be asked. They were to be seized and restrained till the new ones were in power.

I was informed of it, without my wanting to know anything about it, by one of them. I said I hoped my friend Jovellanos, the President, whom I liked, would come to no harm, but he said: "Oh no; he's all right". "How about Ferreira?" "Oh, you had better not ask!"

Among the conspirators was a man whom I could not bear, Padre Maiz - a villainous-looking face, and character to match. He had been one of Carlos Lopes' agents when there was a story invented during the war of a plot against him - as far as I could learn, a pure invention - but a number of wretches turned informers to pay out old spites, and many were horribly tortured to make them confess what they did not know, so they invented things, and made matters worse. Padre Maiz had a disgusting record in all that. One dreadful story there could be no doubt about.

A remarkably beautiful and well-known woman was Pancha Garmendia, and she was accused of being in the plot. When she was brought before him, she said: "Oh, he is an old friend, and I shall be all right!" Not a bit of it! The inhuman brute ordered her to be stripped and flogged, and tied down on one of the great ants' nests! And this was the man who I feared knew that I was aware of the conspiracy.

He thought he would get on best with the party in power, so he betrayed the whole thing to the Government!

My friends got warning in time, and bolted up-country. I could not bolt, and didn't know if the brute had given my name as one of them. I don't know what eventually became of him, but his name was sent to the Pope as a worthy successor to the Bishop who came to an untimely end!

Things went on, and when up-country about my people I used to see Caballero and Co., and was asked by my fighting friend Goiburu to take a letter or two to his lady-love in Asuncion, which I was rash enough to do in the lining of my hat.

I knew that I was suspected, for the brother-in-law of the President, a very good fellow, told me that Ferreira suspected me of being a spy of Caballero's, and I must look out not to get knocked on the head one night by one of his men. I thanked him, and said I must take my chance. Coming back once, I heard that I had better avoid the regular road, so I and Manuel made a round, and crossed the ground where the great battle of Las Lomas Valentinas was fought. It was curious to look over the positions, which my friends had talked to me about, of the very hard-fought field which practically finished up the Paraguayan cause.

As we left it we had to swim a small river, and when we got to the other side Manuel said nothing, but pointed to an enormous alligator which was lying against the bank about six feet from where we took to the water. I gave him a reminder of a revolver-bullet as near his eye as I could aim, and I was then a pretty good shot. Anyhow, he went straight down. Perhaps I ought to have left him alone for not molesting us.

One night with Manuel we had lost our way, and were riding through a forest. He said: "I wish we had a mule with us". I said: "What on earth do you want a mule for?" He said: "Horses are such fools; they will run right on top of a tiger; mules smell him, and won't go near him".

Riding up-country alone one night, I came to an open place which I knew sound ground with long grass, and in the moonlight put my horse to a hand-gallop. He ran right on top of a tiger asleep in the grass. The beast was so startled that he bolted; I think we trod on his tail or his leg.

Things went on, and my friends determined to put it to the touch, or win or lose it all.

They had a curious sort of nondescript force, mostly boys, armed anyhow. I heard of their coming, and with old Horrocks rode out to have a look at them.

My poor friend Caballero was bothered with a very bad inflammation of his eyes, and unluckily I had no borax with me to put him right straight away. He said I must go through with it, man, even if blind!"

The question was, what part was the Brazilian force to play, which was still encamped just outside the town, if there was fighting?

I knew some of them fairly well, but did not want to mix up much with them.

They sent an officer to try to make some sort of terms, and I rode out with him.

Nothing came of it, and, wishing to sleep at my house, I galloped back with him through the cordon drawn round Asuncion.

My friends Caballero and Co. had made a mistake. In talking to them I advised them to attack at once, that night, and try to surprise the place, as Ferreira had gone out with a party to try to meet them, and had missed them. However, they hesitated, which was fatal, and in the night the streets were blockaded with barriers of big trusses of *alfalfa* (luceme) hay done up in large lumps, and what curious cannon they had got were put in position. In a letter given presently will be found a fuller account of this.

The fun began at daylight, and I got into a church tower to see it, but the first cannon-shot passed close by me, and I came down, thinking the place too risky.

The Brazilian troops were drawn up, and their commander said that if they were not molested they would remain quite neutral, and abide by the result of the day's fighting, it being the usual way of changing a Government in South American republics without the farce of an election!

It was interesting and amusing. I was supposed to be an impartial spectator, but I wanted the invaders to win. My friends had placed in one street which gave on the central Plaza a small fieldpiece, which faced a twenty-four pounder in the barricades about two hundred yards off. I could not resist helping serve this. Some of them had got knocked over, but we loaded the little thing nearly to the muzzle, and let drive at them; it leapt into the air and turned right over, but we picked it up and fired again.

The twenty-four pounder seemed loaded with any sort of stuff - I really believe old sardine-tins full of stones - but unpleasant at close quarters.

In some streets commanded by the Government garrison they kept firing at anything or nothing. Some young fellows recklessly attracted the fire by pretending to run across, and then stopping short, but I saw more than one killed by that folly.

I have mentioned the grave but rash piece of swagger of my friend Goiburu.

While riding round to see it all, I found a commanding position and stopped there, but it was too conspicuous, as I soon found, for I attracted the fire of the whole guard of a barricade. Luckily they were armed with new rifles with a high trajectory, and so I and my horse escaped some forty rifles and cantered off. The day wore on, and no impression was made on the barricades. News arrived that Ferreira and his troops were returning, and rapidly nearing the town. Old Major Serano was wounded in the eye, and finding he would be caught between the fires, Caballero drew his force away and avoided meeting Ferreira.

I thought the best thing I could do was to take the part of an innocent spectator, and rode out to see Ferreira and his men enter. I saluted him, but was looked at very suspiciously, and perhaps it was risky, as his men were thirsty for blood. One unfortunate man I knew, a very good fellow, who had not gone away, but who was a friend of Caballero's, was quite near, and the order was given to kill him, which the lancers did at once.

After they had passed I heard my name called from behind a thick hedge which hid a small *rancho*. I found there Marcelina Godoy, who was the lady-love of Caballero. She had gone into the outskirts of the town to speak to him as he came in. She said: "You must manage to get me back' into the town, as I am not safe here, and if they catch me just now Ferreira's men will kill me".

I watched as the evening fell till the coast was clear, and by running and hiding several times, I got her safely home, but it was risky.

After this, things went on much as usual. The revolutionaries had to give up for the moment, and the leaders got away south, and across the river to Corrientes, where they waited a more favourable opportunity, when they turned the then victorious party out.

She was a most cheery, pleasant creature, Marcelina Godoy - had been very pretty, but was getting a little over-plump. One of my enemies tried to make mischief between me and Caballero by telling him that I was making love to her!

She had once saved his life by dressing as a peasant woman and getting a small boat ready, in which he escaped at night when some disturbance was going on in Asuncion, and his enemies had nearly caught him.

My difficulties were getting thicker and thicker. I made one journey to Buenos Ayres to see the agent there of the firm which has sent me out, and try to get some money, for I was in great trouble how to feed nine hundred helpless people.

The well-known Mulhall, owner and editor of the *Buenos Ayres Standard*, had been abusing me and my people roundly, and when I was going down, my genial friend Horrocks wrote to him to say I was coming down to "cow-hide" him, and he added: "If he says he'll do it, you may be sure he will, so look out".

I met him at the gathering of all sorts of men of business which they called "on change", and he was most lamb-like and apologetic, and ready to put anything I liked in his paper, so a *palinodia* was concocted and printed.

Doctors had been sent with the people in the ships. One of them stayed, by my persuasion, and fell ill, and another went off back to England. I got much help from an American chemist in Villa Rica, who was a very useful doctor, and knew the malaria of the country very well. That was the trouble. We used up all the quinine in Paraguay, and I believe that every one of my people, with only half a dozen exceptions, had it. A few died, and some were much weakened. I escaped it; I was too busy to have time for it. My man Manuel was in despair; he said I should wear out. I was as thin as a lathe, and ate nothing but manioca and eggs. *Manioca* is the nicest, most nourishing and digestible of all vegetables.

The Paraguayans make cakes of its flour and cheese called *chipa*. One could live on it and nothing else, and eat it cold or toasted.

Alexander Baillie was very ill, and Maurice was very bad. Billiatt was laid up too. As soon as he was well enough, he left the colony and started for England, abusing me for the want of money and supplies.

I raised money by bills drawn on London, and so managed to get food for my people, but it was becoming impossible work. At last the people at home dishonoured my bills. I had great difficulty in finding anyone to keep my accounts to send home of all that was bought and distributed, and suddenly the Government ordered me to translate them all into Spanish, and deliver the result to them!

Then one day I was accused of some nonsense, and marched straight off to prison - not at all a tempting abode: the same hole used by old Francia, and decidedly insanitary.

The gaoler was a friend of mine, and treated me very well. I had taught him previously to fancy the mixture of champagne and stout which Bismarck was said to patronize.

My friends extracted me from that after a little, but I was forbidden to leave the country, and a guard was put on any ship leaving to see that I was not on board.

I wrote to our Legation at Buenos Ayres, where Frederick St. John, now Sir Frederick, was *chargé*, and he at once interested himself in the matter, and gradually measures were taken to withdraw from Paraguay all who wished to leave, and bit by bit nearly all did leave.

At last, after I had repeatedly represented to the powers that it was no use keeping me, I was allowed to go.

II

The following letters give a few more particulars than I have put in above, and will show the very complicated position in which I found myself:

"ASUNCION,
"*April 19, 1873.*

"DEAR MR. ST. JOHN,

"I was unable, at the beginning of the week, to do more than write you a short letter in reply to your two notes.

"I then tried briefly to explain to you the position, but I will now do so more fully.

"In raising the two loans for Paraguay, conditions were made that large sums should be employed in the establishment of a bank here, in railways, in public works, and in encouraging immigration. This was proposed in London to boom the loan.

"The proceeds of the first loan of one million pounds were so quickly exhausted that a junta was formed in London for the disposal of the second loan of two millions. (It would be very interesting and instructive to know what became of it!)

"With the power to do so I have nothing to do, and the proceedings have been the cause of a Chancery lawsuit between the London firm and Sr. Benitas, the Paraguayan representative now in London.

"The first thing the junta resolved to do was to begin by sending out immigrants to this country, and for that purpose they made a contract with a Mr. Billiatt to collect people, and to accompany them to Paraguay.

"A considerable number of families were engaged under the conditions of which I enclose you a copy, the heading of the form of engagement in all contracts being, 'Between ——, Consul-General of Paraguay, of the first part, and ——, of the second part, and —— of the third part.'

"You will see that in this way the responsibility for anything done is curiously mixed up between them, and it would never be easy to say against which of the two an action would lie for the neglect of fulfilment of any contract.

"In August I engaged to come out here as head of the whole immigration affair, and made a contract with the above-mentioned people in the same form to proceed to Paraguay, and communicate with the Government, and to make all preparations for the reception of the immigrants.

"By the terms of my contract I engaged to 'see that the obligation come under in respect to such immigrants be fully carried out'. I copy the sentence for you to judge how far it has been in my power to comply with their engagement.

"I was further to explore the country, and to report as soon as I should have time; but that period has not yet arrived.

"My written contract does not show clearly that I was head of the business, but verbally I had all instructions as such, and all money and correspondence has passed through my hands as sole agent here. But the London house gave me no power to draw on them, except for the amount of the letters of credit they gave me on Messrs. Terrero in Buenos Ayres, they promising to supply me from time to time with the funds necessary for the support of the colony.

"When I first came they sent me letters for the amount of five thousand pounds, but since then they have left me quite without funds.

"In London, Sr. Terrero assured me that the Paraguayan Government would afford me on my arrival here every facility and assistance, that this scheme was arranged in conjunction with it, and that it would place maps and other information at my disposal.

"I was assured that there was plenty of room in empty barracks, etc., in which to accommodate the people on arrival; that there was any quantity of land belonging to the State unoccupied in the neighbourhood of Asuncion; and that there were splendid sites for colonies on the river. That there were abandoned villages and homesteads in which the colonists could be accommodated without delay; that there were maps of the State lands; and that the use of the railway would be granted free of expense, if required, to assist the colonists.

"I arrived in Asuncion, and at once placed myself in communication with the Government. The Ministers with whom I had to do informed me that they knew nothing of me or of my business; that Sr. Terrero had not even informed them of the immigration scheme, of my engagement, or of any contract which he had made for the Paraguayan Government.

"That he had certain powers given him to negotiate the loan, that the loan was to be used for certain specified works, etc., but that Sr. Terrero had received no powers whatever to dispose of the loan, or to make contracts in the name of the Paraguayan Government. Consequently, in doing all that he had done as to immigration, etc., he had entirely exceeded his powers, and that the Government would in no way recognize his acts.

"I found in Asuncion no maps, and no one who could tell me what was Government land. I found no empty barracks for the reception of people, and I could hear of no land either on the River Paraguay, or anywhere in the neighbourhood of Asuncion.

"I asked the Ministers what I was to do, as nearly four hundred immigrants would arrive in three weeks, and they informed me that I was at liberty to settle them on any Government land I could find, but they offered me no assistance in finding it.

"I collected what information I could here, and set off up the country to look for land on which to settle my people, and I fixed on Itapé, a place on the banks of the Tebicuary-mi, on the road from this to Villa Rica, and four leagues from that town.

"I made arrangements for supplies of food, and for transport, and finding it impossible to find house-room for the people on arrival, I had to trust to the tents that I had arranged in England they should bring with them.

"Three weeks after my arrival in Asuncion, the first instalment of immigrants arrived, about three hundred and fifty in number.

"I found that Messrs. Green and Le Rosignol in Buenos Ayres, who had engaged to transport them up the river, had crowded them into a small steamer called the Cisne, leaving half the baggage to follow as it could, and leaving the tents behind in Buenos Ayres.

"I accommodated the people as far as it was possible, and moved them to Paraguay *en route* for Itapé, to which place they were transported as soon as it could be arranged.

"These immigrants were followed in a month by four hundred more, who I had to dispose of as well as I could, and who are now in Itapé.

"Again, in the month of February, one hundred and thirty more arrived, who I have placed in Ita, not so far up the country. I am sorry to say that the people in Itapé, who have been out here all the summer, are suffering from fever and ague. Nearly all have had it more or less, and are much pulled down by it.

"Among the adults there have been few deaths - about fifteen - but children seem to feel the climate very much, and we have lost a considerable number - about thirty-five.

"More moderate weather has set in the last few days, so I hope the cool wind may do something towards restoring the people. The doctors think they would become acclimatized by degrees; but the first settling appears to be very trying. I am one of the very few out of nearly nine hundred people who have not been laid up here.

"The colony at Ita has been more healthy; but they arrived much later in the summer, and have been better housed all along than the others, their numbers being so much more manageable, and I having got more experience of the country by the time of their arrival.

"When I first came out here I was provided with a credit of five thousand pounds, which naturally was not sufficient for my necessities up to the present time, and everything is most expensive in Paraguay, and my expenses have been augmented by the peculiar circumstances of my position.

"I always expected that the house in London would go on supplying me with funds; but I wrote at the end of December to say that my money was exhausted, and my letter was only acknowledged by them on the 8th February. But though I have mails from England up to the 12th March, I have no news that any steps have been taken to prevent the colony being utterly destitute.

"I have raised money to go on with in various ways, and I have made a contract with the house of Segovia here to supply me with provisions and what money is absolutely necessary for six months, from the beginning of this month, April. As they do it on speculation, their terms are naturally high, but I was only too glad to take any means for the preservation of the colony.

"I cannot say that the terms of the London contract have been strictly carried out, as I have never been able to get a supply of cows and pigs, and do not see any way of doing so.

"With reference to the offer of the Argentine Government to transport the immigrants and to provide for them, I am not yet imperatively driven to accept it, and only absolute necessity would make me take a step that would raise such serious issues in the future.

"The Government here will have nothing to do with us, so it is no use applying to them.

"I went to the President before making my contract with Segovia, and explained to him my position, and he only said that I must do the best I could.

"The money already spent is now the subject of a lawsuit in London, which is the reason given that I am left without any supplies; and if I were to take such a step as to move the colony from Paraguay, the Paraguayan Government would at once decline, in any event, to pay my liabilities incurred in maintenance of the colony, as well as those of the people in London....

"I cannot yet think myself justified in taking a step which would so much further complicate everything, and I wait the result of the struggle among the London junta..."

I told Mr. St. John that I did not feel that I could write to him until he first wrote to me, which he had done.

As to the offer of the Argentine agent to move the colony, I told him that I heard it was only to a spot higher up the river on the other side, where they would be no better off, and in constant danger from Indians.

III

I also give the following letter, which I wrote among others, as it explains more fully the events of the moment:

ASUNCION,
"July 8, 1873.

"DEAR MR. ST. JOHN,

"I am again writing to you, because I am most anxious that you should not lose the interest which you have taken in the immigration to Paraguay, with regard to which I hope that I can write to you both as a private person and as the Minister of the nearest state to Paraguay.

"I am going, in this letter, to speak of the present position of the colony, and of the state of public matters just now in Paraguay.

"In speaking of the colony I shall, of course, be quite ready to have what I say brought forward in England, in case sufficient interest is ever taken there in what has been done in Paraguay for Her Majesty's Government ever to trouble itself at all in the matter.

"With regard to public affairs here, I feel it is so much to our interest that you should know the truth that I scarcely think it necessary to apologize for taking up your time with a brief account of what has passed here.

"Before saying anything about the colony, I wish to mention that I think it very possible that Mr. Billiatt, who was entrusted to collect and bring out immigrants to Paraguay, may have called upon you lately in Buenos Ayres, for he has left this, and is on his way to England.

"I say that I think it possible, but that I do not know, which may sound strange when speaking of a man who came out from England to work with me. But Mr. Billiatt has given me no information whatever as to what he has done in Buenos Ayres.

"From his letters to some of the colonists alone I can judge a little of what sort of steps he has taken. I feel the greatest reluctance in entering upon what appear to be personal matters, but I cannot avoid it to enable you to judge of how things really stand by my further description, and by what you may learn from reliable authority in any other way.

"I must tell you plainly that from the time that Mr. Billiatt first arrived in Paraguay, some three weeks or a month after I did, he has steadily refused to profit by any knowledge I had acquired of the country, either in that short time, or during my four years' residence in the Argentine Republic.

"I am most anxious to urge in the strongest way possible the responsibility which was incurred in sending out those emigrants, and, in case of absolute necessity, that still further steps should be taken for their interest, yet I cannot but regret the way in which Mr. Billiatt has set about this work.

"Before leaving the colony he made a speech to the colonists, in which he said that he should shortly return to Paraguay, and take them all away with him to England.

"If he thought he could accomplish this, I should be extremely glad, for my part, that he should try, and, if possible, effect it, but it was the height of folly to say such a thing publicly to people who wanted encouragement to endeavour to do something for themselves. And the result has been that he has left me with a large number of people who expect to be kept in perfect idleness until his return, about the distant date of which no one could doubt.

"He now writes to various colonists to inform them that, in the event of his not being successful in obtaining the means of transporting them back to England, he has made arrangements for their removal to Argentine territory.

"I have never believed it possible to take the colonists back to England, and I cannot understand where Mr. Billiatt gets his authority from for making terms with the Argentine Government.

"In case the announcement should not be enough to paralyze my efforts to induce the colonists to do something for themselves, he writes to them further, urging them to show no obedience to me, or to Mr. Baillie, whom I have placed as manager in Itapé, and he advises the colonists, in case I endeavour to make them work by refusing supplies to the idle, to band together and take things by force.

"Anything more disastrous to the undertaking and demoralizing to the colonists cannot be imagined.

"What Mr. Billiatt may have really done or said in Buenos Ayres I can only judge by these letters.

"I am ready to encourage every legitimate effort, if necessary, to remove them from a climate which does not suit Englishmen as agriculturists, and from a country whose prospects are so unpromising. But a large debt has been incurred to the Paraguayan Government, and to attempt to remove the colonists without any sort of repayment appears to me to be plainly a dishonest act.

"If the Argentine Government really contemplates mixing itself up in this affair, the Minister will have to consider seriously this view of the question.

"Of course, the compliance or non-compliance of the Paraguayan Government with the terms of the contract with the immigrants must also be considered, but as yet the immigrants cannot bring forward any legal claim for such non-compliance.

"Supplies have never as yet failed, but that has not been through the efforts of the Paraguayan Government to do its part, or of the London firm, but through my having, in my anxiety to carry out the business on account of which I left England, staked my own personal credit for a very considerable sum of money in support of the colony. Whether this money will be repaid I shall now know very shortly.

"The present state of the colony is as follows:

"In Itapé, where the first immigrants were placed, there are now about four hundred and fifty out of the seven hundred and fifty who originally went up there. Of the three hundred missing, about fifty are dead, of whom about fifteen are adults. The great mortality among the children was caused by the admission on board one of the immigrant ships of a child with measles, which epidemic ran through the ship, and caused a large number of children to land here in a condition totally unfit to encounter the severity of a Paraguayan summer, and the hardships of the early life of a settler.

"The other two hundred and fifty have either left the country, or are employed, or are seeking employment, in Villa Rica or Asuncion; some few of these are doing fairly well, but these are men of exceptional trades and considerable ability, who might have done well anywhere.

"In Ita, where I placed the later arrived immigrants, there are one hundred and thirty persons.

"These all came together three months after the others, and I formed them into a colony under the management of Mr. Edward Maurice, younger brother of the Mr. Maurice who came from England in the ship with you.

"Mr. Maurice worked most energetically with those people, and succeeded in really founding a colony. None of the people, except three real London blackguards, who, I believe, must have left England to escape the police, have deserted; they have all built houses, and though they have suffered much from fever, and have never been as well off for supplies of all sorts as their fellow-countrymen in Itapé, they have laboured with a good deal of energy, sticking fairly to their work.

"They have ground cleared for planting, and though they started three months later than the colonists in Itapé, yet they are planting a considerable amount of seeds of different kinds, while in Itapé few houses have been built, and scarcely any cultivation yet begun.

"The reason of this contrast it is impossible to go into fully in a letter, but I have to observe that, seeing the state of things at Itapé, I purposely avoided placing the late arrived colonists under Mr. Billiatt, in spite of the stringency of his contract, which he insisted on, but I placed them at a considerable distance under Mr. Maurice, who, I regret to say, has lately resigned his post, so I have replaced him by a Mr. Frazer, a gentleman of much experience in the country.

"I do not wish to draw a stronger moral than necessary from the existing facts, but I wish to point out that the colony in Itapé was made up of people chosen by Mr. Billiatt himself, that the whole of the stores, implements, and clothes issued to the colonists there were chosen by him in England, and I was nearly always able to supply him quickly with whatever he required out here; while the colonists in Ita arrived when I was very short of money, and have had to put up with what implements I could get them out here, besides which I never issued to them nearly as large rations as Mr. Billiatt considered proper to give those in Itapé.

"I should never have troubled you with these matters but that I find what Mr. Billiatt has been doing in Buenos Ayres, and I cannot doubt that something of what he has said and done must have come to your ears, and I feel that he has acted in a way that could only destroy any hope that might remain of the success of the enterprise which he was most instrumental in starting, and which he came to this country to carry out, while he is only injuring further the unfortunate country, and taking care to lay the blame of everything that has gone wrong on anyone but himself.

"The house of Segovia still goes on supplying me with provisions for the colony according to my contract, and I hope that they will continue doing so for the three months more that the contract has to run; but they are getting very nervous about the payment of their bills, and the next mail from England must decide whether I can support the colony further or not.

"Although matters have been arranged between the London house and the Paraguayan Minister, Benites, in London, I have not yet been able to come to a proper understanding with the Government here. I have incurred a large amount of debt in my own name for the colony, and I do not yet know how it will be paid.

"I consider that the colony in Ita will be able in course of time to support itself, and I see no reason why that in Itapé should not at last be able to do so.

"Mr. Baillie * is doing all he can to revive the energy of the people, and to make up for the mismanagement of the past, and if Mr. Billiatt will only let it alone, I shall be able to see what chance of the people doing anything there is still left.

"In the meantime I suffer from a perpetual anxiety as to the stoppage of supplies, and am waiting impatiently to know what the house in London finally determines doing.

"If you will forgive the length of my letter, I will tell you shortly the political position here, as I know that you have no agent here, and if only for our interest, it seems important that you should know it.

"I need not tell you that the two contending parties in this revolution represent no different sides in politics, but merely men scrambling for power and plunder, as in all South American revolutions.

"The man of the people at the minute is certainly Caballero; but he has shown no capacity for anything beyond the duties of a recruiting-sergeant, and if there had been a man on his side with the smallest military capacity, he could not have failed to succeed.

"Bareiro is a man who had, for a Paraguayan, a good education, and has the advantage of having resided for some years in Paris and London when on the Paraguayan Legation. He is a man of some capacity, very ambitious, and extremely proud and reserved.

"I should consider him the most capable man in Paraguay to take a leading position, but as President he would be most despotic, and his character for temperance and sobriety does not stand high.

"These are the leaders of the revolution; the others are not worth much consideration. Colonels Serano, Goiburu, and Escobar are soldiers of courage and energy, but no particular capacity, and the civilians with them are not worth mentioning.

---

* While writing this book I hear of the death of Mr. Baillie, who has for long been Paraguayan Consul in London.

"This party is notoriously friendly to the Argentine Government, while the party now in power here belong to the Brazilians.

"If Bareiro became President, he would let the Argentines take the Chaco at once, and do for them all that they want; and the Brazilians, knowing this, have naturally worked to maintain the Government of Jovellanos and Ferreira.

"I have no doubt that you may have heard that Rivarola was President here, and is *de jure* so now, but he was put on one side by a little exercise of the divine right of revolution, and Jovellanos, the Vice-President, took the reins of government.

"He is popular enough, as he is good-natured and very easy-going, but he has no sort of talent, and only a good address and pleasant manners to recommend him.

"Ferreira is the man of the day. Not more than thirty years old, but with more energy than most of his countrymen, he has been gradually working his way to power, and I suppose we shall before long see him President. He is not particularly clever, but he has plenty of determination and energy, is very ambitious, and quite unscrupulous. He is very little educated, and served for some time in the Argentine army.

"He is proud, overbearing, and unpopular, but he has pushed one man after another out of his way as he mounts to power.

"He is now commanding the force against the Revolutionary party.

"The other two Ministers are Soleras and Miranda. Soleras has Finance and the Home Office to look after, and is a notorious robber. He is, for a Paraguayan, a decently capable man of business, but nothing more, and is a complete tool of Ferreira, and is Minister of War and Marine and Foreign Affairs.

"At the beginning of Rivarola's presidency, Candido Bareiro - now in revolution - was 'Secretary-General' - that is to say, he did the work of all the other Ministers, who had not then begun to be appointed, and found no great difficulty in getting through it.

"So the Brazilians are with the 'Ins' and the Argentines are with the 'Outs'.

"As to what the Brazilians did when Caballero came to take the town, I will just say this:

"The allies here some time back guaranteed the tranquillity of Asuncion, giving assurances to the Government and to the Foreign Consuls that Caballero would not be allowed to enter the town. On the strength of this the Italian Consul sent his gunboat away, and I believe that it was relying on this that the Paraguayan Government had so few men in Asuncion.

"When Caballero appeared so suddenly in front of the town, there is no doubt that he could have at once entered without any fighting if it had not been for the delay requested by the Brazilians.*

"Had he been suffered to do so, the revolution would have at once come to an end, as he would have been too strong for Ferreira's troops to attack, and there would have been nothing to fight for.

"Caballero offered to allow Jovellanos to remain in office until the legal expiration of his term, and only demanded the retirement of Ferreira and Soteras, against the former of whom the whole revolution has been aimed.

"The excuse given for not admitting Caballero's forces on the eveningf of their arrival was the disorder likely to occur on the late entry of two or three thousand men, but it was fully understood that they were to be allowed peaceful admission in the morning.

"When it became known, however, in the evening that Ferreira was marching in, the Brazilian Minister late at night assured the President that he would use sufficient moral force to prevent Caballero entering, but that if necessary the Brazilian troops would interfere. In the meantime the Government spent the night in making barricades round the Plaza where the Government buildings are, and arming them as well as they could.

"The barricades were made of trusses of *alfalfa*, which were ready pressed and bound with iron bands, and bullet-proof, and the engineer was my friend Colonel Thompson, who proposed and arranged the way of doing it.

"The morning came, and time was wasted in further negotiations to allow Ferreira to get near, and at last the Brazilian General said that, on the promise of Caballero to respect private property, he would remain neutral while he attacked the Plaza.

"The whole thing sounds more like a farce than like reality, but if there had been fighting at night, and if then the Brazilians had interfered, there might have been some very unpleasant events.

"As it was, Caballero did not attack the barricades with real resolution; but he was greatly handicapped by his promise not to touch

---

* I did not, in my letter, tell Mr. St. John that I strongly advised Caballero to march straight in.

private property, as there were flat-roofed houses which commanded the Plaza, and from them he could have killed all the defenders of
the barricades.

"The Brazilians were, of course, playing for the 'In' party to remain in, as most friendly to them, and they played without any scruple as to good faith.

"Of course, I should have preferred Caballero to have won; it
would have helped me out of many of my troubles to have had my
friends in power. As it turned out, as you know, Ferreira came near,
and Caballero drew his forces away without fighting him.

"In reply to what you say about our danger, I cannot say that we
are in danger; but if you can send up a gunboat, we shall be only too
glad to see it, the more so that we have no sort of representative of the
English Government up here.

"The Italian Consul told me that we might hope to see you up
here, but I fear that that is too good to be true.

"I must apologize for the length of this letter".

It would serve no purpose to add copies of any more letters,
which only tell the same story. Things only went from bad to worse,
and at last food at Itapé came to an end.

General Mitre, who I was constantly seeing then, helped me to
send provisions for a fortnight, but I met with nothing but refusal and
insult from the Government, and when I could not gain admittance,
Mr. Baillie experienced the same treatment.

It must be remembered that the immigrants were forced upon
the Paraguayan Government by interested speculators as a boom to
the loan in England, and without even the knowledge, much less the
consent, of the Paraguayan Government.

As they could not revenge themselves on the London people, they
took it out of us in Paraguay as best they could.

I was a short time in prison, and then a prisoner at large, till my
creditors thought their best chance was to send me off to England; so
that was arranged, and I was allowed to go.

Mr. St. John took active steps to remove almost the whole of the
strange collection made by Billiatt, and they were scattered everywhere, a few returning to England.

Then followed lawsuits.

IV

There was a rather well-arranged little club in Asuncion in the old house Carlos Lopes once used. The cooking was very fair, and the wine good and not dear. Nearly all the leading foreign men of business belonged to it, and some of the officers of the Argentine and Brazilian troops in the place.

They had a good supply of very sound light port in the wood, which I found most acceptable after my hard work up and down.

The summer in Paraguay was rather hot, and for six months in the year it was the general habit to take a siesta after the midday meal. The office hours in the Government offices were from six to twelve, and many business places used the same, and did not reopen in the afternoon.

Almost everyone slept in a cotton hammock, made of cotton grown and spun in the country. The hammock was made by stretching strong cotton threads on a frame from eight to nine or ten feet long. I saw one twelve feet long, and from five to almost twelve feet wide. These threads were close together, and were held by interweaving across at intervals of one inch or two inches, sometimes straight across by bands of half an inch to an inch wide, sometimes in patterns. The sides were ornamented by frills of cotton lace, six to twelve inches deep, and cotton tassels.

I have seen a small baby's hammock very fine and beautifully worked. One sleeps generally slanting in it, or even across if the hammock is very wide. The big ones might be called matrimonial ones, and answered to the old family four-poster.

In cold weather, with a thin mattress and a blanket, nothing can be more snug; in hot, with only the cottonnet, nothing cooler. You always carried your hammock with you, and so had your bed ready and always clean. Every room was built with rings in the wall, so that it could be slung everywhere, or in the veranda, which every house possessed.

As to animals, the tiger, or jaguar, is very common, and certainly dangerous, one often hearing of people being taken. In districts depopulated by the war I heard of roads being so dangerous that they were given up.

Tapirs there are, but so shy that they are rarely seen, but when caught young and tamed, nothing could be tamer. I had a young one, about the size of a large pig, still spotted as the young ones are, and the most familiar beast. He would waddle into the house, but was so strong that anything he touched, such as a table, went over at once. Then he would throw himself down with a grunt to be tickled and scratched.

Plenty of opossums of various sizes and colours - one I had for a time, big, strong, and fierce. A man gave it to me, as it killed every dog which came into his yard! But I got afraid of it, and gave it away. It had long claws to climb with, and enormous strong teeth. The little ones were very nice and amusing, but bit at times.

Monkeys, of course, we had; also one or two small nondescript things I have not seen here at the Zoo.

When I first went into my rooms they were overrun with rats, as was all the town after the war. One evening I heard a cat, and found one had come in and presented me with a family of kittens. Then came a second and did the same, and I got so well known among the race that even a third came. My place was cleared of rats, and my kittens were in great request.

Of birds, the macaws were the largest and finest. Alligators swarmed in the rivers, but seldom seemed to touch men.

There were stories of some fierce, mysterious beast by the river which was most dangerous, but I don't think he really existed. Snakes, of course, but not enough to be dangerous; the python was there, but no one minded him. I heard stories of them in the swamps to the north up to ninety feet long!

But snakes and snake-stories are always very elastic in every country. I saw pieces of snake-skin that seemed to have come from an animal at least two feet thick, but one knows how elastic he is when swallowing an animal whole.

In the rivers was the stingy ray, with a nasty spike in his tail to strike with; also a fish that grew up to two feet long or a little more, very thick, with a mouth like a dog-fish.

He attacks everything, bites tongues and noses of beasts when drinking, and my Manuel had a nasty scar on his leg from a bite. I had good reason to know him, for one day when I was having a swim

from my little steamer in the Tebecuary-mi, one seized the upper part
of my leg, and luckily did not get a firm bite, but I had the marks of
fourteen teeth on me for some days!

While I was in Asuncion I had several very interesting talks with
General Mitre, ex-President of Argentina.

He was living in Asuncion, nominally as a sort of diplomatic
agent, but in fact in a sort of exile, as he was hostile to the party in
power. We talked a good deal about the curious system of changing
Government by revolution prevalent in South American States, with
or without bloodshed, but it seems to have become part of the constitutional system of government.

He said he was against the system. He told me that he intended
to run again for the Presidency, but that, if defeated, nothing would
induce him to employ force to gain the supreme power. However, the
road even to power may be paved with good intentions, and not long
after he *did* stand for President, he was defeated, and he *did* march an
army into Buenos Ayres.

I was in Asuncion at Christmas, and went to the cathedral late
on Christmas Eve to hear the midnight service.

It is a very large building, magnificent in the most hideous architecture of brick plastered over and much painted, with two great
ugly towers at one end.

The service was, of course, gorgeous. The Brazilians and
Paraguayans love all the show and ceremony that can be put in. The
Brazilian garrison had a very good band, and this was there to join
the organ, so that the whole thing was really imposing.

Various tunes were played, more or less sacred, but the climax
was reached at the elevation of the Host, when the band burst forth
with the familiar strains of "Le Roi Barbu qui s'avance!" from the
"Belle Hélène".

A very few miles beyond Itapé is the pretty little town of Villa
Rica, rich with trees, and the densest of foliage in and around it - an
ideal subtropical little place.

I found some most hospitable friends there, but had little spare
time to give them; but I half fell in love with a most remarkably pretty, pleasant girl, Rufina Alarcon. I can see her now - very dark auburn
hair, beautiful eyes, and the figure of a Paraguayan girl. Perhaps with
more spare time I should have quite fallen in love. But, dear me! what
an eye her old aunt kept upon us!

A Brazilian friend of mine had a most well-managed cigar-factory there, and I hope he has made a fortune out of it long since.

Near Villa Rica are the celebrated yerbales. They are the groves of the sort of ilex-tree from the leaves and twigs of which the yerba is made. It is the tea of nearly all South America. It is dried over fires, and packed in packages of hide, like huge cushions, sewn tight up, and weighing about a hundredweight.

It is drunk out of little pots, made of dry gourds, called *matés*. Hence it is known generally by that name, and you are asked if you will take a *maté*.

It is not drunk, but sucked through a silver tube with a bulbous end pierced with holes, called a *bombilla*. It may be sweetened or not to taste. It is most refreshing, and splendid to quench thirst after a ride in the dust, and most wholesome - much more so than tea. A very large business is done in this.

The villages (*capillares*) are just as they were formed and left by the old Jesuits - rows of neat white houses in a quadrangle round the village green, with the church in the centre or at the end, and often with a second quadrangle with a market-hall; the belfry formed of four enormous balks of splendid hard-wood timber, with one or more bells; the whole generally in excellent repair and order, where not utterly ruined by the war; the padre still much looked up to by an easy-going, rather superstitious flock, whose morals would perhaps leave something to be desired in a good Anglo-Saxon community.

I must say a word about the orange-trees of Paraguay. They were planted by the Jesuits everywhere, and have flourished in a way I have never seen in any other country I have been in. They grow into forest trees forty feet high. One splendid old avenue between two *capillares* is twelve miles long, and a double row each side. They bear more or less all the year round, and when most prolific I have seen a heap of oranges at a railway-station four to five feet high.

The railway was rather a curiosity, mended and patched - line, carriages, and engines - after the use and abuse of the war. One little engine was the one which ran by Balaclava from the sea to the camp in the Crimea! It now and then ran half the day without breaking down.

The engines had no cow-catchers, a rather risky thing. One day I had been taking a ride with my friend the driver on the engine, and had just got off, and into the last carriage. I was dozing off, when I was awakened by a great bumping, and found we had run over a bullock, and the engine was on its side.

I was well out of it, as one man on the engine had a compound fracture of his leg. I tried to set it, but had little knowledge of compound fractures, though a small experience of simple. We did what we could, but the poor thing died two days after. I heard that a native surgeon took off his leg, so the end was natural.

One thing struck me at the place when the accident happened - the number of centipedes disturbed and running about. They were rather common everywhere. One evening I was writing, and saw my kitten playing with some thing on the floor. I found it was a centipede, some inches long, so I took the liberty of putting my foot on its head, and my kitten at once made a meal off it.

The Guarani language is very curious, and is not well known in Europe, but it is rich in expression. I remember having a long talk about it to that charming omni-linguist, Max Müller, soon after my return, when sitting next him at dinner at All Souls College.

The Jesuits left no books in it, so we could only pick it up anyhow. I amused some spare moments in turning a Spanish Ollendorf into Guarani.

I got to express myself a little in it, but once, when lost by myself up-country, I was very much at a loss to understand the replies to my efforts. Some words sounded long. An egg was *eruguassuerupia*!

As to minerals in the country, there were reports of gold, but I don't think they have come to anything. I think there is mercury, for we found what I am sure was the red cinnabar, but had no time to attend to it.

But the climate and scenery are ideal for a man disgusted with Europe, who wants to escape right away, who has enough to keep him in ease - not much would be necessary there - and who takes with him enough books, etc., to furnish a home.

Though I had more than a year's distraction and worry beyond words, I could appreciate the possibilities of paradise there.

As to health, there is malaria, but not a very bad sort, and the Paraguayans have it to a considerable extent, and soon get over it.

Two English friends turned up for a short time there - my old neighbour on the Pampas, James Trotter, late R.N., and that amusing, versatile traveller and writer, Cunninghame Graham, who has written an interesting history of Paraguay.

The size and variety of spiders one came across was curious. Of course, there were the big hairy tarantulas, whose legs would more than cover a large plate, and who were said to be of a poisonous, biting order; but I never heard of anyone the worse for their bite. I saw a hen go for one one day. He showed fight, but she hit him on the head, and soon had him piecemeal and distributed among her brood.

There is a nasty little red-headed brute, whose bite killed the brother of a lady I knew.

There was a gregarious one, which built an enormous nest, some feet across, and the inhabitants of it looked as large as hazel-nuts. I rode right into one once in the dark, and was all over cobweb and spiders. Most unpleasant!

The enormous wasps or hornets were very tiresome. They built hanging nests from roof-beams and thatch. I used to worry them by taking a gun and putting some powder in it, and, with the muzzle close to the nest, blowing them to pieces in the evening. Once up-country there was a nest right at the top, out of reach, inside the roof of my room, which was bed, sitting, and office room. One night a brute dropped on my head while writing, and I was sore for some time from the result.

I saw some large buildings, deserted, which had been an arsenal during the war. There must have been millions of these stinging things about them.

The piques or jiggers were a great bother. They get under the skin, generally of the foot, and, if not extracted, make a nest, lay eggs, and, if not looked after, loss of limb, or even life, may follow. Constant inspection, sharp eyes, and a needle are necessary, and the natives rub in a little tobacco-ash after the extraction. My unlucky colonists were dreadfully worried by them.

Chapter XII

PARAGUAY LAWSUITS

On my return from Paraguay I found my father living at Worcester, in the residence of his canonry. The house was inside the large square, with grass and trees in the centre, surrounded by the houses of canons and a few laymen, which was called College, and was shut in by an old gateway and lodge, where lived the porter with the sweet name of Dearlove.

The cathedral occupied all one side of College, and the Severn ran at one end. Our house was very comfortable, some of it very old, and it had a very nice garden, which ran up to the cathedral wall.

I stayed there a little, and then went to London. I soon found plenty of occupation in the squabbles and lawsuits which rose out of the unfortunate termination of the emigration scheme to Paraguay. I have never been able to understand how clever and otherwise sensible business men ever conceived such a useless, unnecessary, wild-goose scheme as that.

First a man sued me for breach of contract, saying that he had been promised to be taken to Paraguay, and then located on a farm, and provided with several acres and a cow, besides other things, and now he was back in England, poorer than when he started out.

I proved that I was not in any way personally responsible, so that I was not attacked again.

The whole thing got much talked about, and my old friend Lord Camperdown offered to ask about it in the Lords, and Lord Randolph Churchill the same in the Commons; but as Sir Frederick St. John had, with great kindness and much work, provided as far as possible for the unlucky people, I did not see much use in making the affair more public than it was.

I don't now feel sure that I was right in letting the whole matter drop, but the question to my mind was, To whom would it do any good?

As long as I was out of it with a whole skin and my liberty I had to consider myself lucky, and though I might be called a fool for ever getting into it, and though I left it, as Lord Esher implied after one trial and Lord Bramwell after another "without a stain on my character", like any young ass wrongly accused of burglary, it was hardly satisfactory. But, as the French say, "c'est facile d' entrer dans une cage de lions, mais, d'en sortir!" Even as long ago as Virgil: "Facilis descensus averni, sed revocare pedem, hic labor, hoc opus est!" I gaily entered into the cage, like a young ass flattered by the excitement of a new venture and all sorts of prospects. I remember being told: "Why, if you make a real success of it, they will call you the Paraguayan Englishman!" A little flattery to an enterprising boy goes a long way, and all that was wanted was some semi-philanthropic parade to boom the loan to the gulls of the public, when they might just as well have made a loan to the Esquimaux, with Polar bears as securities!

I only wish I had known as much about it all as I do now! What fun I could have had! But an artificial colony like that was foredoomed to certain failure.

No doubt either Lord Camperdown or that then most energetic, rising man, Lord Randolph, would have made a great sensation by raising a discussion on it in either House; but, personally, I was so weary of it all, and so longing for a rest and an entire change from the subject, that I did not see what good I could do either to the colonists or to myself.

If I could have been transported straight to London when I wrote my letter to Mr. Maurice, I should have been ready to crucify the whole lot of them; but five weeks' steamer to England had cooled down my indignation, and I landed penniless and deeply in debt, with the hands of my creditors hard upon my heels.

Incidentally it came up when Henry James's committee went into the question of all those South American loans, and I much feared that I should be called as a witness about it, but was luckily spared that unpleasant ordeal.

I had the trouble, worry, and expense of two trials on which I was a witness, and had to see that I was well advised and kept clear of any responsibility.

One was brought by a man who had paid something to go out and get a farm, and he sued the London people for breach of contract, and it very much turned on whether I had done all in my power to provide him with all that had been promised.

It was tried before Bramwell, who always made a trial interesting. The plaintiff fenced a good deal on the point as to whether he ever was shown, and so far placed upon, the spot of ground marked out for him at Itapé, and Bramwell said to him in his very blunt manner: "By the way that you are giving your evidence you lead me to think that you are not speaking the truth!" To one of the defendants he said: "It seems to me that it is lucky for you that this is not a criminal court!"

In commenting on the evidence to the jury he was very severe on some of the witnesses, but when it came to my turn he said: "As to Seymour's evidence, you can take it ,from me that he was speaking the truth!"

The other trial was an action brought by some of the people in Paraguay and Buenos Ayres who had discounted my bills drawn to provide food for the people.

Sir Baliol Brett, afterwards Lord Esher, than whom no better judge nor kinder gentleman ever sat on the Bench, was judge.

It was anything but pleasant to me, and I never wish to go through such a time again. I was threatened with all sorts of prosecutions by the agent of the plaintiffs, and that very clever, but I will say very fair, counsel, Benjamin, treated me to a very long cross-examination.

His was a curious career. Distinguished lawyer in South Carolina, he was driven by the War of Secession to London, where he rose to a very high position before he died, still young.

My prosecutor insisted that I should make a statement in court. I told him it would not be allowed, but he raved about all sorts of evils if I would not try.

I got up and asked the judge if I might make a statement. More than one of the witnesses had said that they wanted to clear their characters before they left the box. Sir Baliol said: "Do you too, Mr. Seymour, wish to clear your character I said: "No, my lord; I will leave my character to your lordship". He smiled and said: "You will be very wise in doing so!" He said that if it was to correct my evidence I might do so, but that I could not add anything new.

Everything mortal comes to an end, and I had indeed had quite enough of Paraguay, its loan, its settlers, and its lawsuits.

Beautiful as it is, it is not a climate for English agriculturists. A paradise for gardeners, and the Gran Chaco is splendid for cowboys.

A country in which a change of Government is effected constitutionally by revolution is not one to which to make loans, and a clever native told me seriously that when the people were tired of a President and his Ministers, a revolution was the correct thing. They liked a little fighting, and bore no malice afterwards.

I had returned to live at the old rabbit-warren in Clarges Street, and used the St. James's Club as a home.

Chapter XIII

LONDON: SCRAPES, CLUBS, ETC.

I was a good deal in Worcester, where my father had unfortunately become a confirmed invalid.

The Dean of Worcester was that pleasantest and kindest of men, Grantham Yorke. He had begun life in the Navy, and had married his pretty, delightful wife, sister of Alfred Montgomery, when a young officer, and had taken her in a small ship to the West Coast of Africa. He afterwards took Orders, and later on was Dean of Worcester. His house was always bright and pleasant to visit. The old Deanery is a charming house, standing high above the Severn, with a lawn sloping to it, and looking away over it to the Malvern Hills.

The house is old and rambling, some of it very old.

He died while my father was at Worcester, and was greatly regretted by everyone.

It was during his time that the controversy arose as to the triennial Musical Festival. Lord Dudley, who had done a great deal towards the restoration of the cathedral, though scarcely a very strictly religious man, was greatly opposed to its being held in the cathedral, as it had been, in conjunction with Gloucester and Hereford in turn, for a very long time.

He put great and, as I privately knew, most undue pressure on the Dean to compel him to comply with his wishes.

It all ended with a compromise, and the festival has taken its turn ever since regularly. An effort was made to clothe the artists in surplices, but Sainton said: "I cannot fiddle in a nightgown!"

I was a steward one year, and it was a very pleasant and interesting experience.

Grantham Yorke was succeeded by my cousin, Lord Alwyne Compton, and he and his wife, who had been one of the beauties of London, took a very great interest in their large and charming house.

They began to repair and do it up, but the first result of disturbing the drains was that the butler died of enteric fever and Lady Alwyne was very ill. They went away for a time, and as I was on the spot I had the interesting amusement of routing up all the drains and curious old foundations. Among other things we found a deep well, utterly unknown, covered over. Some of the drains were of the sketchiest nature that I ever saw, but the necessary part was fairly straight before they returned; she, I am glad to say, in excellent health again.

The taste with which they did up that most interesting house must be seen to be realized.

Lady Alwyne's brother, Noel Anderson, was my intimate friend, first at Charterhouse, then at Christ Church, and again in the Admiralty. He was very good-looking, and very popular in London, but was unluckily not very strong, and died young.

I was able, by the kindness of the Dean and Lady Alwyne, to do a service to that brilliant and gifted man, Russell Lowell, when he was minister here. I had the good fortune to know him fairly well, and I found that he was much interested to know something of the house of his ancestors in Worcestershire. I mentioned it to them, and they kindly asked him to the Deanery, to make his pilgrimage to the ancient home of his penates.

My cousin, Lord Alwyne, left Worcester to take the Bishopric of Ely, where he succeeded Dr. Woodford. That excellent man had great learning, but ordinary country life did not come among his acquirements.

A story was told that once, in reading about Nathan's parable to David, he said: "Now the poor man had one *ee wee* lamb". The humorous Sam Wilberforce, who heard him, said: "Why do you pronounce it like that? What do you think it means?" "Oh, it means one *very little lamb!*"

About sheep he knew but little, as this story shows. When made Bishop of Ely, someone said to him: "There is a little farm by the Palace, and you can keep some animals". "Oh", said the Bishop, "then

I will keep a sheep, and have fresh kidneys for breakfast every morning!"

I happened to be at Worcester when there was an unusually high flood. My brother, now Sir Edward Seymour, was there also, and one day we took a boat and, with one of my sisters, rowed down to Tewkesbury. The river was so high that we went clean over the locks, only the lock-house being visible. We took train at Tewkesbury to come back, and, as we were leaving the bridge, saw a crowd watching something. They said it was a small boy, who had fallen off the bridge, and we could see something floating in the distance. My brother and I went in, and when we got to him, found that he was lying on his back, his arms under his head, and his clothes so greasy that they kept him up. He was sensible, and weeping gently! We took him back and delivered him to his friends, only wet. The stationmaster kindly kept the train for us, and we returned rather wet to Worcester. I often wondered what became of him. He was a mischievous urchin, and had thrown stones at Lord Beauchamp's carriage. I think the present Lord Beauchamp bears him no malice.

While at Worcester time hung rather on my hands, so I tried writing a novel. It was not a success, and I do not think that it quite deserved to be, so I will not say much about it, or even mention its name, for it was published under a *nom de plume*. A friend, who thought he would make it go by a startling critique in the *Morning Post*, began with, "This clever but somewhat revolting book!" Save me from my friends! Another wrote: "This book may simply be called 'Adultery made Easy'!" But, compared to the run of novels today, it was nearer one of Miss Yonge's novels in social morality.

Another writing experience of mine was a considerable period with "Tommy" Bowles as assistant on *Vanity Fair*. This experience was amusing and instructive. I had with me, under "Tommy", that clever and most charming companion, Lord Desart. We saw a great deal of each other, and on the evening after going to press always dined together and made a night of it.

I remember one evening we went to the Princess's Theatre, where "The Colonel" had just been put on. We took Coghlan with us to supper at the Lotus Club - that good-looking, cheery man and fine actor. We asked him what he thought of the piece, and he said he thought that it would run for a few weeks, while they got something else ready; but it turned out an enormous success. How very hard it is for the most experienced to judge of how the public will take a piece!

I always think of Coghlan as the ideal of Charles Surface, in "The School for Scandal", in his sky-blue satin suit. He looked so handsome - just what one pictures a "rake" of those days.

The Lotus Club was a Bohemian gathering which had its home in Langham Place, and of it I was a member.

Small-talk, supper, music, and flirtation made the evenings very pleasant. Many of the most charming actresses were members, and many actors, artists, writers, and a crowd of people who were something known, used to meet there.

Fatty Coleman was one of the active promoters of it, and I remember his great indignation the night when he caught a friend of mine kissing his niece rather over-affectionately.

We were amused one Sunday evening by opposition music in the adjoining rooms. That irresponsible, jovial young gentleman, Hughie Drummond, was diverting the audience with the then new song of "Over the Garden Wall". There were, however, a few people who tried to take the club seriously and artistically.

We heard in the next room Mrs. Bernard Beere and Willy Wilde solemnly performing "Sweet Vale of Avoca" as a protest, and its thrilling melancholy, mingling with the cats' yowls over the garden wall, formed a decided contrast!

Hughie Drummond, whose death everyone lamented, was a very good man of business in the City, but of irrepressible spirits in the West. I remember him one night outside the Orleans Club defying the police, sitting on the bar at the top of a lamp-post, and reading Lord Wolseley's book of hints to soldiers and policemen to them as they waited for him to come down.

I was now living in rooms in Queen Anne's Gate, with a very large sitting-room, which had a big bow-window looking north over St. James's Park. Here I was most comfortable, and now and then had a lively supper-party after the theatre.

That pleasant comrade and gifted artist, Chartran, came over to do some work for Tommy Bowles in *Vanity Fair*. I saw a good deal of him, and introduced him as a guest at the St. James's Club. He had rather a weakness for écarté, then played there fairly high, and I fear that his earnings by the brush were rather reduced by the turn of the cards.

Having no painting-room in London, he borrowed my large sitting-room, with its fine northern light, and there painted two or three very clever portraits. I was immensely interested to see the facility with which he painted, and he told me that he considered the French students studied much longer and harder than was the habit with English painters.

I once observed to an artist that the distance between a really good amateur and a moderate professional artist was generally so very wide, and he said: "It would be very hard if it were not, considering that the worst artist has given quite three or four years to study, and that the amateur has had little or no real training". In reality, the good amateurs have worked very hard, but how very few of them there have been! A painter like Admiral Sir Edward Inglefield is very rare.

Of course, my dear old friend Sir Francis Grant only painted for years as an amateur, and, well as he painted, critics always said he would have done better with more early training. I saw a great deal of those two inimitable caricaturists, Pelligrini and Leslie Ward, who did so much for *Vanity Fair*.

Pelligrini was a typical Neapolitan. Genial, humorous, happy-go-lucky, and gifted, he was the ideal of a Bohemian artist and *bon camarade*. He was as good a mimic as he was caricaturist. He could exactly imitate the expression and gesture of his victims, who, he said, he sometimes let off easy.

His English was delightful, and gave a point to his humorous way of putting things.

I went one day into his room, and he took the sheet off a large canvas on an easel with pride, and said: "Is it not 'im?" There was a good portrait of Gillie Farquhar. I said: "Yes, it is first-rate; but why have you painted him in a fog?" "My fellow! You do not understand! That is the thing!"

Jimmy Whistler had set the misty fashion, which I believe many connoisseurs much admire.

Jimmy I knew fairly well, not very intimately. He was a remarkable character, as well as an artist, and very good company - could say very smart things. One day, at lunch, he said something very funny, and Oscar Wilde, from the other end of the table, said: "Very good, Jimmy! Very good! I wish I had said it". "But you will, Oscar - you will!"

Dear old Pelican! He died much too soon. He was humorous up

to the end. He said to his faithful body-servant, William: "William, William, bring me a clean shirt. I go die!"

Leslie Ward I had much to do with, and often helped him to see and sketch the so-called victims, though there were many seekers after celebrity who sought hard to be immortalized in *Vanity Fair*, but who swaggered afterward, saying, "I don't know how the Devil the fellow ever saw me", when they had bothered to sit or stand for their likeness!

Tommy Bowles happened to be away in his yacht when Parnell was to be put in, and I went to call on him with Leslie Ward, and to interview him. He was then little known, but many looked for his future already. I found him a most taking personality. No one who talked to him for some time could fail to be struck by his strength of character and grasp of things.

I wrote the notice of him signed "Jehu Junior", and on his return Tommy said that I had made too much of him, and that I should have rather pooh-poo'd him; but I assured him that I was certain we should see and hear a great deal more of him.

Another acquaintance I made in the same way was Captain Boycott, the origin of the word now used in many languages. He was interesting at the moment, but only unhappy circumstances had made him such a prominent individual.

About this time there existed two most pleasant clubs which I often frequented - the Orleans at Twickenham, and the Orleans in King Street, St. James's.

The country one was started by the well-known and justly popular Sir John Astley, the mate, and it occupied Orleans House, once the abode of exiled French royalty.

Many most amusing parties were given there, and those who were not invited called it "fast", and all sorts of bad names.

It was very well managed, and one could go on the river in the afternoon, or on a fine evening sit on the charming terrace giving on the Thames.

One evening I was sitting there with a fair lady, when some cad from the river began to chaff, and she injudiciously made some reply, which she got back at once with interest; and then to me: "Why don't you marry her, and make an honest woman of her?"

Many pleasant little dinners and suppers have I given at the one in King Street. There one had to write the name of one's guests in a book, but curiosity led to too many members examining it in the morning, to see who the couples were, so that it had to be kept only for the inspection of the committee.

I often used to arrange a *partie carrée* for the theatre, Orleans, or Maidenhead, one of the most delightful ways of spending an afternoon and evening. My male companion was often that genial and eccentric individual, Sir Charles Forbes of Newe.

The importance which Charlie could assume was superhuman, and he nearly always got his own way.

He was going one evening to a ball at Buckingham Palace, and asked a friend to drive down with him in a hansom. When they got to the entrance, the cab was, of course, stopped, but Charley said: "What! Why, you don't know me! I'm Sir Charles Forbes of Newe. Drive on, cabman!" And he got through.

At the Westminster Aquarium the great sword-swallower was putting all sorts of unpleasant things into his "little Mary", and Charley asked him to swallow a very smart cane, with his full name and titles on the gold handle. "Oh no, Sir Charles; I can't swallow all that!" was the ready reply.

The place of all others which I did then, and still do, love best of all is the dear old river at Maidenhead.

Saturday, Sunday, or other quiet days, there is nowhere so charming. Nothing in the world can beat in its way the scenery of Taplow and Clieveden Woods, and that reach of the river, and away up to Marlow.

The scene of Boulter's Lock on Ascot Sunday has become famous everywhere, and no other place in the world can show together so many pretty and so becomingly dressed women.

No one knows what a river-party can be like till they have enjoyed a well-assorted one, and dined there. Then a turn in a punt on a warm evening makes a most fitting finale to a delightful day.

I have often and often lunched and dined at Skindles in the many years past. There are now one or two other hotels, but I prefer my old love, Skindles.

For many years Charley Hammersley and his most kind and hospitable sister, Miss Hammersley, kept open house, first in a prettily overgrown house close to the bridge, and then at Bourne End, and many a time have I been a guest, and met some of the pleasantest of men and women there.

Miss Hammersley used often to get up an eight-oar, manned by some of the best oars on the river, and steer it herself. I was hard to press into that service, as I preferred my own particular friend of the occasion in a punt.

I remember an incident that made us laugh very much one evening. There had come down a party, one of which was the well-known Bay Middleton. Dinner was over, and Bay had invited a very pretty woman, who was perhaps not used to such frisky society, to take a turn in a punt in the cool of the evening with him.

Off they went into the darkness. Presently we heard from under a tree a squeak, and then: "Oh, don't, Captain Middleton! Don't! I'm an honest woman!" Then the deep voice of Bay, who was rather deaf: "What's that?" He was evidently, as the nigger said, "paying her some attention!"

I had a curious experience myself down there. We went down a large party, and after dinner we went on the river again. I and my companion found our company so pleasant that we were quite oblivious as to time. Presently we happened to see the lights of a train going over the bridge, and she said: "I wonder what time it is?" I looked at my watch and said: "Good Lord! That's the last train". She said: "If I cannot get home to-night, I can never go home!" We got to the station, and the station-master said: "If there's an engine with steam up anywhere about, you can have a special". There was one at Windsor, and we ran up very quickly, so no harm was done. But was seven-and-sixpence a mile too dear for half an hour on the river with her?

There was about this time in London one of the pleasantest and most convenient places to meet your friends that London has ever known. I mean Princes Club.

Where Cadogan Place now is was then a cricket-ground, lawn-tennis courts, racquet courts, and the well-known roller-skating rink.

"Everyone" - as they say - belonged to it. There you met all your friends. It saved nearly all the trouble of visiting, and one could make up all the parties and engagements that make life pleasant.

In summer in the open air, and in winter in the "Elephant House", as we called it.

There naturally grew up many jealousies between non-members and members, and later on the rather absurd rule was made that only ladies who had been presented at Court could be members. But the committee were not always insistent that ladies should present their marriage lines - I mean their Court certificates!

I had a great fuss about a very pretty woman who had been so silly as to make enemies, and I packed her and her husband off to make their bows, and then, with the help of my friend Duppy (Lord Dupplin), got her safely in.

One funny story was told of a girl whose mother said to her: "Now, my dear, take off your skates; we must go home". "All right, mother; I'll just have one more turn, and then I'm off!" And so she was, but to Paris with a young gentleman! They were married there, but it ended in the Divorce Court.

Chapter XIV

SCOTLAND

I used at this time to go and stay with my old friend Jock Baird of Knoydart, at his wild place on the coast of Inverness.

It was the centre of the great property of Invergarry, and lay between Loch Orn and Loch Nevis. There was no road within some forty miles of it, so that the only approach to it was by sea, and without a steam-yacht a man there would be completely isolated.

It is true that every fortnight or so the well-known boats up the west coast, the *Clansman* and the *Clydesdale*, used to call in there, but if rough, the landing was a scramble, and once one of my portmanteaux went into the sea.

The first time I went up my host was not married, so we had a bachelor party. He brought up a French chef, and did us extremely well, but the hard work in the hills quite prevented good living doing any harm.

There was not much shooting, as grouse and stags do not go together, and the fishing was very precarious, the rivers running out so quickly; but the stalking was excellent, and the forest very wild and broken, so that it was really hard work and fine sport.

Jock Baird was remarkably strong and active, and had done one or two great feats in distance walking in England, so that he was a tough companion to go out stalking with. We had some first-rate sport, and one day I had the good luck to stalk three good stags and get all three.

We got as near as we could, but the old gillie said at last that we could get no nearer. "It's a verra lang shot, aboot two hundred and fifty yards". Presently one got up and stood broadside on. I got him tight through the heart, and another sprang up, and, having got the range, I hit him in exactly the same place.

The young gillie jumped in the air and clapped me on the back; the old one only said: "Shoove in another cartridge". The third stag did not see us, and came galloping past, and I bowled him over.

When impossible to fish, I and one of the gillies used to walk quietly away and spear a salmon, without regard for that being a forbidden sport, but it was just as good to eat.

People who have never tried may think it easy to spear and land a fish, but they will find that it is not so by any means.

I went to Knoydart later on when my friend Jock was married to a charming wife, and life was very pleasant, and we made long trips in the old yacht *Griffin*.

Towards the end of one visit I had the bad luck, in twisting round behind a rock to get a shot, to put out something in my knee. I had some trouble in doing the nearly fifteen miles home with the help of the gillies over very rough ground.

Next day the yacht was sent to Skye to fetch a surgeon, and a strong young man arrived, who thought that main force would do as well as skill. He had plenty of that, and rather took away my breath by his efforts of muscular power, which were quite in vain. I managed to limp about, but was no good for a distance.

When I got back to London Wharton Hood put it right for me, but it was loose for a year or two, only I learnt to put it in for myself.

I had a curious experience of the anæsthetic, ether and chloroform, which he gave me. I said I did not want it, as I wanted to see what he did, but he said it was so much easier to do on a non-resistant patient.

I heard what he said to the ether administrant, and told him word for word afterwards, but though I knew exactly what he was doing, I could feel no pain, and had no power to resist whatever.

Ether and chloroform, luckily for me, have no after-effect but one of exhilaration. And I got to giving it to myself when I did not sleep well, but once woke up after a twelve-hours sleep with the empty bottle in my hand ! Of course, the wonder is that I woke up at all! It was rather a warning, but what an easy end! I love the feeling of taking chloroform myself, though most people find it stifling and pernicious.

Of course, the Laird had to be very particular in observing the Sabbath, and we paid full attention to the performances of a curious minister.

Old James Baird, the former Laird of Knoydart, had been a great supporter of the kirk, and made to it the magnificent donation of half a million. A large fire insurance!

He was rough and plain-spoken enough. His nephew told me he remembered one wet Sunday when the kirk was very close and "niffy", the Laird from his pew inhaled the perfume of damp shepherds and gillies, and said in an audible voice: "Baad smell they Heelanders!"

I saw one Sunday a row of small boys very well in order, with their hands behind them, and the old deer-hound with us, weary of the entertainment, walked up and licked the face of each in turn, they not daring to resist.

Many stories are told of the peculiarities and remarkable utterances of Scotch ministers, and the following actually occurred.

In the Highlands the collie dogs mostly came to kirk with the shepherds, and at times expressed their impatience of an extra-long sermon by the lashing of their tails on the floor.

They also got the habit, when the congregation rises at the end of the sermon for the minister to give the blessing, of rushing tumultuously out.

One day the "meenister" said at the end of his sermon: "And noo, my brethren, I will give the blessing with the congregation sitting. Not that I mean any disrespect to Almighty God, but just to cheat the whelpies!"

Another day he was preaching about St. Peter and the cock crowing, and he drew this curious moral lesson from the story: "Puir Peter! Puir Peter! This is what comes of keepin' low company, and stan'in' talkin' wi' a common servant girl!"

Another I did not hear may not be greatly known, of the minister who was praying for fine weather, and in the middle came a violent squall of sleet against the window. He turned towards it and exclaimed: "Oh Lard, this is simply ridic'lous!"

But to get rather mixed is not confined to Scotch divines. A man told me he heard an English curate, preaching about the parable of the Ten Virgins, appeal to those present: "Oh, consider, my brethren, which part would you choose to watch with the wise virgins, or to sleep with the foolish ones?"

Jock Baird was not content with home shooting, but made a most successful raid on Africa with Colonel George Brownlaw Knox, and who was so well known in London as "Curly Knox". It was before the days of the Mahdi and the closing of the Soudan, and the Seteet was a most happy hunting-ground of big-game shooters. They made between them a very large bag of elephants, lions, and various other beasts.

Baird also brought home some lion cubs, which I visited with him at the Zoo, but they had quite forgotten him.

Strong and healthy as he was then, his health later gave way, and to my great regret he died while still young.

CHAPTER XV

GUNMAKER AND STORIES

About this time I tried yet another profession, and joined Lionel Gye, late R.A., and my friend Lynedoch Moncrieff, who had retired from the Navy, and had together started in the gun and rifle business in St. James's Street.

I found it very interesting, and learnt all the secrets of the trade at Birmingham and at Liége. We did much business with Scott and with Webley, of Birmingham, whose businesses were afterwards joined in a company, and have been so well known.

We could not complain of doing a bad business, but it takes a great deal of retail dealing to provide profit enough for three men like us to live in comfort. As long as we could get large orders of military arms from abroad it did very well, but that is a very casual class of business.

I used to try every gun and rifle myself at the firing-ground a little out of London, and in showing off to buyers guns of different bends of stock, I soon could adapt my holding to any shape. I think the straightest stocks we ever made were for that first-rate shot and most popular man, Archie Stuart Wortley, whose very clever shooting pictures were so much run after.

I found the big-elephant rifles knocked one's shoulders about a good deal with the big bullet and heavy charges, but the accuracy of their shooting was marvellous. The firing from a rest to insure accurate aim shakes the firer much more than just holding the rifle without one.

We had a tent at Wimbledon in the shooting-time, and gave a prize to be shot for at the running deer.

We were never dull in our shop, as friends loafing in St. James's Street constantly dropped in for a chat.

The following curious incident happened to me while there. That popular man and good sailor, Sir Reginald Macdonald, Chief of Clanranald, known everywhere as "Rim", came in one morning and said: "We elected you last night a member of Pratt's". Pratt's Club is a small and rather select little society made up largely of Guardsmen, which had its home just off St. James's Street.

I thanked him for telling me, and said I had always wished to belong, as I had several friends in it.

A few days passed, and I heard nothing from the secretary so I saw Rim, and told him, and he said he was quite certain of it, and remembered that when my name came up, the Duke of Beaufort, who was chairman, and whom I had not the pleasure of knowing, asked about me. Two or three friends of mine on the committee all said something pleasant about me; the Duke remarked: "He has chosen two curious members for proposer and seconder" - who, though very popular men, were rather remarkable characters - and Rim said that I was elected without the ballot-box going round. Another member of the committee told me exactly the same thing, so I went to the secretary, and there was "Not elected" on my page.

How it came about my friends could not make out, but my eccentric proposers did not bother themselves, and I was not keen enough about it to stir them up strongly.

Gye, who was a very clever mechanic, was much interested in a magazine gun of the Gatling order. We worked at it, and spent too much money over it, to my thinking, but it was no use to compete with Maxim's gun.

That was in the early days of breech-loaders, and hammer-less guns were just then rapidly coming in; this made it risky to lay in any stock, as one improvement after another came along so fast.

I was now living in what they call a maisonnette in Victoria Street. The basement, ground-floor, and entresol of one of the great houses of flats, with its own private door, made up the establishment, and I was most happy there, as it was an ideal place for a bachelor. Many pleasant little dinners and suppers did I have there in those palmy days!

At this time I used sometimes to go in the evening to the head-quarters of the Fire Brigade, then in Watling Street, as one of the pleasant little group of friends of my dear old friend Captain Shaw, and wait for the call to a fire large enough to be interesting to go and see.

He used also to have evening parties now and again, when a dozen or so men and ladies met at his place, and he drove us in two or three large vans round some of the fire-stations, which he wished to turn out for drill, to see if they were up to the mark in speed. We went at full gallop, and ended at Greenwich, where a fire-float was waiting, in which we returned to Westminster Bridge.

The society was always very pleasant, and dear old Shaw had a great eye for pretty, amusing women! I remember one evening a very pretty little woman was there who had a sprained ankle, and she engaged me for the evening to carry her about in our changes of conveyance, which I did not find a disagreeable occupation!

Between business and pleasure I found that life could be a very enjoyable thing as long as "times were good".

I was fortunate enough to see a good deal of very varied society at that time and for the next few years, and I hope I may be allowed to recall a few incidents and stories of well-known people.

Just at this time occurred the following amusing example of the calmness of an intimate friend.

I had gone out of town for three or four days, and on my return I observed in the corner of one of the rooms a small hamper of wine; so I said to my man: "What on earth is that?" He said: "Oh, that was sent by the gentleman to whom you lent your rooms while you were away". I was naturally surprised, as I had done no such thing, and asked him who it was. He said it was a man he had often seen there at dinner and supper, but he forgot his name. When he described him, there could be no possible mistake, for he was a remarkably good-looking, finely-built man, late of Her Majesty's Household Brigade.

It chanced that I saw him an hour or two later in a hansom near Hyde Park Corner, and hailed the driver, and asked for a lift. He made no remark, so I said: "Well, my dear fellow, I hope you found my rooms to your liking?" For once in his life he actually blushed. "My dear Walter, I will explain it to you. A great friend of mine came up to London, and at the Derby time it was impossible to get into any hotel; so I knew you would take pity on us, and not mind the liberty which I took in coming to your man, who, of course, knew me, and saying that you had said I might occupy your rooms in your absence!"

Of course, I could only laugh, and hope that they had a pleasant time - "Bon site, bon gîte et le reste!" - and I said that it was only his honesty in replacing the wine they had drunk which ever made me know anything about it.

He was a most amusing companion, who had led rather an adventurous life, and I miss him very much among departed friends.

I once had a difficulty with a foreign gentleman which might have led to business, and he, hearing of it, said to me: "My dear Walter, if you should need a second, I will come; I know now how hard it is to get anyone to act!"

I was talking about him one day to Sam Lewis, and Sam said: "Oh yes, I like him; he's a warrior-a real warrior!"

One curious character that I used to meet was a versatile and amusing Irishman, very good-looking, and seductive to ladies.

In the early days of the Divorce Court, so ably presided over by that clever and amusing judge, Sir Creswell Creswell, he became so well known that Sir Creswell asked him whether he was a professional co-respondent, as he saw him there so often.

It was there that I was asked the difference between a cor-re-spondent and a co-respondent. One does write; the other does wrong!

A very pretty cousin of my Irish acquaintance told me how she and her brother disguised him as a powdered footman to escape the bum-bailiffs, and put him on the box of the carriage. He was one day describing a billiard match to a friend, who, thinking the story long, said: "And were you beaten?" "Beaten, was it! Beaten! With Tim, that plays a better cue than I do at the table, and myself at the marking-board! Beaten, was it!"

He died in due course at a mature age as a Marquis in the odour of sanctity!

Among well-known practical jokers was Bay Middleton, that very fine rider and first-rate horseman across country, who piloted the beautiful and charming Empress of Austria when she honoured us with her presence in the hunting-field.

Among stories told of him was that in a country-house he made a bet with a lady that he would hide in her bedroom, and she would not find him.

She retired to rest, locked her door, and began her search. She looked under the bed, and, as Byron says, "there she found no matter what, it was not what she sought". Cupboards, up the chimney, no sign of the adventurous better, so she proceeded to retire to rest, thinking he had given it up.

Just as she was getting into bed she heard a voice "Hulloo! How are you? Here I am!"

Her bed was a wide one, and he had got his friends to make him up as a bolster! And she had to pay her part of the debt.

But he was not always so lucky. In a country-house there was a boy who came to the smoking-room in the evening in ordinary evening dress. Bay said: "Now, look here, we don't allow this; if you join us at night, you must wear proper smoking things. If you come again to-morrow night, I shall cut your coat to the proper shape".

Next night down came the boy in the same togs. Bay said, "I told you the penalty", and proceeded with a penknife to alter the cut of a tail-coat.

Someone said to the boy: "You don't seem to mind much!" The boy said: "No, it's Bay's coat; as I passed his rooms I put his coat on".

A story was told that in a country-house the talk had turned on the figure of a man, "all face", as the Indian said, and how he would look as a decorative statue. Opinions differed, so, to make a living proof of the beauty of form, Bay Middleton persuaded a pal, who always fancied his own elegant figure, to join him in a show, and having slipped out of the dining-room before the ladies left after dinner, they posed, when the ladies went to the drawing-room, on each side of the door, clad only in the traditional fig-leaf of their father Adam.

A curious story is told of the result of an argument about beauty of body, and the assertion of somebody that a sculptor never could find a model so perfect that she would serve as a model for all parts of the body, and that it was necessary to take bits from more than one woman. A beautiful member of the party, celebrated through England, scorned such an accusation of her charming sex. That evening the door of the smoking-room opened, and a figure entered in a long black cloak. The cloak dropped, and there stood the lady in all her glory, and said: "Look there! and where do you want any improvement in the whole of that?"

I knew a house where the cheery and facetious host often used to bring the letters of pretty guests to their rooms in early morn, regardless of abuse and snubs. His guest one day was a lady renowned for her splendid figure. My friend waited till he heard sounds of splashing, and then walked boldly in. Madame cried out: "——, you little pig! Well, now you're here take a good look, for you never saw anything so nice before, and never will again!"

Among the well-known characters I used to meet was Alfred Montgomery, one of the best-looking and most well-bred-looking men in London. He had a slight hesitation in his speech, which gave rather a piquancy to the little amusing things he often said. I remember calling one day on a very pretty woman, and she said: "Alfred Montgomery has just gone; he was regretting advancing years, and said, 'I'm so t-t-tired of being old!' "

I nearly had a serious accident as I was leaving the fair lady that afternoon. I ventured to bend down over her in the low arm-chair in which she was sitting to imprint a chaste salute on her pretty lips. She had on her lap a black poodle, who did not at all approve of this, and his sharp teeth missed my nose by about an inch.

The talk turned one day on a hotel abroad, which someone accused of being haunted by insects of a ferocious kind, and a well-known noble lord, not renowned for the extra polish of his personal, toilet, said: "Not a bit of it! Often I slept there, and never was bitten!" " But, my dear - even a b-b-bug must draw the line somewhere!"

I remember the following absurd incident. A very popular and pleasant Guardsman was taken ill in a country-house with what turned out to be a severe brain fever, and the first sign that he was queer in the head was this:

He was too unwell to come down to dinner, and was supposed to be in bed, but he was not.

He had remarked a stuffed tiger in the house, and thought he would have a show. He placed it sitting up in a small place that opened upon the hall through which people had to pass from the drawing-room to the dining-room, got what candles he could to make an illumination, and, having laid in wait till the dinner procession was coming, opened the door, and displayed his striped friend in its strange position with a pipe in its mouth.

A well-known and most amusing man who I often met tried a very poor practical joke on his host, a rather nervous member of the Upper House in Cheshire.

There was a skeleton in the house. I don't mean the proverbial one of some doubtful marriage, but a real bag of bones strung on wires.

This he got hold of, and placed in the bed of his noble host. His valet or the housemaid saw it there, and warned him of the bed-fellow the guest had prepared for him. Next morning at breakfast the host said: "Mr. ——, there is a train at half-past eleven, and there will be a fly for you at eleven. I don't say I shall never ask you here again, but this visit is at an end".

The same sportsman is said, after a week's very big shooting, to have been asked by his most liberal host to tell the keeper what game he would like to take. Someone having given him a hint that he was not likely to be asked again, he told the keeper to send seventy brace of pheasants to his poulterer in London, which went down against his poultry bill.

I remember a very funny scarf-pin he used to wear, like a little hatchment. One afternoon a lady asked him what it was. It seems that he had been an intimate friend of the well-to-do Mrs. Brown of Hamilton Place, Park Lane, whose house was said to have so long blocked the way to opening the bottom of Park Lane. Having paid much attention to her, he had hopes of a legacy when she was gathered. All he got by the will was a small sum to purchase a souvenir, so he had a pin made like a hatchment, and on it might be read "Done Brown", and the date of the lady's death.

Of country-house stories, the following amused me.

A friend of mine had been a regular guest in a very pleasant house, with very good shooting. But one year he was not invited, and, as he was still an intimate friend of the host, he was puzzled to find out for what reason.

Finding an opportunity, he asked his friend why he had not asked him. He was a bit taken aback, but said: "Well, I'll tell you the truth. You see, one of the maids in the house got into what they call 'trouble', and I found that the culprit was my right-hand man, who is invaluable to me, and with whom I could not part for anything. My wife tackled me about it, and, driven into a corner, I played a low trick on you, who are still a gay bachelor! I said that I was sorry to say it was you who were guilty, and now my wife won't have you in the house! " My friend said it was over-playing it rather low down, but it was done, so it was no use saying anything to the wife!

That most kind-hearted and pleasant companion Kenneth Howard related how he was playing whist with the well-known

Duchess of Cleveland, a lady of the old school of manners and language.

At the end of the deal he said: "Honours are *easy*, Duchess". "Honours are what, Mr. Howard?" "Honours are divided - a very common expression, Duchess". "*Very common indeed*, Mr. Howard!"

Kenneth Howard used hardly ever to go out of London, and rather made a boast that he had never been so far out of London as the Isle of Wight.

He used to amuse us by "taking a rise" out of a well-known member of the Bachelors' Club, who was a mighty stickler for appearance and doing the "correct thing". He was also fond of displaying his dignified form in the window looking on Piccadilly. Kenneth loved to come there in an omnibus, stop it just in front of the window, and kiss his hand to the owner of the disapproving eye looking at a member of the aristocracy and of the club "riding" in the plebeian bus!

I remember this incident returning from some race-meeting in a crowded carriage. A seedy-looking individual, just as the train was reaching the ticket-collecting place, suddenly got off his seat, crept under it, put out his head, and said: "Gentlemen, I trust to your honour!"

Another incident, when one of a party travelling without tickets put on a stiff-looking cap, and went to a carriage near, and said: "Tickets, gentlemen, tickets!" and collected the lot, which he distributed among his pals when he returned.

One curious experience was this. In a first-class compartment at King's Cross, in a train from Scotland, as the collector was coming, a man next the window collected the tickets of the five other passengers, and gave them to the collector, who said: "One short!" Everyone protested he had given up his, and the man insisted that he had put his among them, and, though there was no doubt that he had come down from the North without one, there was nothing to be done, and the railway people gave it up.

I am sure my old friend Reggie Herbert will forgive me for relating this humorous trick he played on a travelling companion.

They were coming from some distant place to London, and he dropped his ticket on the floor of the carriage, and Reggie put his foot on it, and then put it into his pocket. When they got near London, his pal said "What shall I do? I have lost my ticket!" Reggie said: "Oh, get under the seat, and I will hide you with this rug". So he did. When the collector came Reggie gave him the two tickets, and the collector said: "But where is the other traveller?" Reggie lifted up the rug, and said: "There he is; he has curious fancies, and often enjoys travelling under the seat!"

CHAPTER XVI

SHAFTESBURY ELECTION

*W*hile I was staying at Worcester with my father, I had a letter from my friend Vere Fane Benett, of Pythouse, who was M.P. for Shaftesbury; and being forced by the Dissolution to stand a contest for his scat, he asked me to come and help him.

We had a most amusing and lively time. To be a "big-bug" in politics has the drawback of publicity in all said and done, when, as the Scotchman said: "There's a chiel amang ye tacking notes, and faith, he'll print 'em!" But in small places elections are sort of family affairs, and nothing gets further than the *Eatanswill Gazette* and *Independent*. You can say anything you like as long as it amuses the crowd, and tends to make them laugh at the other side.

It is much harder to defend a seat than to attack it.

The "outs" can promise to do almost any mortal thing, whereas the "ins" are painfully conscious of failures and of the disappointments of constituents.

My candidate companion had a ready wit, and was often very amusing. We went the usual rounds. Of course, he used to speak first, and then I fired my gun. As he had first go, I could not exactly repeat his sayings, but more than once he would say, "What was that, Walter, that you said about Gladstone?" and then he would borrow my ammunition at the next meeting we went on to, and leave me to invent something new.

He amused me one day by a fine, florid peroration, when he said: "And think, my friends, of those glorious days when, at the great Battle of Waterloo, we fought the whole of Europe!"

When I smiled afterwards, he said it did not matter - very few of them knew better.

Bribery still hung about, but it was a risky affair, and the ballot has always made it an unsatisfactory way of spending money. I have often asked men who have had something to do with it what they thought happened when a man was bribed by both sides. The opinion seemed to be that he generally voted for the one who bribed last, such being the working of the so-called conscience of the free and independent.

I have reason to think our opponents did spend money that way, for, a few months afterwards, I was dancing with a charming lady at a ball in London, who had been interested in the election, and I said: "We felt sure that you bribed, but our agent could never find any evidence how it was done". She laughed and said: "Do you remember meeting me and —— in a victoria one afternoon, when you were riding round with Mrs. Benett? Well, we had a bag of sovereigns in the carriage, and were going round".

The fatal day arrived, and I watched in the streets for agreed signs at the window of how it was going; but alas! the wrong way for us!

When the result was declared, there was a hostile demonstration against the victor, and he and his friends were kept prisoners for many hours by the enemy.

Vere Benett had a basket packed at the hotel with food and wine for the prisoners, which I took to them, being well known to the crowd, and allowed to pass.

We sadly drove home, and as we passed the cricket ground, Vere made us laugh by saying in a sad voice: "And to think how I have run my fat tum-tum up and down on that ground to please those ungrateful brutes!"

Though defeat is always vexatious, my friend bore up, and stood the loss of what once was called the best club in London (but not now) with equanimity.

I have had several pleasant visits at his always cheery and easy-going house since then - the best of everything, and host and hostess kindly let their well-assorted guests amuse themselves, instead of their being, as too often in country-houses, "under orders". Alas! he is one of the many old friends whom I sadly miss.

I hope I may be forgiven if, anent this election, I quote the defeated candidate's lament from some rhymes which I put together in "Howls from the Hustings" after the last election:

"AFTER BYRON.

"Fare you well! Constituents heartless!
    I'm turned out, so we must part;
Sent off like a schoolboy, tartless,
    One last word before we part.

"Could you know my awful brain-rack,
    Canvassing such stupid owls,
Shouting like a cock on grain-stack
    To a flock of gaping fowls.

"Could you know my silent laughter
    At the questions you can ask,
You'd know I shall be glad hereafter:
    You've relieved me of my task.

"Could you know how oft I've voted,
    On hot nights, e'en you would know,
Tho', as thickest numskulls noted,
    'Twas a shame to spurn me so.

"How I cussed to join your football,
    Kicked by every lout in town,
And at bumpkin cricket matches
    Ran my fat tum-tum up and down.

"Popular Candidate, you called me,
    As my rabbit-pies you munched,
And on your silly shoulders hauled me,
    When on my strongest ale you'd lunched.

"But it's done, so no more talking
    I wish your member lots of fun,
Like a young bear first set walking,
    All his troubles just begun".

Henry Labouchere, the versatile and remarkable Member for Northampton, was a great friend of my host the candidate, and amused us much by the letters he wrote, describing the course of his canvassing, and some remarkable posters, among which was one he sent us, very highly coloured, of a soldier tied up and being flogged, flogging in the army being one of the questions of the moment.

I hope he will forgive me if I tell a story related of him when he was long ago a young M.P. - how some elderly M.P., thinking to patronize him, and fancying that he was a son of Lord Taunton, said to him in the Lobby: "I have just been listening to your father speaking". "Have you really? But where?" "Where? Why, in the House of Lords. But why do you ask?" "Well, you see, my father has been dead some years, so I was naturally anxious to know where he might be".

An election story amused us of the very pretty wife of a very well-known candidate who was going round canvassing for her husband. The free and independent to whom she was speaking did not know her by sight, and was not easy to persuade. He said: "They do tell me that he be so precious lazy he can't get up in the morning. Now I don't take much stock of a member like that". "Oh no; I assure you that is not true, and I ought to know, for I am his wife!" "Well, now be you, ma'am? I can only say, if I was his lordship, I s'uld lig a-bed all day!"

Chapter XVII

STOCK EXCHANGE

The gun-making, unluckily, could not last for ever. It was clear at last that it did not pay, and most reluctantly we had to put up the shutters.

I was for a bit once more in my life at a loose end. A friend of mine on the Stock Exchange kindly asked me to come into his office and learn the business, with the idea of taking to it seriously in due course.

I thought it would do no harm, so I attended daily, and learnt a good deal about Contangos, Backwardations, and other mysteries of the "House". Also the difference between a broker and a jobber, though I thought Dr. Johnson's definition of a jobber rather severe, for he calls him: "A low knave who deals in stocks and shares!"

As a clan, the members of the House are as pleasant, cheery, and light-hearted a lot as exist in London. There is an enormous amount of good-fellowship among them, and a great deal of useful, timely help given to lame dogs in a difficulty.

I nearly became a member, having arranged about my sureties, etc., and it was then a rather simpler matter than it now is. Events, however, occurred which caused me to give up that very pleasant profession in good times.

I made some very agreeable friends, and learnt a good deal about a side of life of which the general public, particularly in the West End, know uncommonly little.

I may mention the following curious experience while talking about Throgmorton Street.

Among the men who had speculative accounts open with our office was the secretary of a large trust company, who had a very large salary, and was well off besides. He was popular, and gave pleasant dinners.

I was dining one evening with a broker, a great friend of mine, and he said: "Isn't —— a client of yours?" "Yes; why?" "Has he been going ahead a bit, and lost money, and given you securities?" "Yes, he has". "What does —— say of him?" mentioning a very smart, wideawake man in the office. "Well, he says he is a thief!" He then explained that he owed him about a thousand pounds, and had offered script as security. He said it was security that a man like him was most unlikely to have held, and he felt sure that he was using the funds of the trust.

We talked it over, and he said he must put it before the chairman, who was a friend of his.

This he did next day, and he reluctantly asked the secretary, whom he liked, if he had been speculating and losing. He had to acknowledge it, and when pressed as to the funds, had to confess that he, having the key of the box at the bank, had put his hand in. He named a sum taken, which, when the securities were checked, was, of course, not near the truth. It was a large sum. He remarked: "Well, perhaps it was best you found out. I might have lost the whole lot if things had continued against me".

According to the rules of the Stock Exchange, a broker deals with a man in a position of trust at his own risk; if he loses by him, and tries to recover at law, he ceases to be a member.

This man had dealt with several brokers; some put up with the loss; some defied the directors, and said that if they would not make it good they would make it all public - a severe blow to the company.

The director of the trust who had put in the secretary was a very rich man, and made it good, and very few people ever knew anything about it.

———•◦•———

CHAPTER XVIII

CASUAL STORIES

*I*was always very fond of a day's hunting, and took every possible opportunity of a day with the hounds. And for a man always limited in money, and not a feather-weight, I managed to get a good deal ever since I was nine years old.

My old neighbour in Warwickshire of early days, and always kind friend, Sir William Throckmorton, was for some time Master of the V.W.H. He had a most comfortable hunting-box at Cirencester, and very kindly put me up for a bit of the season. His cook was excellent, and the society very cheery.

Ned Hayward, from Worcestershire, lived and hunted with him, and we used to get four days a week pretty regularly. Hayward and I used to go every Monday with the Duke, as he came to that side of his county on that day, and we got some good gallops in the stone-wall country round Tetbury and Trouble House.

That was in the days of the "Tetbury Goddesses", when that little hunting centre was crowded with pretty huntresses. I have seen more than thirty out, many of them riding very hard and very well, and as jealous as you can imagine of each other.

The Duke was liked, and one may say feared, and kept martinet discipline in the field, which, with such a lot, was perhaps a good thing; but I must say I liked the more free-and-easy ways of the V.W.H. Hunt, and a more patient, sound sportsman than the Baronet could nowhere be found, and excellent sport he showed us; and as to his language, like the Admiral in "Patience", you may say, "Hardly ever".

At another time I paid a long visit to my cousin, George Watson, at Rockingham Castle, when he had the Woodland Pytchley, Lord Spencer hunting the rest of the country. We used to go out with the Woodland when they hunted, and with the Cottesmore on Tailby's other days.

A delightful host and hostess, lively party, charming old house.

One very popular small guest was Driver Brown, the well-known light-weight rider in the Artillery.

One morning, after dancing very late, we were going out, and there was a little frost, which made the ground very nasty. The Driver was going to ride a three-year-old thoroughbred, very fresh. I said something about his mount, but, in his funny voice, he said: "I like young uns; they jump big, and they fall honest".

The dear little Driver was killed afterwards at Sandown, but not riding. There was a great crowd at the station coming away, and he was in a hurry to cross the line. There was a fast train passing behind one standing still, but, being deaf, he could not hear it. Some of us tried to catch hold of him, but he hurried the more, and the engine killed him instantly.

We were amused one morning at breakfast at that most comfortable old house Hanford, where I was staying with the Ker Seymers, by the following. Our hostess said: "Is Joe Maidstone going to hunt to-day?" Someone went to see, and said he found him trying what he called his "jumpometre" - that is, to see if he had the "jumps" too bad to ride, for we had been dancing all night.

His contrivance was to hold his thumb and finger as near together as possible, and if they remained steady and did not touch, he was not too nervous to ride. He was a good fellow and a fine rider, but he died very young.

Snow on that visit stopped hunting, so we improvised toboggans, and unluckily broke one very pretty lady's leg by her man steering into a frozen bank.

Staying with some friends in Cheshire, I was asked one day to ride a horse they had just bought at the Barratt-Leonard Sale. Of course, all the horses there were famous for their schooling. I rode him one day, but the bit did not suit him; he had apparently such a light mouth. I was on him again a day or two after with a lighter bit, but hounds would not run at all - just a short burst now and then.

He was fresh, and it was hard to hold him with that bit; he bored very much. We were with Lord Stafford's hounds, and the well-known M.F.H., Reggie Corbett, was out. I had never met him before, but he was in a good humour, and very polite to me. Then, in one of these checks, my animal was pulling hard, and not easy to stop; but I was not near hounds, or in anyone's way. Mr. Corbett, however, chose to call out: "Damn the fellow! here he is again". This was too much; as soon as I got my beast round, I rode up to him, and I did give it to him. I told him that they were not his hounds, that I was in no one's way, that he could damn his own field with his own hounds as much as he liked, but that I would be damned before I took such language from him, and that he had better look out. He took it like a lamb.

Two or three oldish members of the hunt, seeing I was quite in my right, came up to me and said they were so pleased to hear Corbett getting it for once, that he buried them all, and they did not like to give it back. An old friend of mine was out, one of quite the best across country, and he said: "Oh, it's only old Reggie; no one minds him". So I said that that was all very well for them, but that he had no right to make a stranger ridiculous.

No doubt he was at times humorous, for one day when hounds would not run, a gentleman from Liverpool, whose nose fully proclaimed his ancestral stock, rode up to him and said: "Mr. Corbett, don't you think the hounds——" "The hounds, sir! what the devil do you know about hounds? I should think you knew more about hunting jackals round Jerusalem on a jackass!"

The pulling horse I have mentioned nearly gave me a nasty fall. Hounds were not running, and I was opening a gate; I had the handle of my crop under the latch, when he jumped the gate standing, luckily just before I gave it a push open. My cousin George Currie broke his arm just after by a horse doing the same thing to him. A hard-riding young friend of mine amused me one day by saying: "I have just got a rise out of the Master". He was a very well-known M.F.H., who used to talk to the field like Lord Scampersdale: "You think, because I'm a Lord and can't swear", etc.

This Lord Scampersdale, who was hunting the hounds, was giving a lead to a well-known pretty magnate in the country, and my friend was riding as near forward as he dared. They came to a nasty-looking fence, which M.F.H. got over, and shouted: "Come along, darling; it's all right". Then he saw the sex of the darling, and was not pleased!

Near my home as a boy was Ragley Hall, the fine place of the Marquis of Hertford, with its beautiful Grecian house, in the middle of a magnificently wooded park. I think the views from the house are a perfect ideal of what the charming scenery of Warwickshire can be in summer.

The Lord Hertford of those days was the one who lived in Paris, and continued the magnificent collection of art treasures begun by his father, and completed by Sir Richard Wallace.

We used often to wander about the park, and in winter skate on the great lake.

The Marquis was to the neighbourhood as little known as the Marquis de Carabas, and strange stories were told about him.

One curious one was this. The elderly incumbent of a living in his gift died, and before the news could reach him, or anyone could ask for it, a young and adventurous cleric started instantly for Paris, to be first in the field. He went to the house of Lord Hertford, but was told he was not there. However, he said his business was so urgent that he persuaded the porter to tell him where he could be found, and immediately, in spite of the late hour, proceeded to a house where the Marquis was entertaining rather a lively party.

It was reputed that he sent his name up, and some intimation of his business, and one or two of the party said: "Oh, have him up, and we'll have some fun with him".

Up came the adventurous aspirant to clerical preferment, and introduced himself to the Marquis, who presented him to the company, and said: "You are just in time; we are going to have supper, and I hand you over to that charming young lady there, Mademoiselle Clementine. Make yourself as agreeable as you can to her, and if she reports well of you, I will give you the living!"

Clementine seems to have reported to the Marquis that he was fully fitted to be a beneficed parson, as for many years he held the living, much respected by his neighbours.

I belonged at one time to the Argus Club, the existence of which was for playing baccarat. The members belonged to various professions and ways of life in London, and the play was high; it was not hard to win or lose ten thousand in a night. Though there was every now and then a member rather hard hit, I never knew of anyone really coming to grief over it.

There were now and then panics about a police raid, and one night a member of the force walked in, and said in a severe voice, "Gentlemen, I must take your names and addresses!" and proceeded to do so. Unwillingly several gave their names. One was Snooks of New York, but that would not do, and his friends said: "Don't play the monkey; you must give your real name". At last the bobby came to "Fatty Coleman", so well known as helping to run the Lotus Club. "Your name and address, sir". Mr. Coleman only made use of a powerful and, so to speak, vulgar Saxon word, and added: "Look at his boots!" The peeler had on a pair of smart pumps, and proved to be my facetious friend Arthur Fitch, who had bribed a member of the force to give him the loan of his regimentals, and take some refreshment below, while he played the raid game upstairs.

They used to say of "Fatty Coleman" that he would come on crowded evenings, take a seat, and punt in "dumps", the lowest counter used, and wait for some impatient player to pay him handsomely for his chair.

The Argus at last came to an end, and was succeeded by the Park Club. This at last was seriously attacked by the authorities. A trial ensued, and baccarat was pronounced illegal. While that was in abeyance, écarté was played for three points instead of five to make it go quicker.

A sad event occurred one evening. A boy was detected playing the poussette trick - i.e., placing a stake on the edge of the board, and pulling it back if the game were against him. He was so upset and horrified that he went home and put an end to himself.

This was the trick the discovery of which occasioned such a great scandal in a large country-house.

Among my intimate friends was Captain O'Shea, M.P. Billy O'Shea was one of the pleasantest of companions, with all the amusing qualities of an Irishman.

His connection with Gladstone and Parnell is too well known to need remark, but he amused me one day when speaking of the O'-Gorman Mahon.

I said something about his numerous duels, and my friend looked at me, and said: "But did he fight them?" He told me one amusing story of him.

The O'Gorman was a very big tall man. One night there was a large dinner, and the O'Gorman came out of the dining-room well filled with champagne and whisky. He went to the cloak-room, and said in a voice of thunder: "Give me a hat!"

The frightened attendant handed him the first hat he found, which was much too small, but the giant balanced it on his head and strode off. Up runs a small man, and breathlessly says: "O'Gorman Mahon, I beg your pardon, but you've got my hat!" "Your hat, sir! I asked for a hat, and they gave me a hat, and I'd like to see the man in all Ireland who'd take it from me!"

He told me a characteristic story of his cousin, who was Colonel of a cavalry regiment in the Spanish Army, to whom he was paying a visit.

The Bishop was visiting the town where the regiment was quartered, and had had to severely pull up a padre in the district. The Colonel entertained them at luncheon, and after it handed round some cigars, of which the Bishop took one. When they were offered to the erring padre, he declined, saying, "I have not got that vice", as a cut at his Bishop. But the Bishop, too sharp, said: "Not a vice, a habit; if it were a vice, you would have it!"

I saw a good deal of an American friend who much amused me, and with whom I went to Spain once.

He had been nearly as much in London as in America, and had begun with a great deal of money. Though still young, he had got through most of it in mines, in every sort of gambling and in horses, and the rest! He had been divorced twice, and his third wife I liked, but I saw it would not last. She was a pretty little woman. She is now at her fifth and he at his fourth matrimonial venture.

He fully agreed with the remark a most amusing woman once made to me on the subject of man and woman "getting on" together. "Mon cher Seymour, la chose la plus importante est d'avoir une peau sympathique presque la seule chose!" He said he was once engaged to a girl, but found, on using some of the privileges of the condition in certain endearments, that she had, as he expressed it, "a skin like a nutmeg-grater!" So he broke off the engagement. I said: "What did her father say?" He replied: "Oh, well, he chased me through three States to shoot me, but he did not catch me!"

I have been sometimes asked: "What do you think was the narrowest escape you have had?" Well, I almost think when once in a certain town I was paying a visit at a house in which, perhaps, I was not equally welcome to all the household.

Accidents will happen, and somebody arrived who was not wanted. I had, as they say, to make myself scarce, and in those days I was young and active, and luckily the window was not far from the ground. I scrambled over the balcony rail, and let myself drop on all-fours into the street, and was up and off just in time to escape a flower-pot aimed at my head.

I found after that that my visits to the house had to cease!

Among curious mistakes in what was said is the following: A clergyman was sent for by a sick old parishioner who was not a church-goer, and who was deaf. The clergyman said: "What induced you to send for me?" "What does he say?" said the man to his wife. "He says, 'Why the deuce did you send for him'?"

This story of Rowland Hill, the preacher, may not be much known, but it is too good to be lost.

Feeling less active, and well enough off in money to do so, he "set up a carriage", and drove to the place of worship. A shocked member of his flock wrote to him anonymously to express his feelings, and the following Sunday, when in the pulpit, Rowland Hill mentioned it to his congregation.

He said: "I have received a communication from one of you to remonstrate with me on my pride and vanity in coming to church in a carriage, and he says that I ought to remember that the great Master whom I serve was content in the moment of His triumph to ride upon the humblest of animals. I wish now to express to him my appreciation of his judgement upon my conduct, and to assure him that if next Sunday he will wait for me outside the church with a saddle and bridle, I shall be most happy to ride him home".

There can be no doubt that much of the jealous feeling between church and chapel is social. The squire and ray lord ask the parson to dinner, but not the Dissenting minister. It used to be said that when a Dissenter was rich enough to add a second horse to his carriage, the first place to which he drove was church!

Of apt quotations in the City, I was one day in a lawyer's office, who was also a commissioner for oaths, with my friend Julius Beerbohrn. While we were waiting he was turning over the pages of an Old Testament used to swear Jews. Presently he was much amused on coming across this: "Woe to the bloody city! it is all full of lies and robbery; the prey departeth not (Nahum iii. I).

I was once with him in Paris, and we went to see an old French speculator about something. He talked of a business affair which had gone wrong, and said. "Eh b'en! Mon ami, l'affaire a raté, mais, grace à Dieu! la race des Gogos est immortelle!"

Years ago I remember this on the Warwick race-course. There was a thimble-rigger, who had placed his table with thimbles and pea, and a young, active farmer put down a sovereign as a stake. A pal of the rigger called "Police!" and the man shut up the table and bolted with the sovereign. The young farmer was after him, and gave him a tremendous kick each time he got near him till he stopped out of breath. A looker-on said: "But why didn't you get back your sovereign?" "Ha! ha!" laughed the young fellow. "It was a bad un!"

The following is not a bad story of Sam Wilberforce staying in a country-house. Wishing to be pleasant to everyone, he went to talk to the German governess. It was Sunday evening, so he asked her how she liked the English Church service. Fraulein said: "Very much, and you are so thoughtful that you even pray for us poor governesses". The Bishop was puzzled, and said he could not quite remember where in the service, and she said: "Oh, why, you pray for women labouring with child!"

At Oxford, just before the examination in Bible history, a Don at a certain college got a few men into his room to see how much they knew, and began to question them. "Who was Amram?" No answer. "Who was Abiathar?" No answer. "Who was Jamrac?" "I know", says one young fellow; "he was one of the Johnnies who was cast into the burning, fiery furnace!" (I fancy most people knew Jamrac as the great dealer in wild animals in the East of London!)

Chapter XIX

VENEZUELA

I

*I*t was at the time of the great success of the Callao goldmine in Venezuela that much attention was drawn to the Caratal district in the province of Venezuelan Guiana, and several companies were formed to work mines in the same district.

It was to this part of the world that the adventurous but unlucky Sir Walter Raleigh twice went, fully believing that in some spot there he should find a mine out of which could be taken bright, shining, yellow gold. He had not the least idea of the formation in which gold is found, or of the processes necessary to extract it.

He may have known something about washing for gold in sand or gravel, but of quartz reef in which gold is found in Venezuela he knew nothing. He also thought that there was gold found near the Orinoco, but none has so far been discovered.

Washing for gold has been carried on for centuries, and the origin of the finding the Callao Reef was from a rich washing. A report of a good find got about, and a man surprised some of the washers who were doing very well, and said: "You fellows are working mighty silently" ("muy callao" - provincial for "callado"). He and one or two others prospected, and struck the outcrop of the famous Callao

Reef.

I saw seventy stamps working there on free milling quartz, which ran seven ounces to the ton.

The success of this attracted a heap of prospectors, and several reefs were found, the discoverers of which swore that they were as rich as Callao.

Some promoters in London got hold of a reef called the Chile, which was being worked by Americans. A company was formed to buy it, and a mining expert was sent out to report.

One knows the three degrees of the family of Ananias, as reckoned in the Transvaal: liars —— liars, and mining experts.

The report was very favourable, the company floated prosperously, and I was asked to go out and take over the property for the company, report how things looked, and get ready to receive the manager they were going to send out.

I left in one of the pleasant Royal Mail boats, the *Nile*, and had with me two young fellows, one a sucking mining engineer, and the other an accountant.

We had the usual run to Barbadoes, but very nearly ended our voyage in mid-ocean.

One night I was woke up by the noise of an explosion just outside my cabin, a great smashing of wood, and a smell of fire. There was naturally an alarm, and at first a little confusion.

We found that an empty hold had been used for coal, and the ventilation was bad. The lights of the coal-trimmers ignited the gas, blew up the hatches, burnt the coal-trimmers, and set fire to the straw in the packing-cases smashed up, and the hold was soon well alight.

The wash-deck hose was soon fitted, but the extra pressure now burst it all to pieces, and there was a long delay before new hose could be got out and fitted. Meanwhile the fire was going merrily ahead.

The question was whether the fire would get through the deck which confined it before the water could be got to play upon it.

We had two or three hours of touch and go, and at daylight nothing was certain. The boats, of course, were ready, and the first officer worked splendidly. We were out of the track of ships, but with daylight we sighted one.

We naturally wanted the captain to get her to stand by in case of need, but he refused, and she was soon out of sight. It appeared that it was the last voyage the skipper was going to make before retiring, and if he had signalled to the ship to stand by, the company would have had to pay her, and would not have thanked him. To help in his retirement pension, he was willing to risk the lives of us all.

Luckily the skill and energy of First Officer Rego got the fire under, and we reached Barbadoes. We thought of writing a complaint to the company, and if it had been on a voyage home no doubt we should have done so, for we felt it was most disgraceful. But we were all scattering over the West Indies and the Spanish main, and gave it up.

We were put into quarantine at Barbadoes, for there was a very severe epidemic of yellow fever there.

I and a few others changed into a boat going to Trinidad, as our boat went on to Jamaica, etc.

Among those on board was an American named Fitzgerald, who had, among past adventures, been one of the famous Walker's Filibusters. He was returning to the Callao mine to take charge of it, and had with him a very pleasant little wife, who told me she looked forward with horror to the long journey from the River Orinoco to the mines.

The day we got to Barbadoes the bum-boats came off with fresh things. I had a real tuck-in at luncheon of green things and fruit. I was sitting opposite Fitzgerald, who observed: "Young man, you must have a cast-iron inside to go on like that". I said: "Don't mind me; I'm all right!" But, good heavens! that night I learnt the lesson that one must treat tropical productions with the greatest care; in fact, we seldom ate fruit except in the early morning. It was painful self-denial, but indulgence was more painful still.

No one who has not seen the West Indies can imagine the beauty of everything. The description of it all in Kingsley's "At Last", when he describes his delight in it, gives some idea, but I think far the best description of everything is in that delightful book, "Tom Cringle's Log", by Michael Scott.

Port of Spain, the capital of Trinidad, lies very flat and low, as the water is shoally there, and the land rises slowly out of it.

It is a bright little place with white houses, green shutters, and beautiful trees and flowering shrubs, and plenty of water in the streets and squares.

Dogs abound, and carrion crows did then: they were the valued scavengers of the streets. Now, I am told, the shiftless, lazy niggers have shot them all down, and would give anything to get them back again. They would hardly get out of your way in the street, and used to take a bath in the fountains at least once a day, flutter up to a bough, and sit forlorn with tail and wings laying out to dry.

I have seen one hop round a sleepy dog, and at last tweak him by the tail to see if he were alive or dead.

I found an old Charterhouse friend there, Albert Marryat, nephew of the great Captain Marryat, who was at work on the family sugar property, and he put me much up to the ways of the West Indies.

A mile or two out of Port of Spain is the Savanna, a grass plain nearly round, about a mile across. Partly round it is a horse-shoe of hills, wooded as only hills can be in the tropics. Under the hills lie the Botanical Gardens, and in them the house of the Governor, an absolutely ideal residence in such a climate - large and cool, with a very fine ball-room, and standing in that glorious garden with a splendid view.

The well-to-do men of business and Government servants live in pretty villas round the Savanna, and I found them most kind and hospitable.

The race-course is on the Savanna, and once, on passing through Trinidad, I was lucky to hit off the race week, which was a charming change from gold-mines and Venezuelan troubles.

I once made a trip to the centre of the island with Marryat and Paget, the district surveyor. It is a high hill, and we rode out on mules to the rest-house on the top, a large unfurnished shed, where we slung our hammocks. It was very hot, and I was just over an attack of fever, and thirsty beyond words. We had food with us, but our nigger had forgotten anything to drink but a bottle of brandy, and water was away at the bottom of the hill. I could not resist a go of brandy, which did not get me on far.

That part was famous for some of the largest poisonous snakes that exist, and we had the luck to see one on an old stump as we rode our mules down. He must have been quite twelve feet long, and we gave him a wide berth.

I saw a good deal of the chief magistrate, and among other questions, I asked him how they managed the niggers, as flogging was forbidden? He said it was forbidden except for breach of discipline in gaol, but that most of them were sure to do something wrong, and were at once tied up; and it gave them a distaste for prison life, otherwise so easy to them.

The way to the Caratal mines was up the Orinoco, and land either at Las Tablas or at Ciudad Bolivar. Las Tablas was nearest the mines.

I picked up a Jamaican gentleman of colour who had been body-servant to the mining expert who had preceded us. He was recommended for several qualities, one being a knowledge of the brewing of cocktails; but he nursed me through yellow fever, so I have a good word for him.

The Orinoco has an enormous delta, and many mouths. I think the one we went up is the mouth of the Dragon. As I said of the Parana, these great rivers are very uninteresting: the hills and great forests are far away.

The huts and canoes of the Indians were interesting, and the alligators, or caimans, were, some of them, very large. There was a dirty yellow fellow who seemed an enormous brute when full-sized.

I and my companions went up the river in the same steamer as Fitzgerald, who was going to the Callao mine. She did not stop at Las Tablas, so we had to go on to Ciudad Bolivar, otherwise called Angostura, because the river rather narrows here.

The boat down, which stopped at Las Tablas, did not start for some days, so I and Fitzgerald hired a steamer, and went at once down to Las Tablas.

We saw on one bank the remains of Sir Walter Raleigh's Fort, which he made when he started to find the legendary city of Manoa.

Las Tablas is a miserable little hole of half a dozen houses and a sandy beech, and here we landed. There was more of resource in it than there looked, and we got together some mules to take us up.

It is a dreary journey of over one hundred and sixty miles to Caratal, on the Cuyuni River, the first forty miles very little but sand, and swarms of sand-flies who could bite, and fresh victims bore the marks for long.

There were two awkward rivers to cross, and the greater part of the way was through rocky country, barren, with a scrubby tree with leaves like sand-paper. There was one oasis on the road at Upata well watered and cultivated.

Having got our mules, we started up-country; but one river was so in flood that we had to make a long round to a spot where we could cross it.

To realize the difficulties of the road, I may say that it frequently cost seventy pounds a ton to transport things up to the mines. When one considers the weight of machinery, stone-breakers, stamps, etc., one can realize the amount of working capital required to start a mine.

I was unlucky enough to get a touch of fever before we got to the end. We were caught in a very heavy storm, and I rode into the place where there was shelter just as it was getting dark. I could not eat, and lay down, and remembered nothing for some days.

My party went on and left me to the natives and the tender remedies of "Dr. Sangreda", as in "Gil Blas". When I could stand, I found he had, according to tradition, filled me up with mercury, and every tooth in my head chattered as I moved. I have never known whether he bled me or not.

A pleasant, oldish American named Marsh came down from the mine to pick me up, and we crawled on up to it. He had charge of the mine to hand over.

Guayana, in the gold district, is hills and valleys, the hills densely wooded with the most magnificent timber, and the valleys dark and damp, the hotbeds of fever.

The mine next to ours had had thirteen managers in twelve years, and the burying-place a caution to visitors. I think a photograph of it would have frightened away any intended comer.

I once rode over there, and found every white man in bed with fever, and a nigger running the mill. The walls of the houses looked leprous with damp.

To know what a primeval tropical forest is like, a traveller must go right up-country; most of the West Indian Islands have no forest unthinned. There is no undergrowth whatever: you walk on the soft ground made by fallen evergreen leaves. There are no insects, no sounds. Every life is far above. The trees for fifty or one hundred feet without a bough, but the lianas hang down like cables to the ground. It is dark, and you cannot tell in the least where the sun is, and without a compass you don't know which way to go. There is nothing for man or beast to eat.

An active man could, like the monkeys, climb up to the regions above of birds, insects, flowers, and monkeys. You now and then can see a monkey looking down from an immense height.

If trees fall, or a fire touches the forest, at once springs up the densest undergrowth, and this in the course of many years would become forest, but probably two or three hundred years before the trees were full grown.

The gloom, the silence, and the solemnity of such a forest must be seen and felt to be realized.

A mine in such a country is a rough-and-ready sort of thing, and the living-house generally has a low ground-floor with stores in it, and a floor for living. Ants are a great worry, as, large and small, they pervade everything, even your bed! Jiggers (piques), the insects that get under the skin, and make a nest, particularly in your feet, are a constant annoyance, and *must* be looked after at the risk of losing a limb.

I found the mine was not doing much; I think old Marsh, the manager, who came to meet me, was very sick of it, and was in a hurry to get me and my people to take it over.

It was my first experience of a gold-mine, so he told me any story he liked. There had been a "cave-in" in one place from his having cut away the gold-bearing quartz pillars left to support the roof, and he vowed to me there had been an earthquake. Marsh's earthquake became a joke afterwards.

Some of the young fellows there declared to me that the expert who made the report for us had never been down the mine, and made his report while taking cocktails with old Marsh! It may be so; I have seen many curious mining sights since then.

I remember a young and an older engineer coming to report on a mine. The younger one prepared to go down, and said to the elder, who lit his pipe and sat down: "Ain't you coming down?" "Not I! I know all about it already". When he came up he said: "Well, did you see anything you had never seen before?" and he confessed that he could not say that he had. I have seen, heard, and learnt a good deal since those days, and I must say I should not care to advise friends to invest in a mine unless I had been with the man who made the report. I omitted to do so once when I might have gone, and I have been sorry ever since.

Time went on, and Nicholson, a very clever mining manager, was to come up. Marsh and some of his party cleared out, and Nicholson arrived - a singular character, very intelligent and energetic, but with a slight colonial weakness for the cocktail, but a very pleasant companion.

He also was, like me, unlucky enough to be caught with fever on the road up. I had to go down to Trinidad about some of the business, and met him laid up at Upata, the oasis of which I spoke. We had some talk, and I had to hurry on over the dreary journey, and found him strong again on my return.

We had a latish talk the night I arrived at the mine, and, moistened with rum, I stood under the shower-bath some twenty minutes in the morning to try to cool down; but as the water never was cooler than seventy degrees, it did not help much. I remarked to him that we had taken a good lap of rum, and he said: "What do you mean?" I said: "Well, nearly a bottle and a half". "But, my dear Seymour, what's a bottle and a half of rum between two men like you and me?"

The yellow fever spread up-country, and I was unlucky enough to fall a victim. There was an American doctor at the mines who hailed from Vera Cruz, the home of yellow-jack, and he stuffed me with podophyllin, etc., and with the nursing of my Jamaican body-servant I was soon through it; but it is not a treat, and one feels so miserable one doesn't care which way it goes. Ache all over, headache, and the incipient feeling of Dover to Calais, knowing that if you are sick it is "good-bye". Of course, the Spaniards call it *vomito negro*.

I soon picked up again, and I think the yellow microbes drove out the remaining malaria microbes.

I had rather an interesting walking expedition one day. There was a difficulty in getting enough water for the stamp-mill, so we tried to find a new way of supplying it. We examined and surveyed the hills, and one day pushed as far as a curious little settlement made by a Spaniard some years before.

It was very isolated, but he had a good large low house, and a very good garden with all kinds of flowers and fruits in it, which made it very interesting and surprising in such a lonely spot. He was called El Brujo (pronounced Brukho), the wizard, and the natives were rather afraid of him.

I went to see him, and told him who I was, but he said it was not possible, as *he* (that's *me*) was in bed with fever only a week ago; so I said we were a tough race, and soon got well again.

In a survey going anywhere off the paths, one has to cut one's way all along through the dense undergrowth. You form a line, each one with a *macheté* (cutlass), and take turns to cut the way through creep-ers, etc. The great annoyance is the ticks. One gets covered with them. The only thing to do is, on returning, get off your clothes, and rub the strong rum all over you; that makes them drop off. I have found at least a hundred all over me after some hours in the grass and scrub.

Nicholson soon set to work to put up a good mill and get everything in perfect order. We got on very well together, and I learnt a great deal about gold-mining from him.

One difficulty in making the mines pay was the awful expense of everything. The few Venezuelans about would not work in the mines. All the miners were niggers from the islands, not easy to manage, and asking absurd wages – I have heard of eighteen shillings a day. Poultry and eggs any price. Beef scarce and dear; everything dear except rum!

The gold from the mines was sent down about once a month; the small bars were fitted into the pockets of packsaddles on mules, and a few armed men escorted the convoy down. They took bars down, and brought back money for wages. The bars would be of little use to robbers - they could not get rid of them; but the return gold train was once robbed. The robbers were caught and shot, and most of the money recovered. The amount sometimes carried was large, for the Callao alone could turn out many thousand pounds' worth a week.

It was the only mine that ever really paid; the awful expenses ruined all the others. Many were opened, and it was sad to see the clearings overgrown, the shafts deserted, and the houses in ruins, with thousands of pounds of machinery rusting to pieces.

If in the early days of the mines a combination could have been made of the various companies, and with a line of rail laid from Las Tablas to Caratal, there can be no doubt that that district would still be a paying mining centre. But no community of interests could ever be established, and it was one huge gamble and failure.

One mine, the Tigre, promised splendidly; its white quartz and beautiful specimens of gold visible in lace threads in it were a picture. But, as miners know, splendid visible gold seldom pays; there is not enough to pay for the amount of quartz which has to be crushed.

To non-miners I may say that the ore from the mines in Venezuela is all in quartz; in the Transvaal it is nearly all a sort of amalgam, and quite different.

This quartz is broken - generally in a steam stone-breaker to about the size of road-metal, and then put under the stamps. There are long steel rods, or bars, with a heavy head, and a big bottom called the shoe, which weigh, as near as I can remember, a ton or so. The shoe strikes a die in a mortar-box of iron in which the quartz is constantly renewed, and a stream of water runs through it.

There is above a shaft, with a cam or catch to take hold of the head of each stamp, raise it up two or three feet, and let it drop into the box. It pounds the quartz to powder, which the water carries away.

This runs over sloping tables of copper which are covered with an amalgam of mercury, and to this the gold set free by the pounding adheres. Once a week at least the amalgam is scraped off and retorted; that is, it is heated till the mercury becomes volatile, which it does at a much lower temperature than the gold, so that the mercury passed through a cooler becomes solid, and is used again, and the gold remains behind.

It is the simplest of all ways of extracting gold, and such quartz is called free-milling quartz. The rock in which gold is found is often mixed with impurities such as antimony, and that "sickens" the mercury so that it does not catch the gold; the ore is then refractory ore. There are, besides, riffles, buddles, the cyanide process, etc., which need not be mentioned here.

The noise of a mill of many stamps is deafening, and can be heard far away; but one soon gets used to it, and on the Sunday, when the men have a rest, one quite misses the noise.

There came up to the mine a friend of Nicholson's, by name Susini de Sandoval - a capital fellow, who had been at school in England - and we made great friends.

There had to be some business about the title of the mine done in Caracas, so we travelled there together later on.

I had business in Ciudad Bolivar, the capital of the province. It is not an exciting place to live in, but the river runs very rapidly by it, and makes the air fairly fresh, though when I was there the thermometer stood at over a hundred most of the day, and the yellow fever was raging.

While I was there an enormous electric eel was caught, nine feet long.

The town is chiefly known by its name of Angostura, which it gives to the celebrated bitters made from the Tonka bean, and known all over the world.

At times from the mines people went to Angostura to catch the steamer, at other times to Las Tablas.

I had one unpleasant landing at Las Tablas. I had in Port of Spain bought two half-broken mules, which had come in a drove from Kentucky, as we were short of them at the mines.

I was by myself, and as I kept my good clothes in Trinidad, I only had with me my saddle and saddle-bags.

The steamer reached Las Tablas about two in the morning, so I got into the boat with the cords to the headstalls of the beasts in my hand, and the sailors "hove" them overboard. One came up under the boat, but none the worse, and I towed them to land, and the boat left me.

While saddling up one damp animal, I was aware of a wretch of a Custom-house officer anxious to know my excisable goods. The idiot asked me for my revolver, and I was getting so out of patience that if he had tried to take it he would certainly have got the contents of it.

I got away from him and reached a house I knew, and after breakfast started on my solitary and dreary journey. The mules were out of condition, and one of them "jacked up" halfway through; however, I got to Caratal on the other.

II

The coast of Venezuela is often very fine, rocky, and mountainous. The ports of Cumana and Curupano are well sheltered, and have fine scenery, and forests down to the water's edge.

La Guayra, the port of Caracas, lies right under the mountains, which go straight up for ten thousand feet. The town lies round a little bay, but the port was quite unprotected till the breakwater was built by my dear old friend Frank Lowther.

There is plenty of water for ships, but it is full of sharks - which don't prevent the native boys being constantly in the sea.

It is piping hot there, as the mountains keep off the air, but it does not seem to be very unhealthy, only the habit of constant "cocktails" tries some constitutions. Mine has, luckily, always been proof against that mixture.

While I was in La Guayra some changes were being made in the sea-front, and the old dungeons were, I cannot say pulled *down*, but *up*, for they were dismal holes, known as Las Bovedas (ovens), from their shape, with a hole at the top for admission of prisoners, light, air, and food, and exit of prisoner if he survived. An old Spaniard living there, who had more than once found admission, said to me one day (he kept a cocktail bar): "They are destroying my old home!" It may very well be that Frank Leigh and the Rose of Torridge were shut up there before they were brought out to make a Christian holiday at the stake.

The distance from La Guayra to Caracas is six miles, but as Caracas is three thousand feet above it, the road is over twenty miles long, and the present railway about the same.

The railway was being surveyed when I was there, and it was finished in due course. The then President, Guzman Blanco, to stop competition with it by the old cartmen, suppressed and ruined them all by his decree.

There is a path over the mountain to the capital, called the Indian path. When Drake took La Guayra, he aimed at the capital. A traitor showed him the Indian path, and while the garrison were out to meet him by the road, he sacked and burnt the town with the usual amenities of the patriotic filibusters of those days. When the traitor asked for his reward, Drake hung him to the nearest tree, and returned to his ship - or ships - by the same path.

I walked down from Caracas to La Guayra one moonlight night by the path, which was not really difficult, though it is true I slipped over the edge once, and was caught up in some bushes. But I nearly came to grief at the end of my walk.

The shortest cut lay across the glacis of the La Guayra Fort. I was sneaking noiselessly across it, when I trod on some loose stones, and went sliding down with a clatter. I at once saw the black, ugly mug of a sentry just above, with his musket pointed, who sang out "Alto! Quien va?" I at once said, lying on my back: "Amigo! Don't shoot!" In that undignified position I interviewed him, and persuaded him to let me rise from among the scorpions and thistles unshot, and find my way to supper at the club.

It was risky, for the sentries always have ball-cartridge, and like loosing off. One night, going home late across the Plaza, the sentry challenged, and a very nice Venezuelan with us made some jocose remark in plain Spanish. The sentry loosed off at us, and it hit him in the knee, and he was lame for life.

Caracas is a pretty, well-built, and well-arranged town, never hot, lovely climate, magnificent views, and every sort of thing will grow there. There are roses in masses every-where. It has all that latitude 8 can give, and none of the drawbacks - no fever and no epidemics. Well watered, for the mountains go up seven thousand feet higher, and the ridge of high land runs for miles both ways. The pineapples are as cheap as apples here, and very good.

The road and scenery from Caracas to Valencia are magnificent, and in temperate climate all the way. The road runs for some sixty miles by the Lake of Valencia, which is surrounded by grand hills, and the large islands, with their small mountains, are like fairyland.

The scene at sunrise is simply perfect as one rides along - small bays covered with the Victoria lily, whose leaves run to six feet across, and swarms of every sort of water-fowl among them.

The soil is perfect, and the sugar-cane grows profusely in every flat spot. The hill-sides have very many coffee plantations, than which nothing is prettier, and the humming-birds seem to have a special fancy for the coffee-bushes. The Venezuelan coffee, sold generally as Porto Rica, is among the very best of sorts and flavours.

The Venezuelans are a most cheery, good-natured race. One is well received everywhere. I gave up carrying a revolver; it seemed needless. They have a curious weakness for internecine warfare, but seem to bear no ill-will when it is over. As it is difficult to reward all the heroes, the rank of General is common, and I was offered that proud distinction for some slight service; but, thinking it could only be useful to sanction my getting an expensive fancy uniform, which I should only wear at some ball - not at our Court - I gracefully declined the honour. But "El Ilustre Americano", Guzman Blanco, conferred upon me the high order of "El Busto del Libertador Simon Bolivar". It carried with it the right to wear a large order on my manly bosom, and a very pretty rosette. Once, in Paris, I got the rosette at the shops in the Rue de la Paix, where they sell the insignia of every honour in heaven and earth, and elsewhere, perhaps, and I placed it in my buttonhole, and swaggered down the boulevard. I met one or two friends, who smiled so sarcastically that I placed the button in ray pocket.

There is a good hotel, and a very fair opera in a fine house, where one saw some very pretty women. The club is a fine large house, with a big garden. Of course, like nearly all foreign clubs, it is chiefly for card-playing.

I met there a strange American, who was always dressed in a queer long frock-coat, white waistcoat of a certain age, and red tie, with black pants. He asked me to play écarté for small points, which I did. He played very indifferently, but mostly won. He one day asked me if I would go with him to a house where they played baccarat. He said: "I will take the bank; you sit opposite and collect the money, and watch one tableau while I have an eye on the other, to see that there is no hanky-panky". It went all right, but I observed that when there was a good stake on, my friend turned up an eight or nine with a marvellous precision.

The party seemed at last to have had enough, so he said to me in English: "Rubbishing lot! We'd better off it. We can get no more out of them". So we said good-night, went off, and shared the "swag".

I played écarté with him afterwards, and always lost. I said to him: "It's no use my playing you. You play a very poor game, but always win. I don't know how you do it". He said, "I hardly touch the cards, as you see", but I said that that was exactly what I did not see!

I found later that he was a famous professional gambler, who had played his way through Mexico and Peru.

When I was in Caracas later on, he asked me to join the baccarat party again, but I was sick of it, and was then too well known to get mixed up with such a set.

The President, Guzman Blanco, has been too well known to need much talk of him. He understood finance enough to make himself the Chancellor of the Exchequer, and his pocket the Treasury!

He made a corner in brandy-bought up a huge consignment, and put on a prohibitive duty. Mr. Lloyd George might take a hint!

He made a corner in milk by buying up cows, and preventing others coming, so milk rose in Caracas.

He married one of three very pretty sisters, and considered that, like the patriarch Jacob, he ought to have the run of the family.

One very pretty one objected, and when he intruded upon her in her lightly-clad siesta hour, she up with her pretty little foot and gave him such a kick that he fled howling!

Some of those charming little women had lovely feet. One I knew actually wore doll's shoes! She was small, but a pocket Venus.

I came across a type that I did not know still existed in the West Indies. I believe they are the pure race of the old Caribbee Indians - a pleasant, copper-coloured race, with a very fine skin, not very dark, long hair, and with features as well shaped and finely cut as any European. As far as I could see, only the darkness of the skin was different to an Aryan type; more delicate features than the Semitic. I met one girl with such a pretty face and figure! I mention the race, as I don't remember hearing it ever talked of. As far as I can make out, the Spaniards did their utmost to exterminate them, for they were no use as slaves.

The farthest west I saw of Venezuela was Puerto Cabello - such a pretty, well-shut-in little port. Everything small, everything neat and attractive. Trees to the water's edge, and all looking so comfortable and peaceable.

There is a large fort above, with a very deep, wide, dry ditch. I went up to see it, and was shown it as the place where some hundreds of miserable Spanish soldiers were kept prisoners after the great Simon Bolivar had finally defeated the Spaniards, and put an end to their rule.

The final great battle of Carabobo was fought not very far from there, and was chiefly won by the Irish Brigade, which was recruited from the British Army after the peace in 1815-16. There are now in Venezuela families descended from those soldiers, most prosperous and well-to-do.

Valencia is the town a few miles inland, in the high land - a pleasant, prosperous place, where I made some friends. I rode from there by the Lake of Valencia, which I have mentioned, and on to Caracas - a four-days ride.

In Caracas I made great friends with General Pulgar, who was a great character. He was the head of the Out party, and the rival of Guzman Blanco. Blanco was not a warrior, Pulgar was most particularly one. He had distinguished himself by his reckless courage in some of their revolutionary wars, particularly at Puerto Cabello, where he stormed the fort at night.

He and his men wore nothing but their trousers, and in the scrimmage in the dark used their cutlasses wherever they felt clothes. He had a most sanguinary picture of it in his dining-room in Caracas; also he had one of a canoe fight in the Meta River, which swarms with alligators. The picture makes the water red with blood, and the gigantic reptiles devouring the wounded and drowning men in dozens.

Pulgar talked much with me about the frontier between Venezuelan and British Guiana, and was anxious to have it settled. He said that if, as he expected, he was the next President, he would do everything he could to arrange it, and was quite willing to stick to the old treaty, by which the boundary gave the watershed of the Essequibo - which took in that of the Cuyuni River - to England. This would have given the Caratal gold-fields to Great Britain.

He had extensive property there, and felt that, if a railway were made from Demarara to the gold-fields, his property would be most valuable, for it was impossible to get the line made in Venezuelan territory from the Orinoco.

I wrote to a friend at the Foreign Office, and asked him to send me a copy of the treaty, which he did; but he said that he had spoken to the head men there of the chance of a settlement, and they said that Gladstone was in power, and that he neither knew nor cared a rap about Venezuela, and that any effort was waste of time.

I feel sure that then, with Guzman Blanco or with Pulgar, a far better treaty could have been made; but, as I learnt still better later on about Delagoa Bay, the British Government never helps on any frontier settlement till they are forced to do so. All our vast territories over the world have been won by private enterprise: the Government only comes in when forced to protect private British interests already won.

Of course, that is the right course, but both in Venezuela and in Delagoa Bay the Government hung back too long, and let others take advantages which were ready to their hand.

England was peopled by pirates and adventurers - Danes, Norsemen, and what not. Their descendants have filibustered all over the world, and, having seized on various places, have forced the Home Government to accept them as part of the Empire.

Our present Government is contentedly waiting for Germany to filibuster England.

I cannot say that I had a bad time in Venezuela, barring fevers, for I had a great deal of variety, saw much that was most interesting, and picked up a good deal about gold-mining from my friend Nicholson, who was an unusually clever man, with large experience.

He might have done anything but for his weakness, which cost him in the end his life, for he shot himself with my gun, which I had left at the mine. He was mourned by many friends, and by me not least of them.

Before that he had returned to England, and seemed likely to do very well, but went back to Venezuela, and a habit of stimulants is hopeless in a hot colony.

I was interested in a mine while he was in London, and asked him if he could go and report on it. He said he had not time, but added: "My dear Seymour, with what you have learnt from me, you can make a better report on it than most of those fellows!"

I did once make a report, on which a company did very fairly well, and the promoter unblushingly put "M.I." after my name in the prospectus! But I did not get the then not unusual thousand pounds fee for it! That was in the halcyon days of promoting.

Everything mortal comes to an end, and I took ship from La Guayra, but after a bit of a delay there. The steamer had evidently broken down, but there was no telegraph then, and I waited three weeks for the next boat. I went for many long rambles up into those fine mountains, with glorious scenery. It was curious in what out-of-the way spots, high up, I found large orange-trees in full bearing.

The boat, when she did arrive, was small and full, and we went on for four days to Port of Spain, with over seventy passengers for just over thirty berths, and it rained a good deal. I was the only Englishman on board.

I stayed a little in Port of Spain, and there, with my friend Sandoval, boarded an intercolonial boat to pick up the European boat at St. Thomas's. I was very glad to see some of the islands, particularly Martinique. They are all beautiful in their way, so one need not compare them.

Mont Pelée, that did such awful mischief, looked the most innocent hill that ever was set eyes on.

The half-caste women of Martinique are splendid creatures - tall, well set up, and know it too!

I was talking to the Consul about the tobacco, and he said: "If you want something strong, buy one of those big cigars the women smoke as a curiosity; but you will never get through it, it is much too strong". And so I found. It is very curious that both there and in Paraguay the women should smoke such much stronger tobacco than the men.

St. Thomas has a splendid harbour, but is a dull little hole. It is the home of hurricanes, and a wreck or two well inland showed what had been done; also a brass gun, said to have been blown a long way by the wind.

It is lucky for Trinidad and the mainland that they are too far south for hurricanes to touch, from some strange cause. Earthquakes they do have. I ought to have felt one, but I was driving along an awful road when it occurred, and when we reached a post-house, we found everything in great commotion. "Whatever is the matter?" "Did not you feel the earthquake?" "Not a bit; the road quaked us so the whole time, it was all the same to us".

The following facts are not without interest:

I have never heard much mention of the enormous cotton-trees which grow on the islands and mainland. They are very fine to look at, and grow to an enormous height. I have never heard of a measurement. Their great branches bear a sort of cotton, but it and the wood are quite useless. The wood is soft and pulpy. You drive an axe in, and it sticks fast, and the wood is hard to burn. The ancient ones are raised from the ground on arches of enormous roots covering a great space of ground, and looking most singular. I have heard an engineer say that it was cheaper to deflect a line of rail than to cut one down.

A curious feature of Port of Spain is the quantity of oysters which there are, and they are very largely gathered by men in flat boats, creeping along the shore and picking them off the boughs of the trees dipping into the sea. It sounds a traveller's tale, but is a fact.

On the Orinoco was pointed out to me a spot which held out very long during the civil war, known as the "Seven Years' War", and spoken of as a sort of heroic age. It was reduced by this barbarous expedient: smallpox broke out among the assailants, who placed their hospital to windward of the port, and just out of range.

Near Las Tablas is a very great waterfall on the Caroni River, which falls into the Orinoco; but everyone passing is too busy to bother about it. It is very high, and very grand, and the noise and spray can be heard and seen for miles.

The sand-flies on that horrible road to the mines must be felt to be believed in. They get through any net, and bite worse than mosquitoes. I came down from the mines once in a hurry, as orders came to register all the mine titles in Caracas. I started on a small mule to go the one hundred odd miles against time to catch the boat. I meant to buy or hire another mule on the way, but it was not possible, so I fed my little beast well, and watered him well inside and out, and he had to go on. The last forty miles he shammed tired-it is nearly all sand, and very hot. At last we came to the end - a slope of about two miles to the river at Las Tablas. He pricked up his ears, gave a loud bray, said to himself, "Thank goodness, it's over at last!" and cantered down to the village. We caught the boat by two hours. One hundred and sixty-three miles in fifty-two hours was not bad for the little beast, and the heat. Luckily for him, I, usually thirteen stone, six foot two, weighed less than eleven stone on starting after malaria and yellow fever. I slung my hammock on the boat, and slept for twelve hours.

My companion Sandoval amused me by a story of how he got rid of an unwelcome cabin companion on one voyage. He had asked the purser to put him in another cabin, but he would not, so the first night he had a fit, as he said: "I raved and foamed so that my companion was frightened to death and fled. I don't know what became of him, but I had the cabin to myself for the rest of the voyage".

What followed my Venezuelan travel was this:

In due course Guzman Blanco, having made his pile, thought he had had enough of it, and did not stand again for the Presidency; but the greedy, jealous adventurer could not stand the idea of Pulgar's coming into office, so, being still in power at the time of the election, he nominated Crespo, and, by putting a guard of soldiers on every ballot-box, he elected him, Pulgar being by far the most popular candidate.

Personally, Blanco was afraid of Pulgar. The latter told me that Guzman would never see him alone. He was afraid he would pull out a six-shooter and wipe him out.

The usual sequel followed, but this organization of Guzman and Crespo made it very hard to get up a good revolution in the country. A ship to bring a resolute band of filibusters was wanted, and to import a good supply of arms.

My friend Sandoval was engaged for the job, and I was asked to have a hand in it; and having nothing to do, I thought it would amuse a few idle days.

We were to equip a ship in Europe, and join our friends at Curaçoa. Money was forthcoming, and a man named Michael, of Jewish and partly English extraction, turned up, who had done business before with some of the same men in Venezuela. He was in the ship line of business, and his enemies said that his father and he had made a good bit by insuring rotten old ships which did not turn up again.

He professed to have the ship ready, but we could never see her, and it was all a queer business; but when you have the Foreign Enlistment Act hanging over your head, you have to risk something. He wanted a good bit of cash down, and we demurred, and sent a telegram to our friends to know if we could trust him. They foolishly economized words in their reply, and we understood that we were to give him the money, on receipt of which he offed it to Paris, to which place I pursued him; but it was like butter and the dog's mouth with the money.

I consulted my old friend Montague Williams, but he said: "It's no use your thinking of the law: the next thing would be, I should get a brief to go for you under the Foreign Enlistment Act".

So the Michael episode ended, and another ship was got which I had little to do with, which was luck for me. The whole affair was a failure', and there was a squabble about paying the ship's crew. This drew attention to it all, and some of my friends were engaged in what an American gentleman called "serious litigation" under the before-mentioned Act, and one or two of them ended by sharing the fate of brawling suffragettes. So I was well out of that affair.

Chapter XX

HENRIETTE MINE

*H*aving returned from Venezuela, I formed a connection with the city and with companies, and was rather mixed up with a very clever, enterprising man, Charles Crespigny.

I was at first very innocent as to the formation and promotion of companies, having had so far no more to do with them than to go out to some wild-cat country in their employment, such as Paraguay and Venezuela; I now saw something of the working internal machinery of the bogies.

I will give a curious specimen of the animal.

There came over to London from Leadville, one may say Denver, one Dave Moffatt. Some called him the "mining king", or some such name, but he was a great boss at the mining game, and became a power, and then very rich.

He had in his pocket the Henriette Mine. This was a silver-lead mine of Leadville. It was announced as something wonderful, and the British investor was expected to swallow its shares "right away".

Dave brought with him two or three followers, all rather of the Wild West order, but one was a very clever artist. He had lived and painted mostly in the West, and knew all ,about Indians and buffaloes. Also he had stayed in Salt Lake City, and painted the beauties of Brigham Young's seraglio.

I asked him casually one day if he had any "fun" there. You should have seen his face. "Fun! One had to live the strictest of lives there, in and to bed early! It was a reign of terror. The 'avenging angels' (we call them bobbies) were always after you; and any scrape, and you were never heard of again!" His sketches of the West were charming - I mean on canvas.

As we were to make a pile out of Dave, we had to be civil and amuse him, but it was uphill work.

Of civilized amusements they knew nothing, and whisky in quantities was the chief instrument of pastime. It was rather tiresome, but my rough life training made me impervious to late hours and deep draughts.

We took them over to Paris, but that was rather a failure. Naturally they knew not a word of French, and no life there, however much Bohemian, had any charm for them. They looked upon claret much as Mr. Jorrocks did, and champagne said but little, and I was very glad when we saw Calais and Dover again.

Meanwhile the company was formed; the mining expert was sent out by the best-known firm of mining engineers in London; a splendid report was published, and all went well.

The public came in gaily, but not quite enough, and a little "faking" had to be done. As I was an innocent, I was used as a dummy, and my banking account showed a surprising amount of thousands of pounds as passing in buying shares.

The working capital was subscribed; letters of "allotment and regret", as they are called, were sent out, and on things went boomingly.

I may say, for the instruction of the innocent, that "regret" means: "We regret that, all the capital having been subscribed, we cannot accept your subscription, and therefore return it". But only too often the regret comes a little later, and is on the part of those whose money has been accepted!

A mining manager went out, work was started, and the manager reported that the mine was worked out, and that he could not find a mag of silver in it!

Then came regrets, and howls.

We were frantic with Dave, who was safe back in Denver, and we swore all sorts of impossible vengeance.

Now comes the most curious part of the story.

Dave repented, said he had played it very low, and gave back the purchase-money, so that most of the subscriptions were repaid.

The next question was, How on earth did —— and Co. ever give such a report?

Dave Moffatt and Co. confessed with much laughter how it was done.

The "expert" had examined most carefully, had taken samples according to every rule of the game, had locked and sealed them up, and prepared to depart. The Denver crowd gave him a great "send-off" dinner, made him royally drunk, put him to bed, took his samples, keys, and seals, substituted very rich samples from elsewhere, and, having fastened them up, sent him off with a cocktail and a headache to New York and London!

But the moral is still to come.

Dave and Co. had another look in at the mine, made a rich strike in it, and ended by making a big pile out of it. So might our manager have done if he had been sharper and luckier.

I heard of a curious mistake made by some Britishers in that part of the world as to "location" of their mining property. Their manager went out to start the concern in due form. He put up houses, sunk a shaft, set a stamp-mill going, and, just as the whole thing was getting into full swing, a quiet-spoken Yankee gentleman came down to the mill from a house hard by, where he had been living, and said to the manager: "Wal, sir, this is very good indeed of you to start a mill going for me! " What in thunder do you mean?" says the manager.

"Wal, you see, you have mistaken your location. Your reef is away over the hill yonder; this here is mine. Here are the plans and titles!" And there was no getting out of it.

Good Yankee stories are short and to the point. One of these men amused me by telling what he heard one day on the rare event of his going to church.

A man came out after an eloquent, touching sermon, and went up to a neighbour he had quarrelled with years before. "Here, old hoss!" says he, "give us your hand; I've heard that sermon, and I've got religion, and I feel that mean I could shake hands with a dog!"

Another story amused me of the Kentuckian who was enlarging on the enormous "head of snakes" that he had seen in one tree. A stranger said: "I knows Kentucky all to pieces, and you never seed that amount of snakes in one tree!" The argument grew heated, and at last the snakeman said: "Wal, if there weren't a hundred head of snakes, there were fifty, and I'll fight before I bate another snake!"

Among American stories, this may not be well known this side the water.

A darky preacher, discoursing to his flock on the Fall of Man, gave this version of it:

"And Adam, he was in de garden in de cool of de evening. And de Lord sed to him, 'Adam, Adam! war's My green pippins?' And Adam sed, 'Your green pippins, Lord? I ain't seen no green pippins!' And de Lord sed, 'You ain't seen no green pippins! What's dem apple-chewin's in de grabble-walk? Just you pack up your fig-leaves and git!' "

This is an absolute fact. When the population was so frightened by the earthquake at Charleston, South Carolina, a darky minister was heard praying: "O Lord, dis ain't no child's play dis time; don't You send down Your Son to help us, but come Yourself!"

Too many American story-tellers are too long-winded. They give you the name, date, family history, and place before getting to a story you heard at school.

I saw something of the boom and gamble in electric light shares, when "Father Brush", as the Company was called, and his "pups" were to the front, and I was lucky enough to make a bit in it. Some of my companions tried promoting one or two electric companies, but they did not take on, which was sad. However, I had but little to do with them.

Chapter XXI

PORTUGUESE COPPER

C opper was very much in fashion just then, and my friend Julius Beerbohm had come back from Portugal full of stories of veins and deposits which were to rival Rio Tinto, and Mason and Barry.

Always ready for an adventure, I went out with him, having arranged with some people to find capital if a well-known expert reported favourably on a certain mine. I then made my first real acquaintance with Lisbon, and with the Hôtel Braganza, which was to be my home on and off for some years.

That particular mine was not a success, nor were two or three others which we worked. Gradually I learnt my lesson in copper-mines, but experience is the hard and only master.

The southern provinces of Portugal are not attractive hardly any mining districts are. The rich and often beautiful part of Portugal is north of the Tagus. I got to know these southern parts only too well, and have been over them again and again in carriage, on horseback, and on foot.

I think the Algarve is as dreary and stony a place as can be found anywhere.

There is plenty of mineral copper, and also very good iron, but the copper veins are seldom thick enough, and the ore workable enough, to really pay. There is some very good iron ore, and if only there were coal near to it, or if the iron ore were nearer the sea, it would be a very good spec. to work it.

I made the acquaintance, and then the intimate friendship, of

Jean Burnay at that time, and we lived together for some months a little later.

He was a most amusing companion, spoke French perfectly, as many Portuguese do, and could take off curious Spaniards and Italians capitally in their own languages. English he gradually picked up too. His cousin Henri Burnay has been for years one of the chief Government financiers of Portugal.

Jean was a widower, and his father-in-law, the Viscount Daupias, was one of the richest men of business in Lisbon. He was a most hospitable man, had a very good cook, and I was always welcome at his table, where I dined over and over again. He had a large collection of pictures of very various merit, but a few really good ones.

I once went to stay with him at a pretty villa he had on the sea a little south of Oporto. We bathed a little, but it was very rocky, and the heavy rollers made it dangerous to swim out, and I could swim fairly well then.

One morning in Lisbon, when I used often to bathe in the Tagus, I took a boat with me, and swam across to the other side. It is about two miles, but the tide is very strong, and when there is flood-water coming down the whirlpools are rather dangerous. Byron speaks with satisfaction of having swam across the Tagus as well as the Hellespont.

While I was staying with Daupias there turned up as his guests Cardinal Vanutelli and the Bishop of Coimbra, both enormously tall and very fine-looking men, and most agreeable.

Vanutelli was then Nuncio in Lisbon. He was very popular, and very much admired by all the ladies.

A story was told of him that one evening at dinner he was sitting by a very pretty woman, much *décolletée*, and with a beautiful diamond cross upon her fair white bosom.

She observed that his eyes wandered a good deal in that direction, and said: "It is a very handsome cross, is it not?" He replied: "Ah, madame! Je ne regardait tellement la croix que le Calvaire!"

That delightful poet Campoamor turned the little compliment into charming verse.

The other divine who came with them was a very small man, the Bishop of Bethsaida, who I often met in Lisbon. He was extremely amusing. He told us how he was one of the envoys sent to Italy to bring to Portugal the almost child Princess, daughter of Victor Em-manuel, as bride to King Louis.

We asked him what she was like then, and he said: "We thought she was the ugliest little monkey we had ever seen!" But she much improved as she grew into a woman. Poor child! she had to leave behind her, I think, all her Italian attendants, and took no fancy to her long-legged husband. She scribbled with pencil or diamond on door or window: "Comme Louis m'ennuie! Comme Louis m'ennuie!"

She grew into a comely, stately lady, and looked very queenly in the celebrated royal emeralds.

I saw the sardine fishery while staying there. It was at a little place further south, where the shore was shelving and without rocks. There was an immense seine-net with very wide meshes at the mouth of the bag, and very fine at the point. The mouth was quite four hundred yards across, and very many cords attached it to two cables.

The net was taken out to sea and spread, and the ends of the cables were fast on shore. The upper side of the net was floated with corks, the lower was leaded.

The net was left till it was seen that there was a shoal of sardines between it and the shore. Then the hauling in began. I saw as many as thirty bullocks hauling at the cables.

When the net was high and dry the purse of fine mesh was cut open, and out came thousands of sardines. These were soon carried off to market, or to the curing and tinning places near. I don't think there is a better fish in existence than the fresh sardine.

No one who has not seen Oporto has any idea what an attractive spot it is, and very few Englishmen have seen the great beauties and variety of scenery of the Douro.

The granite-built churches of Oporto and their carved granite adornments are very remarkable and fine.

The port-wine merchants are a very pleasant society, and very hospitable, and the lodges (logias), as the immense wine-stores are called, and the gigantic vats are most interesting. It is all above ground.

I may mention here an old gold-mine which a few years later I had some interest in, and which was reopened as a spec. It was a few miles up the Douro - Rio do Oro (River of Gold), and had been very largely worked by the Romans down to water-level, which stopped them.

We thought that if it were worth their while to work it so extensively without blasting-powder, and with their primitive means of extracting the gold from the ore, it must be worth putting pumps in and reopening.

The water was pumped out, and the ore was mined and milled, but, alas! it proved much too poor to pay even with all modern science.

It showed how valuable gold must have been then, and how cheap labour.

It was in a hill - one may say mountain - on the bank of the Douro, the situation delightful.

The workings were most interesting: the galleries as narrow as it was possible to work in, and rock-cutting economized in every possible way. What a time the slaves must have had there!

I visited one or two other gold-mines about Spain, one in a very secluded part of Guadalajara, but though very interesting, there was no ore worth working. I also had a turn at tin-mines, and with a couple of friends put up enough money to give it a fair turn.

We got a very clever young engineer who had been some time doing tin in Cornwall, and I devoted a few weeks to going round with him to all the tin places we could hear of.

I cannot say it was a tour of luxury, but he put up with it very well; only a wet afternoon in a loft over a mule-stable was not an inspiriting place in which to write, eat, and sleep.

We took great pains to try and find something that seemed promising, but could find nothing that gave any prospect of paying more than for just native scratching the lodes and for local hand-washing.

Tin there is, and a good deal of it, but the veins are what the Yankees call "knife-blade" ones, and the alluvial not in quantity enough to pay for mechanical washing.

There were small companies working in two places, one French, where we were very well received, and shown everything, but we found nothing we could recommend to serious people in England.

I saw some wild scenery, and was surprised to find how common wolves were in places. Walking one night to where I was sleeping with a native, we passed a sheep-fold, and he said: "A wolf took a sheep from there last night."

We had a run through Galicia, which I was interested to see, much of it very pretty country, and I had picked up enough of the Gallego dialect to get in. When fertile there the land is subdivided into the most minute properties, over which the people are always squabbling, and a man who has never had a lawsuit is thought very little of.

The people are desperately superstitious, and the local saint is like a tribal deity.

I heard one story of two small districts on the coast separated by a small river. One day a man who wanted something came across, but was told nothing could be done, as it was the *fiesta* of their saint.

He used one or two forcible but not polite words about the saint, whereupon his worshippers "fell upon him that he died".

Litigation - as the Yankees say - followed, and when the defenders of the reputation of the saint were asked for their defence, they said to the presiding magistrate: "Look here, sir, this man might have used this language about the Holy Virgin, or one of the Apostles - that would not have concerned us; but when it comes to our saint, who brings us the fish, and the crops, and the sunshine, that was too much, so we killed him". Then the magistrate said: "Well, perhaps after all you are right; you may have acted quite properly, so there is an end of the matter!"

The following is a specimen of their "hand-to-mouth" piety. A man crossing a very bad torrent by a narrow plank, and wishing to stand in with both parties, said, as he crept across step by step, "Dios es bueno, y el Diable no es tan malo" (God is good, and the Devil is not so bad!), which he repeated to please both till he got across; but, once on firm ground, he exclaimed, "I spit upon them both!"

Travelling in out-of-the-way parts of Spain and Portugal, one now and then put up with the local padre. It is an understood thing, and in the morning one gives a good tip to his housekeeper.

One now and then comes across a man of some intelligence, but most of them are very ignorant and very narrow-minded. Their private character is often what in more civilized parts would be considered very shaky, but their flocks don't take any stock of that at all.

In Brazil they were a very queer lot, as Lady Burton had to acknowledge, and in the Argentine and Paraguay they have themselves told me some very curious stories. I knew the padre at Frayle Muerto in the Argentine, who was a well-educated Italian, and who seemed to have left Italy for some good reason not disclosed. He was a clever and most devoted worker during the cholera epidemic, but he made no secret to an intimate of his goings-on with some of the fair members of his flock.

Speaking of ecclesiastical matters, I was amused at Salamanca, in a curious old church I was looking at with a friend, by the sacristan, who I asked about some venerable man buried there, who I spoke of as a saint. He said: "He is not a saint yet, but I think he soon will be; they tell me his papers are nearly in order!"

CHAPTER XXII

AVILA TO SALAMANCA

While I was working at the Delagoa Bay Railway, I kept looking for something useful to be at, and heard, when in Madrid, of the projected railway from Avila to Salamanca through Peñaranda de Bracamonte.

It seemed a good project, and I, with my friend Julius Beerbohm, went into it seriously. A good-looking, very amusing, very shifty Chilian, named Cardosa, living in Madrid, had it in hand, and some of the others were kittle - cattle to work with; but in Spain one must take things and men as one finds them. When something very startling turns up, they only remark, "Cosa de España!"

They are a curious race to live among and work with - charming manners, the stateliness of which is mistaken for stiffness of character, whereas they are most genial and jolly when one lives with them.

My old friend Sir Clare Ford, the Ambassador, was quite right when he said to me: "I find this reported standoffishness is all humbug. If you want to get on, poke the men in the ribs, and pinch the women's legs!" And he was quite right.

But, alas! they were very hard to trust. They mistrusted each other, and naturally all foreigners, and this one found most disappointing, and often disastrous.

We made our headquarters in Madrid, and took a flat of several rooms in the Calle Florin, near the Cortes. Our friend Robert Carr, a clever lawyer, came out, and we set seriously to work.

Surveys, questions of finance, of estimates, and of contractors took up time and labour.

I had to be a great deal at Avila, the point where the line was to leave the North of Spain, and passes through Peñaranda to reach Salamanca direct, and so cut off the long round by Medina del Campo.

Avila is a strange old place, the walls enormously thick and strong, and in places high and perfect, and over nine hundred years old. The lower part of the town is in ruins inside the walls.

It is a dog-hole of a place, dismal to live in, and the hotel (!) left everything to be desired, though kept by an ex-cavalry officer, an extremely good fellow.

The cathedral is very interesting, part of its massive walls forming the city wall.

There is a very curious, very old church there, lately restored by the Government - for the Government now does much for ancient buildings - and these and the cathedral I examined closely in this way, for I am, when alone, a poor sight-seer.

I got a letter from Sir Clare to say that a great friend of his, a most agreeable man - Mr. Mocatta - was coming up, and would I show him everything?

I found him as pleasant a man as ever I had met, and that he had taken a great interest in the Jews in many parts of the world.

He spoke a curious dialect of Spanish fluently, and I asked him what it was. He said that, after the horrible cruelties of Ferdinand and Isabella, when they exiled the Jews from Spain, the exiles had always preserved the knowledge of the Spanish language, that very many Jews spoke it, and that he had got on with it in all sorts of places. I remembered that many years before the Spanish Consul at Jerusalem told us the same thing.

With this pleasant companion I examined the town carefully, and when going round the cathedral, the sacristan was very ready to show more than I had seen before. Pressed by my companion, he carefully locked the door of the sacristy, where was much church plate and some beautiful vestments, and opened a well-concealed secret closet. There was seen a large and exquisitely worked silver shrine, which I found that very few people had seen.

When inspecting the old church, we were told that it was built to the memory of a Christian Roman soldier martyred there.

The man guiding us, to my companion's amusement, showed us

a hole where lived a serpent which had come out, and for long guarded the body of the martyr. He added that a Jew who saw the miracle
of the serpent was so moved that he became a Christian, and helped
to build the church.

The legend in Avila was that the town was never taken by the
Saracens: that once all the men were away, and a body of Saracens attacked it, but the women put on armour, and made such a show of
defence that the enemy drew off.

The country through which the railway was to pass is not at all
difficult-flat or rolling, with no serious earthworks or bridges. It is
fertile, and has been called the granary of Spain and the granary of
Castile. The antediluvian system of agriculture, however, ruins it -
the same crops year after year, and scarcely any top dressing.

Trees there are scarcely any - everything cut down for firewood.
I one day asked the alcalde of a place why they never planted trees,
and he said it would need a guard night and day to preserve one tree!

The main roads under Government are excellent; as for the by-
roads, like the snakes in Ireland, there are none. There are tracks,
stony or muddy according to the soil, and that is all. There are the
equivalent to road-rates, but none of the money ever reaches a road;
the man who let it escape his fingers would indeed be thought a fool!

The village may lie a couple of hundred yards from the sound
high-road, but the moment you leave it you plunge into mud axle-
deep.

When negotiating for local subscriptions towards the railway, I
visited some very curious primitive places. In one we were received
by the local Town Council of about twenty members. They were all
dressed exactly alike in black cloth-short jackets like the bull-fight-
ers, open waistcoats, and narrow ties in a slip-knot, and the ends fastened down in front; black trousers, tight above, loose below, and sort
of pumps for shoes; flat, low-crowned hats; clean-shaved, except a
tiny bit of mutton-chop whiskers.

They were the most solemn assembly that I was ever before. One
could see the same Spain of three or four hundred years ago at a
glance.

They listened, and were very attentive and polite, but there it
ended. They no more wanted a railway than they wanted the moon.

They viewed us as having our own axe to grind and pocket to fill,
as did an old fellow I heard of at a meeting in Glasgow.

The railway companies there wanted Sunday trains allowed, and a friend of mine was put up to show the benefits of them to the townspeople. He eloquently contrasted the open hills and glorious air with the slums and grubby streets, and sat down much pleased. Up gets a canny old Scot, and this was all he said: "This he said, not that he cared for the poor, but that he was a thief, and carried the bag!"

My friend got about as much change out of it as we did out of those old fossils.

I said to the advanced Liberal alcalde of Peñaranda that I was so interested to see those old dresses and customs, and hoped they would not change; but he said he thought it shocking that it could still exist in the nineteenth century.

At one place near Salamanca, when we were at luncheon, as we were going our rounds, we were waited on by a fine young woman, whom some of my party seemed to know well, and who had lately had a turn in a convent. The Spanish chaff was what they would call *muy salero* (very spicey), and she was quite ready for it, and the light it threw upon the "goings-on" in the convent where she had lately been would have startled the good old St. Theresa, who lies buried so near, and who had been so concerned in reforming the morals of the converts of her day.

There is a stone about a mile up on the hill from Avila to mark where the saint kicked off her shoes to testify against the evils of Avila when she returned to Alva de Tormes.

I just missed a great festival at Avila to celebrate a centenary or something of the sort of St. Theresa.

Her effigy at Alva de Tormes was brought over with great ceremony, and our facetious Chilian friend Cardosa gave us a humorous account of the whole thing. He said some of the people were uneasy at leaving the two St. Theresas in the cathedral together all night for fear they should fall out.

The presiding padre gave him an old bone to kiss, but he said, "Must I really kiss it?" And the padre smiled, and said he would let him off.

The great difficulty of the line was how on earth to cross the tremendous rocky valley and hills between Avila and the more easy country beyond to Salamanca.

I went day after day with our engineers, but it was evident that it would be a very heavy and very costly work; we could find no way to make it simple.

The result has been that, like other things in Spain, the rest of the line has been made, but it has never been connected with the northern at Avila.

I spent many a dreary day and evening at that little dog-hole Peñaranda de Bracamonte, whose name is as large as itself.

The inhabitants were civil and hospitable, according to their lights, but though I often went to their houses in the evening, I never had a meal in one all the time I was there on and off. Spanish hospitality is complimentary and sketchy; you don't get fat on it.

I was dining one night with Sir Clare Ford, and the other man there was the Madrid agent of one of the greatest European banking houses. I was speaking to Sir Clare of my experience, and he said: "What do you mean? Why, I could dine out every night in the week if I liked". I said: "Yes, and at how many houses? The Duke of Alva, the Duke of Fernan Nunez, and a very few others keep open house; no one else ever gives a dinner-party. And the other guest, with years of Spanish experience, said: "Mr. Seymour is quite right". I have given dinners in Madrid, and they would come and drink heaps of champagne, but never gave a dinner! One must remember one thing - that most of them are very poor. There is no trade or manufacture of any sort in Madrid, and there are no well-to-do men of business - a few very rich great nobles, and that is all.

The *fonda* was a queer little shanty. It was rather of the nature of what is called a *casa de huespedes*, a house where people are taken in and done for-boarding-house.

There was a common table in a very small room, which had two closets off it, each large enough to hold a bed, and with glazed doors, and no ventilation of any sort. Here slept two *huespedes*! (guests).

There was one window, and in cold weather (and it could be very cold) there was a brass dish of hot charcoal under the table in a wooden frame.

The edge of this was the favourite lair of a mongrel red puppy, of the sort that the Yankees designate a "yaller dog" in contempt. Now and then we smelt singed hair above the aroma of garlic, fried oil, and *bacalao*, then a howl, and this was the pup, who in his dreams had rolled into the hot ashes. He looked very patchy as winter went on.

With the ancient city of Salamanca I made an intimate acquaintance. The oldest thing about it is the old Roman bridge, and I should think that the natural perfume of the town must be nearly as old. The Salamancan native might say, as did the returning exile to Edinburgh: "Ah, dear Auld Reekie, I smell ye again!"

I drove into Salamanca one day with some Spaniards, and at the hotel we went upstairs. I nearly fainted with asphyxiation till I could get to a window and put my head out. The natives roared with laughter, and said I did not understand the native breezes. And yet I was not new to it!

At the hotel there was one stove in the long dining-room, the iron tube chimney of which ran the whole length of the room. This was only lighted at meal-times. In the rest of the house a few dishes of charcoal were all the warmth known. I arrived there once out of a driving snowstorm; the only warmth was a room with a large round table, under the centre of which was a *brasero* full of ashes, all the chilly guests sitting round with legs and arms under the tablecloth!

The field of the battle, some four or five miles out of Salamanca, was interesting. It is locally called the battle "de los Arapilles" from two round hills there, which were the centre of the fighting.

Against these Wellington concentrated his forces, putting the unlucky Portuguese troops in front, as they wanted a lot of driving on.

I had a talk with an old woman who, as a young girl, saw the battle. She remembered the sufferings of the French wounded on the hot night after the battle, to whom the Spaniards would give no water, they hated them so. It was in June.

She was full of the brutalities of the French soldiers, and told me how the Colonel of a French regiment treated the alcalde of the place (who had displeased him) in the same way that, as Byron says, the Sultan of Turkey and the Popes of Rome treat their chief attendants and great chapel-singers.

The University of Salamanca has long since disappeared, and I could not help thinking of the great sermon I had heard Dean Stanley preach at Oxford, foretelling the fate of that great centre of learning if she allowed ecclesiastical narrowness to stop every sort of advancement in knowledge and science.

Only one or two schools for boys still hold on there, the wretched boys of which were loafing about the streets and cafés of the place.

I asked a friend why the Spanish schools were never in the country, and he said: "Because the professors and masters would not for a minute put up with the dulness of a rural existence".

Of the many bull-fights, big and little, which I saw I don't think I need say much; they are too well known. The skill and pluck of the men I learned to appreciate, but the brutality to the horses always disgusted me. They said that that part was necessary to take the edge off the bulls before the men could safely tackle them. But I regret to say that I found the people, both men and women, enjoyed the barbarity of it. Accidents there were; I have seen two men killed, and more badly hurt.

If one expressed any feeling for the horses, all that they said was: "No vale nada" (It is of no value). Cruelty is a word not understood in too many countries, in the Latin ones especially. The people would enjoy the gladiator shows just as much as the Romans did.

At local affairs sometimes bullocks and cows were let in for the populace to bait. A cow is very dangerous, very sly, and charges with her eyes open; the bull generally shuts his.

I once saw a little boy caught by a bullock and tossed very high; he fell over its tail, and got up and ran away laughing.

But if they were too poor to have more than one bull the agony was prolonged as much as possible, and small boys were brought up to stick a knife into the still breathing animal, to give them courage, as they said!

They are a strange race, and, I cannot but agree with Lord Salisbury, a decayed nationality; I don't believe it possible to revive them. The causes of decay are a much-vexed question. Religion may have something to do with it, but did the religion make the character, or the character make the religion?

One strange thing is that even among the most apparently well educated - I say apparently, for, though very showily educated, as many of them are, it is absolutely on the surface - they are mostly professors of Free-thought on religion, but have a strong substratum of superstition.

A man tells me he is of no sort of religion one day, and next day I see him kissing the Bishop's hand, escorting him into town, and letting off fireworks in the day-time to his honour.

He speaks of the "Iglesia Catolica Apostolica Romana" with a bow, and, while he says he believes nothing, would go to see me burnt as a heretic just as gaily as he would go to the Plaza de Toros!

Social morality troubles them very little; the Eleventh Commandment, "Thou shalt not be found out", very much.

The conversation is of the same freedom that I fancy it was in the days of Queen Elizabeth, and could only be repeated in la *lengua Castillana* and to Spaniards.

A woman is looked after in the same sort of way that she was centuries ago; she is considered compromised if a man has a chance of being half an hour alone with her!

For a foreigner to pay an afternoon call was then almost an unknown thing. It may have changed.

If you get Spanish women out of Spain - they are often most charming - they are very different, and more like the ladies of other nations; it is the men who are the bother to one in Spain.

Spanish men have a curious jealousy of foreign men in Madrid, whether diplomats or whatnot; the tradition is that they must not have the chance of being intimate with their women.

One unfortunate thing of the women is that they hardly ever read. You scarcely ever see a book in a Spanish house. They are all desperate talkers, but it is mostly chaff, flirtation of sorts, and nonsense.

They will get up the most childish, elaborate, practical jokes like this:

A few of them at Biarritz agreed to play a prank on an American there who wanted to hang on to their set, and of whom they were wearied.

A sham secret society was formed with midnight meetings, fearsome ceremonies, and blood-curdling oaths of fidelity and obedience.

A traitor to the society was discovered; he was tried, and condemned to death. Lots were drawn for his murderer, and of course the lot fell on the luckless Yankee.

The victim was decoyed one night to the Spanish frontier; he was seized, the bag of blood was placed over his heart, which was well guarded, and under dread of instant death the transatlantic assassin did his bloody work.

He made his escape from the French police, and the victim went back to supper in Biarritz! I could give the very well-known names of the conspirators.

Pretence bull-fights are got up at picnics, particularly in Andalusia.

I had the following experience at one of them:

After our luncheon a young bull was let loose in the yard, and I had to do *bandarillero* with a coat as *capa*. The brute dodged me round the support of a shed, and I was soon on my back with him pounding at my ribs. Fortunately his horns were short, and a very young one butts with his forehead, not with one horn, but it is not enjoyment all the same!

He was pulled off by the tail, and I was rather sore, and very dirty.

I said it was all very well to roar with laughter, and they said: "Oh, you would have laughed if you could have seen your long legs kicking at his nose!" I had to dance with the *muchachas* for a long while after, but was very stiff next day.

They related the story in the town, and said that in reality after luncheon I saw two bulls - the wine bull and the real bull - that I escaped the wine bull, but the real bull caught me.

Some of the girls (of sorts!) will now and then tuck up their skirts and join in the fun, but very rarely. I only personally saw one, and as she was running away the beast gave her a tremendous lift behind, but luckily lifted her over the barrier, and she was not much hurt.

I was made a member of the Veloz Club in Madrid, but I did not use it much, as there was little to do there but play cards, and I was not just then in a humour for that.

The dining-places in Madrid are very few, about three; they are very fair, and we used them pretty often, but when we had our own house we got a fair cook, bought up the remains of the wines sold off for the hotel at Huelva – some very good, all very cheap - and gave pleasant little dinners to young diplomats and some very pleasant Spanish young fellows.

So time passed on, and the company of the Avila and Salamanca Railway was launched in London.

It went to a certain degree, but not very successfully. The works were begun and finished between Salamanca and Peñaranda, but money ran short, and the line has never been completed to Avila.

At the end I was an older, a more experienced, and a poorer man. That was all!

Though I lived a good deal in Madrid, and had many friends and acquaintances, and was also made a member of two clubs, I knew very little of the ladies of Madrid society.

Of course, I had not much spare time, but my experience of it was that, polite and cordial as Spanish men seemed to be, they did not want foreigners to know in the least intimately the ladies of society.

What we call morning visits - which mean afternoon ones - seemed unknown, except, perhaps, among a very few Spanish ladies who had lived enough out of Madrid to get into foreign ways.

As far as I could make out, the Spanish lady who is Spanish in her habits runs about in the house in much the state she gets out of bed, only with a wrapper of sorts on, the thickness depending on the thermometer, till she dresses for the afternoon. The meals are all excessively casual, a guest rarely coming, except a very intimate relation. If they went to church early, they mostly wore a mantilla, but made no toilette whatever. I am speaking of thirty years ago.

In the afternoon they made themselves smart, put on too much powder, and drove out. A carriage was a necessity, however poor. Any sort of pinching must be done to have a smart dress and hat and a carriage.

A story was told of a conversation heard in the Retiro. A lady told the coachman to drive round again, and the answer was: "No, mother, I cannot; I am tired out. I am going home. Up all last night waiting for you at the ball, I have had enough of it!" - a dutiful son in coachman's livery, for the credit of an impecunious family!

I went to two or three great balls, which were well done, as they were in the very great houses. There were some very fine jewels, but not as much beauty as I expected.

Spanish women strike the new-comer much, but there is rather a sameness in their looks after living among them. But their eyes, of course, are generally splendid, and they *do* know how to use them. A dead white skin, generally as smooth as polished ivory, mostly pretty little feet, and, when young, often delightfully developed figures, which, alas! go terribly to pieces very soon. Want of exercise and love of sweets put on weight much too quickly.

They are naturally bright and quick, but generally very unread and ignorant. Of course, I am speaking of the absolutely Spanish ones, not those who have travelled.

I went to a ball at our Embassy, which was much considered, on account of the liberal supply of supper and champagne. Nourishment for the animal is little thought of at Spanish houses.

Early in the evening there was a large supply of cigars and cigarettes in the smoking-room, but large and hungry pockets soon made a clean sweep of everything!

The Embassy then was originally the old palace of the Grand Inquisitor, and there was a disused passage under the street to the dismal and horrible dungeons of the Holy Office.

One could not help thinking of the brutal, bloodthirsty followers of St. Dominic, who had for centuries held their orgies across the street, revelling in the shrieks and groans of helpless men, women, and children, all, as they said, to the honour and glory of the Christian God of love and mercy, because the poor wretches did not agree with them about some nonsensical doctrine or dogma, invented by man, and which meant little or nothing to anyone.

The more one lives in Spain, the more one feels that it has never recovered from that baptism of blood, flame, and torture, and that fear and distrust are still the inheritance of the people, who are as superstitious as the obi-worshippers.

The problem oft discussed was, as I have said before: Did the character of the people make that religion, or did that religion form the character of the people? I don't think even the most liberal-minded Spaniard ever quite shakes off an inborn sense of fear and distrust. Their swagger of free-thinking sounded so often to me like a thing put on to disguise their natural fear of something, they could not say what.

Chapter XXIII

DELAGOA BAY RAILWAY

*I*t was in the year 1883, while I was in Lisbon, interested in copper-mines, and in daily intercourse with my amusing companion Jean Burnay, that my connection with the Delagoa Bay Railway began.

He had talked to me now and then of the concession which the Portuguese Government proposed to give for a railway from the port of Lorenço Marques, generally known here as Delagoa Bay, to the north-east frontier of the Transvaal.

The line in itself was only a short one of some fifty-two miles, and would pass through a country without known agricultural or mineral value. It could therefore never even pay working expenses. But, with the continuation which the Transvaal Government was under treaty engagement with Portugal to construct from its frontier to Pretoria, it would form part of a trunk-line so much shorter than any route either from the Cape or Natal as to make successful competition on the part of the British colonies impossible.

At this time the great mineral wealth of the Transvaal was unknown, and the Pretoria Government, which had been obliged to borrow money to pay its few officials, was in no condition to build or subsidize the Transvaal section; while the Lisbon Government, on its side, could not afford a subsidy, although it was ready to give a liberal land grant and harbour privileges at Delagoa Bay.

It happened, however, that I had heard from some mining friends that gold had been discovered in the Lydenberg district, and I at once made up my mind that it was not likely to be confined to one

particular district in a great and unexplored country, and that therefore the despised railway concession might turn out to have great value. When, therefore, Burnay one day mentioned to me that a great
friend of his, Senhor Chagas, had just been appointed Colonial Minister, I said to him: "If your friend will give me the concession, without a money subvention, but on liberal terms otherwise, I will take
it". That same evening we interviewed the Minister, and I came away
with the concession in my pocket, so to speak.

Returning to England, I found that the concession was much easier to obtain than the money needed to give it effect, and I had tried
every probable source in vain, when I happened to meet in St. James's
Street my old friend Colonel Francis Baring, to whom I mentioned
my difficulty. Said he: "I know the very man for you - a superior sort
of American promoter, who is forming a company to mine in the
Transvaal;" and thus it was that I became introduced to Colonel Edward MacMurdo, who for some years was somewhat of a conspicuous figure amongst City financiers.

MacMurdo, who, to do him justice, had won his rank on the bat-
tle-fields of the Civil War, and was built on big lines, both mental and
physical, possessed quite remarkable foresight and breadth of view in
financial matters, untiring industry, and great personal magnetism;
but the fine qualities were marred by an extraordinary vanity, which
was fostered by the group of satellites whom he loved to maintain
around him until it almost amounted to a disease.

When I called upon him, he carefully listened to my story, made
a few notes, and then, turning to me and removing for a moment the
big cigar which was eternally in his mouth, he laconically said: "Mr.
Seymour, the value of this line is political as much as commercial. I
will build it".

On that very day we began to arrange the "caution money" of
£15,000, which had to be put up, and from then onwards during five
years I passed the greater part of my life backwards and forwards between London and Lisbon.

In those days there was no Sud express train, and I have had to
pass the three nights sitting up in a crowded carriage, and during the
three days I only got a hurried splash at a tap for a wash, and a hasty
meal at some station. What a luxury the *wagonlits* and dining-cars
seemed later on!

While MacMurdo and I were in Lisbon, arranging the formation of the Portuguese company by which the concession was to be worked, there appeared at the Hôtel Braganza, at which we were staying, President Kruger, with two of his Ministers, Schmidt and Detoit. They had come for our concession - the money for which they had arranged at Amsterdam - and were furious when they heard that it had already gone elsewhere. They alternately bullied and wheedled the Colonial Minister either to take the concession away from Mac-Murdo or to give them a parallel railway (although our concession gave us a monopoly), but Senhor Chagas indignantly rejected both proposals as "dishonourable". One morning the three Boers suddenly left for Paris - so far as we knew, defeated; but I was filled with misgivings when old Maria, our head chambermaid, called me aside in a mysterious manner, and described how, in passing MacMurdo's bedroom door in the early morning, General Schmidt had indulged in a few steps of a breakdown, while the usually sombre President had "put his thumb unto his nose and spread his fingers out".

We were shortly to learn by a little experience that their jubilation was well founded, the fact being that they carried away with them a "secret memorandum", signed by the Foreign Minister (to whom they had gone after their rebuff by the Colonial Minister), which gave them the right to build a steam "tramway" parallel to the railway, in case its construction was not carried out with what they might consider due diligence. Imagine Sir Edward Grey giving such an engagement after its refusal by the Colonial Secretary, and without the knowledge of any other member of the Cabinet, or the King himself!

This "secret" document was unscrupulously divulged by the Boers, with the object of preventing MacMurdo from raising capital before the concession ran out, so that they might come into the reversion which had been promised them. Once in Brussels, once in Paris, once in England, the construction funds had been promised, but on each occasion the capitalists withdrew from the negotiation on account of the tramway promise, of which "confidential" information had been allowed to reach them, although its existence was each time denied by the Colonial Minister, who, with his colleagues and the King, remained in ignorance of its terms for some four years, until a copy was furnished by the Boer Government, none having been preserved in the archives of the Foreign Office.

At the last moment, so to speak, when only some ten months of the concession remained, a strong group of English capitalists agreed to brave the Boer opposition, and to raise the needed construction funds by an issue of the debentures of an English company. They were very insistent that the concession itself, which was then vested in a Portuguese company, of which MacMurdo held practically all the shares, should be transferred to this company, but I warned them that the Portuguese Government would never sanction such a breach of the terms of the concession, and their very astute lawyer, Mr. W. Capel Slaughter, pointed out that their object could quite well be obtained by keeping alive the Portuguese company, and transferring to the new company the shares which MacMurdo held.

Making, at their urgent request, yet another visit to Lisbon to see what could be done, I found, on my arrival there, a most grave and perilous state of affairs. So powerful had Boer influences become, and so certainly was it assumed that the construction funds could not be obtained, that a decree rescinding the concession had *actually been signed by the King*, and was awaiting publication in the official gazette.

I explained to the Colonial Minister the favourable turn which our prospects had taken, but I found him - as I expected - inexorable that the terms of the concession should be strictly complied with in relation to the Portuguese company, and so emphatically a *persona non grata* had MacMurdo become that it was only after convincing him that the management of the English company would be in the hands of an independent and highly reputable board of directors that I was enabled to cable to London that the line was cleared for the debenture issue.

The issue was promptly made, the debentures being liberally subscribed, and I had packed up and was about to start on my return journey, when a long cable was handed to me which indicated that our ship was likely to be wrecked at the very moment when it seemed safely in port. The wrecking this time appeared to have a Portuguese rather than a Boer origin, as my cable informed me that in the leading morning papers there had appeared a semi-official statement, evidently emanating from the Portuguese Financial Agent in London, to the effect that the position of the company was irregular according to Portuguese law and the terms of the concession itself. In the face of this declaration the directors were naturally hesitating to allot, and subscriptions were being withdrawn, so that, unless a prompt contradiction could be obtained, the whole issue would collapse.

Not a moment was to be lost, as it was already late in the evening, so I hurried off to our lawyer, a very able man, but a politician, and a viveur who wanted money. I found him playing billiards at his club, and ruthlessly dragged him out. He was receiving a large fee, half of which I had paid him, and when I had made him understand that his getting the other half depended entirely on what he could do within the next three hours, he developed a really remarkable energy, and started an immediate chase of the Minister through all sorts of curious, un-Cabinet Minister places, until at length we ran our quarry to ground. Then my companion pointed out to him, with great vehemence and eloquence, that the action of the Financial Agent would reflect on the Minister himself as a breach of good faith, a national dishonour, and so worked on him that he then and there drew up a cable to London, which we saw despatched ourselves, ordering the Agent to officially declare that the position of the English company was quite legal and in order.

It was broad daylight before I got back to my hotel, but the situation was saved, and the allotment took place without any further hitch.

The fury of Kruger when he found that the line was to be under British control was unbounded, and the Portuguese Government was bombarded with despatches which accused it of want of good faith in not publishing the already signed Decree of Rescission, and issuing a new concession to the Boers, as promised, and which categorically declared that, as long as the fifty-two miles remained in English hands, the continuation on Boer territory should never be built, so that the smaller enterprise would have to die of starvation.

Meanwhile the construction of the line was pushed on with a vigour and ability which the inspecting engineer, Major Machado, reported to his Government he had never seen equalled, the requirements of the concession being, he said, largely exceeded, in order to give greater stability to the line, with the result that within the time allowed the line was opened for traffic; and the Portuguese Governor, at the inaugural banquet, was equally complimentary to the company. The prospects of the company now appeared to be rosy in the extreme, but its directors soon found to their cost that they had quite underrated the resourcefulness of their wily old foe at Pretoria.

About the time that the English company was formed it was discovered at Lisbon that the plans which had been originally drawn up by the Portuguese engineer, and which had been handed to the concessionaire as those of a line, to the "Transvaal frontier", fell short by at least nine kilometres; but this mistake was not pointed out to the concessionaire until about two months before the line as originally planned was completed, when the Portuguese engineer astounded his English colleague by handing him the plans of the additional section of nine kilometres, which presented more engineering difficulties than all the rest of the line, at the same time admitting to him that the point marked on the frontier was a purely hypothetical one, as no frontier had ever yet been delimited.

The company, on being advised of this action, promptly made representation at Lisbon to the effect that they were willing to comply with the terms of the concession, and build to the frontier, but that to do that it was necessary that the Government should agree upon a frontier-point with the Transvaal, and then notify the company where it was. The Government recognized this request as reasonable, and at once cabled to Pretoria, asking that an engineer might be sent to meet the Portuguese representative, and fix on the frontier-point. The answer to this was that, until the concession had been taken from the English and given to the Boers, *no frontier-point would be agreed to*, and a most peremptory demand was made that the concession should at once be forfeited.

As the result of this pressure, the Portuguese Government issued a Royal Decree that the nine kilometres should be built to the point which was not the frontier, and that the work should be completed within the absurdly unreasonable period of eight months, of which four were in the bad season, when work was impossible.

Finding protests useless, the company faced the situation with such remarkable vigour that the construction was in good train to be completed within two months after the expiration of the prescribed term, which was to expire on the 26th May, 1889. MacMurdo cabled to Washington, asking for the intervention of Mr. Blaine, the Secretary of State, and the English board appealed to Lord Salisbury; and, as the result, the British and American Ministers at Lisbon used their friendly offices to obtain a few weeks' grace, which could harm no one, but were informed that a promise had been given to the Boer Government which could not be broken. The matter was further complicated by the sudden death of MacMurdo in the beginning of May, and the directors then sent for me, and asked me to undertake a last journey to Lisbon on their behalf. To this I reluctantly consented, but on reaching Lisbon I found, as I anticipated, that nothing could be done and I at once returned to London, and so reported.

Unfortunately, my association with this enterprise, which had lasted for more than six years, and was now ended, entailed upon me a great deal of hard work and anxiety, without a corresponding reward. The weak point of MacMurdo, as I have said, was his excessive personal vanity, and he never forgave me because, when I found that his unpopularity at Lisbon was likely to lose him the concession, I had deemed it wise to keep him as much as possible in the background, and to push his interests in the name of the new directors, who were favourably known to Ministers. As I had made no hard and fast written contract with him, he was able - and did not scruple - when we came to a settlement, to show his pique by paying me much less than the amount which was properly due to me. So, also, he successfully used his influence to prevent my going on the Board of either the Portuguese or the English company, where my presence was desired, because of the special knowledge which I had of the railway complications and of my good relations with the Lisbon Government, and also that I was the only man who personally knew all the men in Lisbon we had to work with.

I greatly regretted this, as I really thought I could have helped to brush away some of the misunderstandings which it was the great object of the Boer party to foster between the company and Lisbon. The ultimate fate of the railway was disastrous in the extreme.

On the very day that the eight months expired the concession was cancelled, and the railway forcibly seized, the Government, in answer to the protests of the English directors, coolly suggesting that they should seek their remedy in the Portuguese courts.

The American Government, however, took up a very strong attitude on behalf of MacMurdo's widow, and insisted that Portugal should immediately restore the line, or pay adequate compensation to the American Government direct. Lord Salisbury then fell into line on behalf of the English debenture-holders, and eventually the amount of compensation to be paid was left to be fixed by three Swiss "jurists" to be appointed by the Swiss President. The result of this easy way of shelving responsibility by a Government towards its subjects has been a good object-lesson to those thick and thin upholders of arbitration in all cases of dispute.

The desultory way in which the proceedings were allowed to drag along by these good gentlemen became a public scandal, and spoiled for ever the arbitration business as far as Swiss lawyers as arbitrators are concerned, for although the matter could have been comfortably completed within two years, no less than ten years elapsed between the reference and the decision!

I was well au courant with the progress of the arbitration by reason of my friendship with some of the counsel employed. The British leader, that accomplished linguist and lawyer, was E. M. Underdown, Q.C., who had a knowledge of Roman law, and also of modern Continental languages unique at the English Bar, but who was better known to me as a charming raconteur who had lightened many weary hours in Spain with a succession of most excellent stories. His junior, MacIlwraith, at that time young and briefless, had studied law in Paris, and spoke and wrote French perfectly, and his conduct of the case so gained for him the favour of the Foreign Office that he is now Sir Malcolm MacIlwraith, the judicial Adviser to the Khedive of Egypt.

The American counsel were my very old friend John Trehane, an Englishman by birth, who had practised at the San Francisco Bar, with the celebrated "Colonel Bob" Ingersoll, who was understood to be as sound as a lawyer as he was eloquent as an orator, and in connection with them a ludicrous thing happened. After their appointment it was discovered that the proceedings were to be in French, of which language the eloquent Colonel understood not a word! The whole burden of the ten years' fight therefore fell on the shoulders of Trehane, who by common consent proved more than equal to it.

The long-delayed judgement, when it did come, was a condemnation of the Portuguese Government, but the damages awarded were ludicrously small, and the subject of general indignation. It was evident that the arbitrators had been quite unable to grasp the business aspects of the matter, and that a fatal mistake had been made by the President in confining his choice of jurists to his own compatriots, accustomed only to dealing with local issues and small values in a secluded country.

Nothing in the history of the line was more remarkable than the ignorance and indifference of our Government as to its political and strategic value as contrasted with the keen appreciation of the shrewd old man at Pretoria. Kruger's great fear was that its control should pass into the hands of our Government. As we have seen, he was angry enough when he heard of the formation of the English company, but he trusted to starve it out by refusing to construct the extension, or to bully Lisbon into cancelling the concession. In 1888, however, he heard from his friends in London that the purchase of a controlling interest from MacMurdo was under consideration at the Foreign Office, and this news threw him into real consternation, as he knew that the long purse and political power of the Imperial Government would foil either the starving or the cancellation policy. Something had to be done at once, and Van Blockland, his Minister at the Hague, and Oyens, his banker, hurried to London to see MacMurdo. As the result they cabled to Pretoria that they believed British offers were being made, and that they both advised the purchase of the control for £1,100,000. Before the matter had gone much further, however, the question was raised in the Lords by Lord Rosebery, who urged a purchase in order to forestall any similar action by Germany; but the Government replied that they had determined that it was rather a matter for the South African colonies than for the Imperial Government. This danger being removed, Kruger breathed freely once more, and kept his money in his pocket. It is certain that if at that time Lord Rosebery had been Foreign Secretary instead of Lord Salisbury, this country would have been saved the thousands of lives and millions of money spent on the Boer War, for with every railway from the sea in British hands no war supplies could ever have reached Pretoria. Nor was Lord Rosebery's prevision that the control might pass into German hands at all fantastic, for just before MacMurdo's death an offer of £500,000 was made by German bankers and refused. Had it been increased, and had he lived to accept it, how difficult would have been our position at the time of the Kaiser's telegram to Kruger, and, later on, when we were actually at war!

Chapter XXIV

DINARD

*C*annot pass over without a line the many weeks of easy happy life
that I spent at Dinard.

Each summer I used to go and join a most charming little society of intimate friends there.

Some years back it was little known to any but a few French families who went there for *les bains de me*r, and a few English ones who
had found out its quiet charms, and persuaded some quietly-disposed
friends to join them.

In the early days there was no dressing up, no show, no unnecessary expense. Everyone knew everyone. The young people could run
loose from infancy to twenty; there was no Mrs. Grundy, and no need
for her.

This may meet the eye of one of the band of eight to ten damsels,
of from ten to fifteen years, who always hunted in a pack – tennis-
court, pastry-cook quite regularly, and swimming; the evening Casino was hardly in their line. They were known as the "Desperadoes"!

Bathing-parties, shrimping ones, excursions to the oyster-beds at
Cancal, and nightly dances at the quiet little Casino.

It was the ideal social little watering-place, and, wonderful to tell,
scandals were as near as possible unknown.

There was a pleasant little club where mild poker was played,
and a little later the ladies had their poker club. But - that was at the
beginning of the change.

The rich, the dressy, the fast grew envious; the snake walked boldly in. Eve trimmed her fig-leaves with expensive lace, and Adam followed example, spending money on the lace to trim the ladies' leaves, and other things as well.

But the early days were delightful, and if I find readers who recall the mornings by the sea, and in it, and the afternoons often at the tennis-court - whence "Baby" Gore worked his way up to the championship of England - or in short trips to Dinan, and along the coast, they will agree with me that rarely has such a haven of rest and easy society been found.

The young people had it nearly all their own way, and were very censorious of the elders, among whom they classed me, though I would then hardly allow it.

It was all right as long as one was useful to teach them to swim or arrange excursions, but they viewed forty as the age of Methuselah, and the limit of all the tenderer sentiments.

I had to pass the ordeal one day at midday breakfast. There happened to be there a lady who had been one of the more than pretty women of that time, and who to men of my years was still admitted as prettier and more amusing than all the younger ones.

We happened to have gone for an early walk in the lovely summer morning, but not unperceived.

The *langouste* had just arrived (the chef had translated it to English on the menu as "Long goose"!), when one of the young ladies began: "We saw you two this morning!" Another: "Yes, we saw you. What on earth can two old things like you want with going out flirting like that!" However, she was charming, and I thought myself as still passably efficient and agreeable.

We had there that greatest of amateur swimmers, Major Knox. Forty-nine inches round the chest, a great athlete, his powers in the water were remarkable, and when he would, his methods of teaching were extraordinary. He used to accompany Captain Webb in his training swims before he did the Channel. There was a race-course, but it became unfrequented. The officers from Dinan used to come and gallop round, but at last, in a race of obstacles, six gallant warriors in uniform, all standing up in their stirrups, came at the bank and ditch, six pairs of crimson overalls were in the air, and six horses galloping off with six empty saddles! The Commanding Officer forbade any repetition of such a scene of six voluntaries!

We went one day to a farm to see the goose-plucking. One

damsel said to a plucker: "But don't they mind it very much?" The plucker answered, with a sigh: "Ah, mademoiselle, nous avons tous nos malheurs!"

Those who so often went in and out of St. Malo knew well what a dangerous coast it is, and none of us will ever forget the awful shipwreck of the *Hilda* in that snowstorm on Chausé, and, among so many others, the loss of Gerald Wellesley and his charming wife, both of whom were part of the old Dinard family party.

No one will ever forget that most hospitable and kindest of hostesses, Mrs. Spencer Chapman. She died much too soon!

One often hears of the typical *chien de faïence*, but seldom sees him inspire fear. But one afternoon I was walking with a lady past a villa, on the garden-steps of which were two very fine specimens. A peasant-woman was hesitating in the gateway, and I asked her what was the matter, and she said: Je n'ose pas d'entrer; j'ai peur des chiens!"

Chapter XXV

BURANO - ROME

I had rather an interesting trip to Italy about some drainage and irrigation works.

There had for long been a project for draining a marshy district in the neighbourhood of Ferara known as the Burano. If completed, it would bring into cultivation a large extent of rich land, and the water could be utilized.

That wonderful man Napoleon, when he ruled that province, had turned his attention to it, and if his rule had lasted his orders would have been carried out, and the works completed. As it was, some work had been done, and then the project was abandoned.

Someone had taken it up, and had got some sort of promise of a Government subsidy or security. The question was, What were the correct terms of this State aid?

A telegram arrived in London to say that they were most satisfactory, and I was asked to go out and complete the contract. I went with a very able lawyer and an Englishman interested with the Italians in it.

It was June, and hot summer, so Rome was sultry. I saw various people, but there seemed to be some hitch in the terms of the subsidy which could not be cleared up.

We worked hard in Rome, and then went to that desolate hole Ferara; its streets were indeed "wide and grass-grown".

The water of the castle moat was thick green soup, and it all looked as though no works could ever wake the place up again. While things hung fire we ran on to Venice, always delightful; and the bathing at the Lido was perfect - sand like satin, and water like milk. I love the heat, and so enjoyed it; but my legal companion, though a very good fellow, was not the ideal one I had with me later on when visiting the Queen of the Sea.

To the opera in a gondola, and back to supper in the same - that silent, dreamy, may I say romantic? - well - conveyance. Old Dizzy called the hansom-cab the gondola of London!

We gave up Ferara as no go, and returned to Rome.

I and my lawyer came to the conclusion that the telegram had been concocted between our English companion and a man in a certain position who we never could see. They certainly got some ready-money out of it from England between them, but it seemed hardly worth all the trouble. Our suspicions were confirmed by our friend one day asking to see the telegram which the lawyer held. He got hold of it, and we saw him no more, as he was off to Sicily, leaving word about a telegraphic call on business.

My lawyer said to me: "What are you going to do? "I said: "Leave the people really interested to tell me exactly on what terms they will make a contract".

The manners of these gentlemen were perfect, but every time we got near business, and seemed inclined to agree, they thought that they were being "jockeyed", and made the terms harder. At last they came to a very hard bargain, but one just possible to carry out. I said, "All right", and off we went to London.

Home in a hot July is not a treat, and there is nothing on earth to do in the evenings.

We got some let up by runs to Tivoli, Frascati, and Naples.

On my return political things took a bad turn, and Italian funds went down to such a degree as to make a bad bargain impossible.

My people said to me, "What are we to do?" So I said, "I will write the letter". I wrote in their name to say that Mr. Seymour had exceeded his instructions, and that it was not possible to carry out the contract.

The Italians applied to my friends at the Embassy, but did not get much change out of them, and I learnt that in my absence I was tried and condemned to some penalty which I have never suffered, though I have been in Italy since then.

I had another amusing trip to Rome on business, which, however, did not make my fortune.

An elderly pleasant Frenchman professed to have the authority to place some Roman municipal bonds in London. The story seemed plausible, so I was asked to go with him to Rome.

He was a pleasant, intelligent man, and things went smoothly. We put up at the Hôtel Minerva, and I was much chaffed at locating myself in the headquarters of the Neri. But my companion's friends were rather of the Neri connection.

One drawback was that the men I had to deal with confidentially knew neither English nor French, and my Spanish was of little use, and then, my Italian was of the smallest quantity. The thing was to be so secret that an interpreter was not to be used.

We talked and negotiated a lot, and the terms were excellent, but the strings of those sort of things were being pulled by very powerful financiers in London, and it was impossible to do anything really. There were men in Rome who would have liked to be free to strike new ground, but their hands were tied too tightly.

I made the acquaintance of a very able, interesting man, Signor Evangelista, for years on the staff of the Tribuna. He was liberal and anti-Papal, and he much interested me by his views of the powerful, centuries-old system of the Jesuits, and the Vatican. He pointed out to me that, whereas governments and dynasties depended so much on men and the lives of individuals, the Papal system was a thing of itself, wonderfully cleverly originated and built up, and carried on from generation to generation, regardless of changes in the dynastic face of the world and the actions of individuals.

The greatest events, revolutions, wars, and catastrophes scarcely ruffled the face of a system which intrigues and ambitions of those who had taken part in its course through ages had never been able to disturb.

Chapter XXVI

CITY - WEST AUSTRALIA

*F*inding myself "once upon a time" unoccupied, I thought that, after having worked for a company or two in the "wilds", and helping to promote the Henriette Mine, I would try what that much - maligned profession of promoter was like myself.

It may be remembered that Henry Labouchere, in his "Journal of Veracity", once humorously gave a description of joint-stock companies, not, perhaps, of the A I class. He observed that a board generally consisted of half a dozen members - five fools and one knave! And it was to join the astute collectors of such groups that I once again took my way to the City.

It was just at the time of the West Australian gold discoveries, and it seemed most propitious for the energetic promoter to reap a good harvest in the expected boom.

I joined two old friends, neither of them British-born, though both had become thoroughly at home in the City in various branches of finance.

I will not say that we started with a large capital, but we did not take large offices to spend money ourselves, only to induce others to do that for us.

We felt like the man who took a pupil to instruct in business, who was to give him a couple of thousand pounds on the ground of his large experience, and he was to work with him for two years. The young man said: "And what shall I have at the end of that time?" He replied: "Well, you see, at present you have the money and I have the experience; at the end, I shall have the money and you will have the experience".

There were plenty of splendid gold outcrops going; in fact, the difficulty was to pick and choose, and it very nearly amounted to putting the names into a bag, and blindly picking out the one to work.

Someone not badly defined a gold-mine as a hole in the ground into which you put gold, and out of which you take water.

I kept the great Beglehole in my pocket, so to speak, for some days. He was the prophet of Kalgoorlie, and could eat good dinners and put down strong drinks alarmingly. I believe one of his good qualifications was that he could punch the head of any miner in the district, and he looked as strong as a bull.

We had through our hands more than one of those mines which have since turned out very rich, but under his advice we proceeded to promote a company to work a fine outcrop which he said he fancied most - the name does not matter.

The report was verified, so to speak. The purchase price was fixed, part in shares, part in cash; a great point made in every prospectus was that the seller was willing to show his confidence by taking so much in shares, and not all in cash! whereas too often the cash was far more than the speculation on the unworked mine was worth, and some of it, of course, found its way back to the promoter as expenses and profit. It is a queer game at the best of times.

Then there is the underwriting that has to be well paid for, and that came out of the purchase money.

Then came the "cusses" of the underwriters when "let in", and the non-paying up of the weak ones. Then the "making the market" - the brokers, who naturally wanted their bit.

Then, again, the allotment day, with the awful moment for directors, and still more awful for promoters, to see if the public has come in.

Then, if the public has come in very badly, the struggle to get the directors to go to allotment is the next thing.

If they are strong directors, and the subscription is very poor, they refuse, and the promoter is in tears, and bad words, and loses, at times, a very large bit.

Occasionally, of course, an issue is oversubscribed, and the rejoicing is accordingly great.

A notice to the papers follows "that letters of allotment and regret have been sent out". As I have observed elsewhere, the regret is frequently on the part of the board and promoter that the subscription is so poor, or is later on felt by the subscriber, when he finds that there is not enough gold to make a thimble.

When there are so many uncertainties, so many queer people all on the make, to deal with, it is not very hard to understand why some become a bit unscrupulous, and some leave scruple, and what those who are done call "conscience", altogether out of the question.

The way rival promoters treat each other is at times outrageous.

We were once working with one of the best-known men from the mines, who at the moment carried great weight, and we had a bargain with him to which he kept.

A man whose name, out of the City, stands now very fairly high asked one day if he and a friend could come into our office and talk about a certain property, apparently with the idea of joining us in the promotion. We made no difficulty, and they came.

There was some discussion, and they managed to get our man on one side, and have some words with him.

When they had gone our man said: "What do you think they proposed to me? They offered me one thousand pounds down to leave you, and come to their office tomorrow".

Of course, if I mentioned the leader's name - he is still alive - he would say it was a lie, but nevertheless it happened!

In a game of "Devil catch the hindermost", can it be wondered that some sail very near the wind, and some reach the next stage, whatever you like to call it!

It is easy enough for a very successful man to be honest, just as Becky Sharp observed that it was easy enough to be honest on five thousand pounds a year!

We had our ups and downs, but never hit on a great success. As a matter of fact, there were no immediate great successes.

There was a good deal of gambling in the shares, and many made something, and, of course, just as many lost, and the losers howled much the loudest!

It takes a good while to sink a shaft, and make all the adits, drifts, etc., necessary to open a mine. The mill has to be put up, and water must be there, and for very long that was just the thing absent in West Australia.

Nearly all the mines, even the eventually richest, were under-capitalized as to working capital, and had to be "reconstructed". The weak holders and the disgusted ones dropped out, and a few old subscribers and the new ones made their money after long delay.

From what I saw I believe that few of the original subscribers at par ever got more than fourteen shillings in the pound for their shares.

People said: "There, look at the shares at five pounds! If you had only held on! Quite true, but they were the prizes in the lottery which make folks subscribe to mining ventures. If there were no prizes, there would be no gamblers. With regard to West Australia, those who held on to any one mine's shares through weal and woe were few and far between, and nearly always had had to pay reconstruction money.

How many went down to half a crown, then sixpence, then nothing! when one might say, as the Yankee mine-gambler observed to a friend to whom he had recommended a speculative investment, but who had held on: "I congratulate you on a fine permanent investment!"

I had some little hand in Transvaal mines, but not very much. As to mines, I once, years ago, had an offer that might have landed me in wealth. A dear old friend asked me to dinner one night to meet some friends. They were Cecil Rhodes and one of his most successful colleagues. Afterwards he said to me: "Now, you are not doing anything very profitable here in London; if you take my advice, you will go back to the Cape with those two young fellows; I feel sure that they are going to make a success. I will arrange it with them if you like to go". They did make a success - De Beers, Consolidated Goldfields, etc. I, unluckily, was not impressed enough; I did not go. I cannot, years after, remember why. Perhaps I was in love for the moment. Some such silly reason.

Mines began to cool down; there was either too much or too little water, or the gold or the manager were refractory - often both - also the public began to get shy. I had not been quite among the lucky ones, and I may observe that far fewer promoters make any real amount of money than people think. Perhaps if I had had a Jewish ancestor I might have had more flaire, and more power of sticking to money when I made it than I had.

Attention was drawn to gold in British Guiana, the same sort of country that I had known when in Venezuela, and not very far away.

We got some men to be interested in that, and launched a mine on the world, which by report was very promising.

I named it the "Sir Walter Raleigh", in memory of the great adventurer in those parts, whose half-brother, Sir Humphrey Gilbert, was among my ancestors, hoping that between the two it must turn out rich. But it did not. Another frost!

Then I had a venture in a theatrical syndicate, of rather the musical order. In that I gained a varied knowledge of the engagement and management of chorus-girls, as well as of prime-donne. I made the acquaintance of May Yohe and some of her friends, and had a few suppers, and one or two parties on the rivers; but for that I was much too old, and could not begin that life again.

There was precious little money to be made out of it, so I wrote it off as only another experience in life, and I marked it, as a friend used to mark such things, "N. G." - No good.

I cannot say that my life was disagreeable - far from it: perpetual movement, plenty of excitement, the best of living, and many charming friends in the West End to make up for the "nasty jars" in the East.

Chapter XXVII

EGYPT

Some friends of mine, who had had a good deal to do with the preparations for making the railway from Suakim to Berber, and had sent railway material to Suakim, were most anxious to be allowed to make the railway as soon as Lord Kitchener had so decisively defeated the Mahdi.

I was asked to go to Cairo, and see what chance there was that the Egyptian Government would agree to an English company constructing the line.

Having got things as far as possible in order, and having collected all possible information, I went to Cairo and saw Lord Cromer. Nothing could exceed his courtesy and attention, but he said that the Government had quite decided not to allow any companies outside Egypt to work Egyptian railways or other projects connected with the Government property.

That was, therefore, the end of any railway project.

I also had a commission to try to buy for a London syndicate the new Savoy Hotel just started by that most able and enterprising man George Nunkevitch, but that astute financier Sir Elwyn Palmer had been too quick for us, and the contract with him was on the point of being signed when I arrived and saw Nunkevitch. I, however, had a most pleasant three or four months in that mixed and floating population which makes up t he society of modern Cairo.

I was anxious not to leave without doing something, so I had much talk with those interested in the steamers and upriver hotels, and with two of them laid out a certain plan of action. This has since been successfully carried out, but again Sir Elwyn, as soon as he heard of it, cut me out - said they could do without English money or help; and I was, so to speak, kicked out. Of course, some of them might have thought of the combination, but so far they had not, and I felt naturally sad at my disappointment.

I had not been in Cairo for nearly forty years, and it is hard for anyone to realize the change since then. Shepherd's Hotel was then a wooden barrack standing by itself, with no houses near it. What is now the Esbiquieh Garden was then a depression in the ground, often damp, the resort of donkey-boys and stray Arabs, with a couple of wood-built French café-chantants in it, to which we used to flock nightly.

The city of Old Cairo was some short distance away, and there was not a single modern-built house to be seen. The Hôtel du *Nile* existed in the town, and was, I think, half a European building.

Everything then was entirely Eastern. Boulak was the port of the dahabiehs - that interesting, romantic vessel in which parties of from two to four started up the *Nile* for two or three months of quiet and seclusion.

Now all is noise, confusion, steam, Cook's tourists, as populous and unromantic as the Thames at Putney. There is still, however, a great charm over it all, but none of the air of mystery of those days.

The eternal parties and dancing at the hotels become very wearisome to any but the very young, and a tram-omnibus to the Pyramids is the climax of disillusion. The Pyramids are there, and the Sphinx, and the first-recorded king gives his name to the Mena House, but only the air of the desert blows as fresh and pure as ever.

I could not get up to the Soudan, as Lord Kitchener would not give passes to people with no business there but it was very interesting to hear on the spot about the campaign, and meet so many who had been through it.

Lord Grenville was just leaving, and I was most glad to meet the charming and hospitable Lady Grenville - alas! for the last time - and renew our acquaintance of years back.

I received great kindness and hospitality from Colonel and Mrs. Harvey, he being head of the police, and saw with him two curious scenes.

One afternoon I went with him into his house, and he was wanted on the telephone. He told me a murder had just been committed in a drinking-place in the Fishmarket, the lowest part of Cairo - and that is saying much - and that he must go: would I go with him?

It seemed that a half-tipsy Norwegian sailor had been stabbed in a squabble by the Greek who kept the boozing-shop. He, as far as I could make out, kept denying it; then Harvey said to his men: "Seize him!" He and his wife fought like cats, but could get hold of no weapon. Then we adjourned to the nearest police shelter, and the case was gone into. The victim seemed to me not quite dead; but no one seemed to mind much about him, till at last a surgeon came; but there was little life in him, I saw, having seen men knifed before.

Such is the confused state of things in Egypt that it needed these languages: English, Arabic, Greek, and Norwegian, and, as the official language was still French, though there were no Frenchmen there, French too.

I asked what would become of the murderer, and made out that he would be handed over to his Consul, then transmitted to Greece for trial, where he would soon be let out!

The other case was a raid on the gambling-houses.

Now I could not for my life see why gambling should not go on in a place like Cairo, but the police said they had orders to put it down. Harvey asked me to go and take stock of the three houses, which I did, and reported results.

It was arranged that they should all be raided at exactly the same hour, and I was to introduce Harvey into the one which was suspected of having a table which did not run fair. As I was known by sight, he came in with me easily, in smart evening dress, with a beard on, and we sat down and played a little.

I sat by a very well-known American - a very tall, well-built man named Pat Sheedy, who was a great patron of the prize-ring, and whose judgement in boxing matters was much respected in New York. I had met him before at some boxing competition, and we had some talk, but we had not then the faintest idea that he was a partner in the gambling-house.

As agreed, I got up just before the minute of the raid, strolled round the room, and got near the door, and the moment the alarm was given below, seized hold of the iron door to prevent its being shut.

There was a rush to do this, but the marble floor was very slippery, and one or two men went down with no sort of difficulty, and then the police rushed in.

I walked back to the table, and Pat said to me: "A police raid, I suppose?" I said: "Yes; I am sorry to help spoil your evening".

I noticed that he had turned perfectly white, which astonished me in a man of his experience in the Bowery in New York and such-like places, but the reason was clear enough later on.

The roulette-table was taken to pieces, and it, and what other accessories and money that could be seized, carted off to the police-station.

I was the only sufferer, for, in the scrimmage - I could not say when, in the warmth of it. I got a blow on my toe, which so smashed the nail that I was lame for some three months.

Next day, in overhauling the table, there were found two steel rods running from one end of the table to the roulette-board. One compressed the division so that a ball could not enter the enclosed numbers, and the other joggled them in case the ball lodged. It was very ingeniously contrived and artistically carried out. An accomplice was to sit at one end, watch on which side most of the money was, and regulate the course of the ball accordingly.

Under the table, written clearly in pencil, was this:

"I have stood over the man making this for more than a week, and now it works well, but I would not take the trouble again for a thousand dollars.

(*Signed*) "PAT SHEEDY".

No wonder Pat, knowing of his remarks under the table, was uneasy.

Nothing, however, could be done to him in Cairo, and I don't suppose that the report to the New York police, or probably Tammany Hall, was taken very much notice of!

While there I had the pleasure of being present at the marriage of my third cousin, Miss Blunt, daughter of the well-known Wilfrid Blunt and Lady Anne Blunt. It took place at Zeitoum, just outside Cairo, Neville Lytton being the bridegroom, and Lord Cromer giving away the bride in place of her father, who was in England, there being on such an occasion no question of old political differences between Wilfrid Blunt and Lord Cromer.

Some little time before, I had been much interested in the City by the question of mineral oil on the Red Sea Coast, and as to whether something could not be made by working the supply.

I had then got hold of all the information in London, but the report was against it, and it seemed not possible to revive interest in it again. There were, however, about the whole thing such curious circumstances that some of us did not believe that the report was honest.

The spot of the outflow is in a very awkward place, with no fresh water near, so that any work there would be expensive.

That enterprising monarch, Ismael, was not stopped by such a trifle, and sent a ship and all things necessary to explore the supply.

Of its existence there is no doubt. It seems to run under the Red Sea, and also flow out in Arabia opposite. A well-known petroleum expert was in charge, and it is believed that he made a practical examination by proper borings. Certainly his report, which I have read, said so, and the men with him are supposed to have agreed to that.

However, many were not satisfied, but the difficulty of the situation, and the care he took to stop up any holes or borings made, rendered it impossible to resurvey it without great expense.

The story told is that the American Petroleum Ring had no idea of a supply being opened so near the East as the Red Sea, and paid him liberally for the report he made, paying, it was said, two thousand pounds a year to him for the rest of his days to hold his tongue, which he did; for he is now dead-peace be to his ashes!

The Geological and Mineral Department gave me every facility to look up the whole history of the expedition, and knew of the story about the report.

Well, perhaps some enterprising people will try again. The Fashoda affair was in full blast then, and a story went the round of other consulates where I used to visit that the very young attaché, who was unwisely left in charge of the French Consulate at such a moment, was so overawed by the imposing personalities of those who called upon him that he sent up to the unlucky occupant of Fashoda the message which they strongly advised him to send, which was naturally the one they wanted sent.

What stories some of those old palaces in grand Cairo could tell! One was current about the Kasa Ali, now the Hôtel Semiramis; but it was still the curious vast pile of many courts and chambers when I was there.

It had been the house of Ismael Pacha's mother, a despotic sort of lady whom even the adventurous Haroun al Raschid and his faithful vizier might have hesitated to intrude upon.

Stories were told of young men being decoyed into that vast and mysterious spider's web, but those who the queen-spider once set her claw upon were never seen or heard of again.

A fine-looking young German was induced to enter, and some days after a wretched half-dead creature crawled to the German Consulate. From his account he had been taken to the great lady, and royally entertained for some days, then she grew tired of him; but unlike the great Catherine, who was generous to all on whom she had cast an eye of favour, she had the poor wretch reduced to the condition of her many attendants, and thrown into a ditch running into the *Nile*, to be washed away in its dark waters. He managed, however, to struggle out of the river and crawl to the consulate.

A great complaint was made, but the unlucky man could not be mended up, and it ended in such pecuniary consolation as might be being paid, and the Khedive's mother warned to behave better.

A ridiculous story was told of Ismael himself. It was when he was wasting thousands on machinery of all kinds. He heard of the charms of the famous actress Schneider, and had a curiosity to see her, so he said: "Send to Paris for Schneider!"

Now there were in Paris just then two Schneiders: one the famous "Grande Duchesse", the "beloved" of Royal Highnesses, and the other a great inventor and maker of machinery.

Ismael's secretary, having machinery on the brain, sent for the male Schneider instead of the female!

Word was brought to His Highness: "Schneider has arrived". "Tell Schneider to take a bath, and come and see me at once!"

The message was conveyed. In vain Schneider said: "But I have just had a bath!" "Never mind; Son Altesse is very particular: you must take another!"

Arrived at the palace, the Khedive at once saw the mistake, and gave a large order for machines; but the unlucky secretary, who could not turn the man into a woman, caught it hot and strong.

———•—•———

CHAPTER XXVIII

PULITZER AND BAR HARBOUR

I

Having returned from Egypt, and the people in Cairo having carried out the project which I had proposed and drawn out, I found that they had left me out in the cold without even saying thank you.

I had managed to keep it from Sir Elwyn Palmer, as I knew that if he thought it a good thing, he would shut me out at once; but by the chattering of one of the men, who was informed of it too soon, he did hear of it, and said: "We don't want Seymour, or any London men, and will do it ourselves". It has been a great success, so I said strong words at being shunted.

Once more unoccupied, a friend of mine told me that Mr. Pulitzer, of the New York *World*, was in London, and wanted some Englishman to come with him, and help him in various ways. My friend said that, though eccentric and peculiar, he was a very able man, and could be an agreeable friend and companion.

About his energy and ability there was no question, but what he was as to the rest my story will show.

My occupation was rather undefined, but I found Pulitzer in London by no means hard to get on with, and there seemed every prospect of our becoming friends. I wanted to see something of life in the States, and to be with a man of his position, great wealth, with a house in New York, and a large villa at Bar Harbour, seemed a good opportunity.

I stayed with him at the house which he had near Virginia Water, and we rode every day in Windsor Park. His eldest son Ralph was with him, an extremely nice boy of about twenty, still at Harvard, and I found him most pleasant to get on with.

Pulitzer's eyes had given him great trouble. He could not see to read, and but little when out in the daytime, though he never was nervous in riding. To a man of his restless energy the loss of sight was a great trial, and it created a feeling of sympathy for him, and a readiness to put up with his impatience. I agreed to go with him, and we joined the Majestic at Liverpool.

Joseph Pulitzer had come from Poland, as I was told, and though well enough educated, landed in New York with little or none of this world's goods. He showed with amusement the bench by the old battery where he slept the first night he was in New York.

He was in the cavalry during the latter part of the war, and then took to journalism - I think, first in St. Louis, but it was the World which made his great success and fortune.

He told me that his St. Louis paper brought in enough to make most men feel wealthy.

The following letters written to England by me at this time will give an account of how things went. They have interested me to read over at this distance of time, and possibly they may others.

"R.M.S. 'MAJESTIC',
"Monday, 17th July, 1899.

"I send you a line from south of the Banks, as I shall have no time to write from New York, as we shall go straight through to Boston and Bar Harbour. I rather foresee a queer life and experience from what I see so far. As for our trip, the weather was dull and calm to Queenstown, then the night a little rough, but not to matter, and then dull and rainy. To-day a very fine one, sunny and fresh air.

"The ship is, of course, very fine, but the pace is not so great as in the Cunarders and the Germans.

"Our party is J. P., Mrs. J. P., Ralph P., and Dr. Hosmer, who has been with J. P. nine years. He was one of the editors of the New York

Herald, correspondent of it in the old war, and in Paris during the siege. A man full of 'information', but not interesting. He is my stable companion, and snores to wake the dead, and plays a good second to the fog-horn off the Banks at night. However, my nerves are sound, and he don't signify. There is Butes, the secretary, a slight, pale individual; he is subdued to almost absolute silence. On board he is a victim to the sea in the last degree. I suppose he has an individuality, but so far I have seen no signs.

"He and the doctor are part and parcel of J. P.; so also are Dunningham, a very intelligent and quick valet, who orders J. P. about, and J. P.'s chief butler, of the name of Townshend, a very useful man, and so far I hit it off with them.

"There is also one Coates, the editor of the *Evening World*, a bright, pleasant fellow, who has been all his life a journalist. He amuses me, and has given me a curious insight into the nature of J. P.

"Mrs. P. is a curious study, and I cannot quite make her out. As time goes on I may be able to make more out of her. The boy I told you I like; he is very cheery and natural, and works both father and mother very cleverly.

"J. P. has seeming 'lets up,' and a sort of bonhomie, but it is only veneer. In his heart he is all and utterly self; that is the secret of his success. He is by nature a slave-driver, and will drive them pleasantly when in a good humour, and the other thing when in a bad. I can now see why no one can live with him unless of the nature of Butes and the doctor, who have wives and families somewhere!

"As for the friend and companion he talked of, he no more wants it than you want your footman to be your companion. To live with him one must put up, or else there would be a row, which would bring things to a sudden end, which I do not mean it to come to, at any rate for a good time to come. I mean, if possible, to endure through the three months; at the end of that time we shall see.

"I have on board made the acquaintance of a very pleasant and clever man, Colonel McCook. He came from Ohio, and he was one of nine brothers who were in the Northern Army. His father was killed at the age of fifty-four, and seven of his brothers fell in the war. He had seven cousins in it, not one of whom was touched. I hear the family is known as the 'fighting McCooks'. He is now in the firm of Alexander and McCook, who are the great Company - or, as they call them, Corporation - Lawyers of New York, and he is a very well-known man. He represented the United States at the Coronation of the Czar, and knows London and Europe very well. He was offered three places in the Government by McKinley, but preferred to keep on at the law. It seems that the *World*, J. P.'s paper, had a most violent attack upon him when there was an idea of his being a member of the Government. J. P. claims that he prevented his being in the Government. McCook tells me that he had refused office long before the *World* had any attack upon him.

"It amuses me to listen to the talk between the two there is no comparison in the brightness or clearness. J. P. cannot answer any of McCook's arguments.

"McCook tells me that, in spite of Mrs. J. P.'s family and connections, there are few ladies of position who will speak to her, and that here on board there are those, like young Pierpont Morgan, who won't have anything to do with her. Of course, these are things which one only learns gradually. In talking to McCook, J. P. says he is not responsible, and being absent, don't know what the paper does. I begin to realize that the paper is only an appeal to the lowest classes, and is not even taken by the more respectable people. I doubt not I shall learn more as time goes on.

"The vibration makes my writing worse than usual. I don't know if that affects J. P.'s temper, but he is very hard to put up with, and makes one feel as though one had done something to offend him.

"I find he has tried every one of the men of any standing on his paper to stay and travel with him, but they all return.

"I shall see how things are at Bar Harbour, and if the worst comes, I shall have had a strange experience to add to my varied life, and shall have seen a new country, which I always wanted to.

"I like McCook and his wife very much; he has curious views about the Philippines, etc. He would get rid of them to-morrow if possible, and is fully persuaded that they will be passed on to Great Britain before long. But how to arrange it? He thinks the time is coming very fast for Canada to join the United States, and he proposes to give Manila, etc., as a sort of exchange. But do the Canadians want to join? I doubt it. J. P. doubts, and one or two intelligent Americans on board with whom I have talked doubt too. Of course, McCook is on the 'inside track' with regard to Government affairs, and talks very openly, not being an official.

"He is all for a consolidated United States from the North Pole

PULITZER AND BAR HARBOUR 261

to the Nicaragua Canal. He says against colonies like the Philippines that 'the constitution of the Republic does not allow it to govern inferior races as such, and insists that they must become citizens, which is at times impossible, whereas Great Britain can and does govern inferior races arbitrarily'.

"I shall leave this open in case there is any event to tell you before we run into New York about 5 p.m. to-morrow. It is very warm and muggy to-day, a foretaste of what New York will be like. Good-bye for the moment.

"Wednesday.

"We have a most brilliant day, and have passed Nantucket Light at 3 a.m. We expect to run in about 3 to 4 this afternoon.

"The temper of the boss is better to-day - that is all that can be said. I find the name of the house is 'Chatwold', Bar Harbour, Maine".

"CHATWOLD,
"BAR HARBOUR,
"Sunday, 23rd July, 1899.

"I posted my letter to you on board the Majestic just before we got actually into the entrance to the harbour.

"The entrance is striking without any particular beauty of nature, but the approach to the narrows, with the trees and villas on each side, makes that very pretty as far as trees, grass, and neat houses go.

"The striking feature when New York City comes in sight is the enormously high houses close to the end nearest the sea. They look like the towers of churches or public buildings, instead of places inhabited to the top, and fortunately for New York they are not a monstrosity of ugliness, like Queen Anne's Mansions.

"For size and extent the wharves and warehouses beat anything in other ports, as no country has a great capital a seaport. Of course, London has its port, but it is a muddy river, and no one can see it - and best not to.

"The ship was most ingeniously twisted into a narrow dock by putting tugs to 'butt' the end round with padded bows.

"The Custom-house was hot, very noisy, and very badly managed, the utmost of delay and unpleasantness being the rule.

"They all protest against the spoliation of home-coming Yankees, but the tailors and dressmakers are too strong, and, though the tax brings in no profit to the Government, it pleases the tradesmen to annoy those who buy in Europe, and no wonder. I make out the differences in prices something huge. A suit of evening clothes, costing at the utmost £10 in London, is £20 in New York, and, they say, don't last long. Of the cut I can't speak, but they all abuse it.

"The streets are wide and clean - anyhow, in summer. Of Broadway I saw but little, but Fifth Avenue is certainly a very striking street, beginning with shops, and running up to great houses, clubs, and hotels.

"The Vanderbilt houses reminded me of the Marquis de Carabas. When one asked about nearly every fine house, it was a Vanderbilt; if not a Vanderbilt, a Gould or Astor.

"J. P. has a house - No. 10, East 55th Street, not far from the park. It was, of course, all in curl-papers, so we could not judge properly of it, but it seemed to me to want space, and to be all done to show how much carved oak, heavy chairs, and tables, and pictures, and odds and ends, could be crowded into the space. Of the pictures I could not speak; they were covered with cloths.

"The entrance to the park is certainly fine, and it seems well laid out, and trees, etc., good and well cared for.

"We got in about 5, went to the house, and dined at Delmonico's at 8. The party was J. P. and Mrs. P., Ralph P., the doctor, Butes the secretary, one Merritt, a World leader-writer, and Ledley. He is a sort of factotum of J. P., and never so happy as when far away from him.

"The dinner was certainly good, all but the coffee.

"After dinner I went with Ledley to the station, to see that things were right, and then we took a short drive in the park. It is well lighted, and a charming place on a warm night. *That* is well done.

"He talked much to me of J. P. He gave me some hints as to how to get on with him. He said he gets on with no one at first, but if they can survive, that he gets used to them, and is not hard to manage; and, really, he can be managed, and likes to be, but not by strangers.

"Mrs. P. manages him when there, but takes no trouble to conceal her temper and annoyance. I must say I hope Ledley will come up here; he is a gentleman, and would make things easier.

"Well, we 'trained' at II o'clock. We had a special private car, which we found was old, and very shaky and noisy. The only pull of it was that it was changed at Boston on to the line north, so there was no need of changing. This suited J. P., who took a sleeping-draught, and remained in his bunk till late Thursday.

"The bed was comfortable - better than the wagon-lits on the Continent - but I think the berths, etc., on the Northern English lines better, but was told this was a very old, bad specimen of a car.

"Darkness prevented my having much impression of anything till near Boston, where we arrived at 6 a.m. I and Ralph left the station and walked to a hotel close to the Central Park, and had breakfast. I got an idea of the town, but only vague. It looks older than New York, and good and bad streets are jumbled up together. Then we took the underground train to the Central Station. That is very good-wide, light, clean, and fresh, all electric, and run in separate cars; I must say a great improvement on London undergrounds.

"The Central Station is fine, with many platforms, into which the trains back side by side; it is, on the whole, well done, and easy to make out. I think better than London, where one has those underground passages, as at Paddington. The number of trains in and out was very considerable. We left at 9, and ran over rather interesting scenery, first being sea, then inlets, then country with much water. The rivers pretty, and all full of logs. The country houses all of wood, and mostly small, but neat. Farms, all of which looked small, but with signs of energy. Of course, one is struck with the want of tidiness and finish of England, but I believe much less so in North England than out West. Lunch at Portland - i.e., I did. J. P. remained in the train. Mrs. P. and the doctor remained at New York, and Ralph left us at Boston to go to Gloster, to read with a tutor.

"Of course, there were no visible strong drinks, but I was told after that if I had asked for whisky, it would have been brought in a teacup.

"We left Boston at 9, and got to Bar Harbour terminus at 6.45; then steamboat to the little town on the island, and two-miles drive to this.

"I was struck with the number of pretty lakes we passed - some a good size, with sailing-boats on them. The trees seldom fine. I expect all the best have been cut down. One thing I remarked in Boston and along the line - the anxious, careworn look on old and young: all in a hurry, nearly all thin, and with a hungry look. Beauty I saw none all the journey. They all give one the impression of hurry, worry, and too much competition. This is an island some twenty miles long and sixty-five round. It has two 'mountains' of the same height, all rock, with pines here and there. There are many islands about, and the views very pretty and varied. It seems this was first a French Jesuit settlement, then English, and was of importance in the old whaling-ship days, and was bombarded by England in 1814.

"The house here is a large, straggling villa. J. P. bought it and added on at both ends, so it is a regular rabbit-warren. He has a tower of his own to live in - library below and bedroom above. I have not been up yet to see the view at the top. The drawing-rooms are a sort of passage-rooms with no doors - not comfortable. They are big and prettily furnished with taste, low in height, but so far an air of never being lived in. Mrs. P. comes on Tuesday; she may change it all. The dining-room is good, forty feet by thirty-four (about); rather low, with beamed ceiling and red satin walls, and white paint on doors, cupboards, etc.

"The house is right on the sea; you could throw a stone from J. P.'s tower into the sea at high-water. The view is very pretty of ocean and islands. Small lawn and seawall, and good gravel tennis-court - never used, I believe. Also a swimming-bath, good size, warmed, as the water is too cold for any bathing in open sea; also too rocky, except in one small sandy spot three miles away.

"Bedrooms mostly poor, sacrificed by a fool of an architect. Mine has window close to floor, mostly lean-to roof. Plenty of bath-rooms. The food good, and decidedly good French cook. Coffee, of course, bad. Wine good. Waiting very fair.

"The family consists of a sort of housekeeper - a Canadian lady of years and grey hair, pleasant and bright - and a sort of German governess.

"The children are Edith, fourteen or fifteen, a tall, handsome girl, very bright and pleasant - should grow up remarkably good-looking; Constance - whose name they will pronounce as French - a fair, rather pretty girl of eleven, who says little; Joseph, a nice strong, active boy of about fourteen, very good manners and pleasant, good-looking in a way; a baby of two and a half - a boy - much like the others. There is just a trace of Jew in them all. J. P. was examining them the first morning, as far as he could see, and, feeling Constance's nose to make out the shape, said: 'Is it like mine?' Edith exclaimed, 'Oh no; not so bad as that!' and then lamented her sudden exclamation.

"I am glad the children are so pleasant; it makes things easier in many ways. J. P. makes a lot of them when there. The baby declines absolutely to be kissed, and howls.

"J. P.'s temper has improved, but he is difficult to please. As I wrote you, his idea of a friend and companion is one to be at his call whenever he wants him, and to work constantly at papers, periodicals, and books, to impart to him in walks and rides. It is a thinly disguised slavery. I mean, anyhow, to go through with the time here if possible, and see what happens. I may get used to it. We had a ride yesterday, and most likely will this afternoon. We had a heavy thunderstorm on and off all Friday; to-day it is fine and pleasant. The weather here is quite cool - cold the evening we arrived, so I got a bit of a chill I have had to get over. I must say I am remarkably well - too well for this dull, monotonous life. J. P. thinks he likes conversation. He doesn't. He wants what he calls 'concrete facts', and now and then to give an opinion in long sentences, and is surprised if one differs from him, and when I think it worth while I tell him so, anyway. But I can see where men break down, and the cause of it.

"Mrs. P. comes on Tuesday - day after to-morrow - and old Charlie Fearing on 1st August. I never thought I would be so glad to see his cheerful red face and stout body. One never knows!

"Well, I seem to be getting through most of what I have to tell, but, as I told you, I mean to make a mixture of a journal and remarks on the people and country, so you can read as much as you can, and then file it. I much wish I could have some of my old letters to various, written from South America and Lisbon, etc. They are better than any diary, as letters have the inspiration of the recipient, which a journal can never have.

"I am wondering if I shall feel at all at ease, and not as though I were playing a new part, and one I do not understand myself in. However, if I accept the dollars, I must put up with the job to be carried through, but I never thought it could be so distasteful to me.

"Of course, what makes it so is that though J. P. does not mean to offend, he does so from ignorance and the habit of ordering people about for years.

"As far as I make out, they see nothing of the society of Bar Harbour, so I fear I shall make no acquaintances, or have any let-ups of that sort; but time will show, and I think Mrs. P. must have some sort of friends here. Goodbye for the moment. Lunch-time.

"*Monday Evening.*

"Since I wrote the weather has grown delightful; the air charming, just warm; the scenery is very pretty. The whole place is pleasant, and if only J. P. were possible, it would be well enough.

"I cannot make out what I am doing here, and expect to wake up and find it is not real. 'Que diable fait-il dans cette galère?' That I keep asking myself.

"I have ridden with him over most of the island near, and that is pleasant enough, but he is the hardest man to talk to that I ever met or heard of. He is really *all* in his paper and politics, and *such* politics! He interests himself in drawing out his son Joseph, who is bright and intelligent - asks him his opinion of the *World*, and so on. Was horrified to find he rather preferred the opposition paper, the *Journal*, once run by his much-detested brother Albert, who is never mentioned. Asked why Joseph thought the *World* improved - as he said - Joe said because it has left off saying, The *Journal* said this, the *Journal* said that - showed up that man, that grievance. Because J. P. always kept telegraphing: 'Advertise yourself. *Say* the *World* drove out that man, etc.; the *World* drove Alger to resign'. Out of the mouths of babes and—— He hears one cause of the offensiveness of his paper.

"Just now the chief editor of the *World*, Van Ben Hysen, a Chicago man, is up here. He is *enduring* J. P., who treats him as a schoolboy instead of a man of very considerable abilities and experience. *Offensive* is not a strong enough word. Van Ben may regard it all as a sort of penance he has to go through to retain his place, and then goes back to New York, and is independent.

"This evening he dined here, and a remarkably clever, agreeable man, Dorr, who is a lawyer, country gentleman, nursery gardener, and a literary man combined. Comes from Boston, and speaks in short sentences very much to the point, and very little accent. He argues it out with J. P., and has much the best.

"What the uselessness of wealth to a man can be is shown here. J. P. has ruined nerves, health, and sight in making a million dollars a year, and now he is *very rich*. He has no amusement of any sort. No interest but in the paper, which he now cannot read; and in politics, in which he is so violent. He is frantic that he has worked to push out

Alger only to get in a Corporation lawyer like Root. He is absolutely against 'expansion', imperialism - i.e., the new colonial possessions. He *says* it is cowardly of the *World* not to have gone hard against it, and blames the editors, when a word from him would have made them do so!

"There was an argument at dinner as to what papers should do - how far they ought to lead and instruct opinion, how far only to give power. He is all for *news*, also abuse of enemies. He thinks nothing of leading articles - 'Editorials', so called - but he seems to have little gift that way. But as they only libel everyone, it does not seem so much to matter. Three-fourths is a personal abuse called criticism. A man's face and figure and voice, a woman's also, is public property.

"One thing struck me. He so much admired in Chamberlain's talk and speech its conciseness - all to the point, no glory of the British Lion, and to stop when said. In spite of that, he would talk ten minutes at a time, and never end, repeating an argument over and over. Van Ben did not like to interrupt. I now and then got a word in, and Dorr, who knew his subjects well, had to rush in to get any hearing.

"They call it all *politics*, but it is *personal feeling* as much as anything.

"Well, it is getting late; I will not begin another sheet, as I mean to close this to-night, and catch Wednesday's mail - a pretty fast one, so you will get it in a week.

"Mrs. P. comes to-morrow".

II

"CHATWOLD,
"BAR HARBOUR,
"Thursday, 27th july, 1899.

"I will begin another letter, as a week has passed since we got here. The chief impression of life here is its utter monotony. Mrs. P. has arrived, but that makes little change. I see her at lunch and dinner, and she retires about 9.30. I find her pleasant enough, but I don't know more of her. Most of the time is spent in spars with J. P., who finds fault with every mortal thing. Nothing ever pleases him, except now and then for a minute.

"Of conversation he understands nothing. He asks endless questions like a schoolmaster, and is irritated if he does not get instant and very clear answers. Then over and over again one may make a remark to him, and he never answers it. He is fond of asking you to look up some subject of the day, and then doesn't care one bit to hear more of it. The silver question and 'trusts' are the two great things at the moment. On board Colonel McCook talked of the silver, and incidentally of the committee which sat in England to consider the Indian rupee matter. Colonel McCook had the report of it, which I borrowed, and J. P. asked me to master it enough to explain it, and as it much interested me, I easily did; but he has never cared to hear one word more, and *I* do not believe that he understands the question one bit. He is clever enough not to give himself away, seldom expresses an opinion, but always asks questions, and calls everyone a fool who is not an encyclopædia and Whitaker combined.

"It is no use telling him anything unless you can go into every particular, and give him chapter and verse. Of an '*Abstract*' idea he knows nothing, and only cares for '*Concrete*' facts. His son Ralph was often chaffing him about it. I am sorry he is not here; he helped to lighten things.

"The old doctor has come up, so we are a complete party. He takes J. P. much off my hands. Butes, the secretary, is a most desperate hard worker, and understands him after five years; but he ends in utter self-repression, and has no life of his own. He is young – thirty-five - and has a wife and child, who are just going to arrive, when he will sleep at an hotel. I like him, and he helps me to get on with this impossible man.

"I get up at 7.30 to 8, and go for a swim with Joe, who is a very nice boy. It says much for Mrs. P. that the children are all quite charming. I think, also, the having to make such efforts to please their father makes it easier for them to please the rest of the world. Breakfast about 8.30; the housekeeper, Fraulein, and girls drop in, also Butes and Dr. Hosmer, and we have a little general talk till J. P. comes down. To-day early, but generally 9.30 or later. Then one has to *make* talk to keep him going, and, if the papers have come, tell him the news. It does not matter who he has heard the news from, when I go out with him later he catechizes me on it again to see if I have read all the current twaddle of Yankee politics. He does all he can that when not with him one shall be at some work for him! He has an idea after breakfast that he will ride at once, but so far never does. The morning goes, and luncheon at 1.30. J. P.'s appetite never at fault. Then Butes retires with him to read letters, and he is by way of a sleep.

Then a ride or walk at 4.30, 5, or later. Dinner 7.30, never punctual, and he mercifully goes to bed at 10 or soon after. I pity Butes...

"Yesterday we had the end of twenty-four hours' down-pour. To-day is perfectly lovely, and this is a beautiful part of the world certainly. The views are always changing. There is a brilliant sun and fresh crisp air, just what one wants. The rides are pretty, but, of course, not very varied.

"I have personally got J. P. less upon my nerves than I had, but I still ask myself, 'Que diable', etc. I am neither secretary, butler, guest, nor any mortal particular thing. But I don't know how to call my soul my own. However, I dare say I shall see my way better in a few days. I do not believe I could by any possibility continue the life. I think one would lose all individuality and independence. I cannot, at my time of life, begin as an upper servant, and to such a man!

"Well, having got to the end of the sheet, I will stop for this morning.

"Saturday.

"I will finish and send this off. The weather is perfect - sun and fresh breeze. Yesterday I had a sail with Joe in a nice sailing-boat, but this morning the mast carried away, so that is over for the minute.

"No change whatever. It is a queer life: its utter objectlessness is its trouble. However, I mean to see out the time here, and, after all, that will soon pass, and I have been through worse ones, only I don't see any exact end. My vague idea is to see out the time here, and, when in New York, look round and try to find some opportunity of turning my past experience to account. They are forming every sort of thing into companies and "trusts", and I may be able to see one which wants English connections, and if so, may do some useful stroke. Then J. P. may make up his mind to return to England and take a house. We shall see.

"I have seen no neighbours, so have no news. My reading of the American papers does not enchant me with Yankee journalism. *All* personal; the society part intensely so. Describes every woman as though she were so much goods in a shop. I wonder that, after all, there are as many nice people left. It is amusing to hear J. P. object to it all, when he and his paper are the life and soul of that style of thing.

"I believe we shall have a visitor or two, but I don't know of what sort. Old Fearing comes on Tuesday, and I rather look forward to him as a let-up. I shall be amused to see what he makes of J. P.

"As an animal life it is not bad, but I don't know myself, and feel as though I were in some other man's shoes and skin. It is, of course, quite different to what I had been led to expect, and J. P., on his best behaviour in England, is another man to what he is in his own den up here. Not that he means to be unpleasant, I think, but he is as the Lord made him.

"I get through some reading, which may 'improve my mind' in my old age. I am trying Justin M'Carthy's 'Reminiscences'. Such rot - so much words for so little result! I feel it the more on trying to condense it a bit for J.P.! Poor man, it must be very trying to be nearly blind! Of what use all his wealth?"

"BAR HARBOUR,
"Sunday Evening, 30th July.

"I am beginning another letter because I want to put down my impressions while they are still fresh.

"There came to luncheon to-day General Wittier, a man of more or less sixty. He was in the army in the old war.

"He went out about a year ago as Commissioner to Manila, and he gave us his views very plainly about it all.

"He showed how the United States Government had drifted into the possession of the Philippines, with no fixed policy ever on hand for one minute.

"Dewey fought and beat the Spanish fleet because he could do nothing else, and then, what next to do no one knew.

"At first it seemed that the Americans seriously intended to help Aguinaldo and his people to hold the country and to rule.

"When Aguinaldo had taken part of the Spanish lines and the American forces asked him to give up the position to them, it was done on the understanding that when the American army left, that position should be given back to them, showing that then the Americans seriously considered themselves the friends and allies of the Philippinos.

"There was there no idea of the Americans coercing the Aguinaldo party and taking possession of the island.

"General Wittier thinks that it was incapacity on the part of the General Otis, and a want of any plan at home that let things drift into their present state. He had had much communication personally with Aguinaldo, who is only thirty, and a remarkably able man. He is rather puzzled to make out how he knows as much of things as he does, and how much he depends on others for information. I make out that he is a pure Malay, not a half-bred. General Wittier says they are a most intelligent race, good men of business, good accountants, and quite capable of a Government; that the island produces more tropical products together than any other spot-sugar, tobacco, cocoanuts, with all their varied uses, and the fibre of the cactus; that the trade is capable of great increase; that at first the natives welcomed the Americans as a relief from the bad and cruel government of Spain. He represents the Spaniards as horribly cruel - more so than what I have ever seen in South America (but, then, of course, Spain itself did not rule there).

"He thinks that the forces might have been incorporated with the Americans, and that many were fit for non-commissioned officers. That, with the example and experience of England before them, they could have clearly seen what should have been done - how there ought to have been a capable civil Governor sent as soon as possible, and an effort at some clear plan of government made. That the natives saw that it was only to fall into the hands of Germany and France, etc., if the Americans at once withdrew, so they were ready to make friends. But there was no plan, no scheme, and a most incapable General in Otis.

"That now they hate the Americans worse than the Spaniards. In spite of all that, he believes it is still not too late, but he can see no hope of any change.

"The Government cannot, or will not, face it either way - will not decide on a plan of government, and try to conciliate the natives, and will not, on the other hand, make up their mind to the overwhelming forces necessary to crush the natives.

"Otis is incapable and indolent. He can do nothing for the health of his men, allows the natives to make and sell the most poisonous spirit in the camp. The sanitary regulations of all sorts neglected. Never himself goes into the country, and knows nothing of it. Always refuses to meet or try to treat with natives. He himself had an interview with Aguinaldo unknown to Otis; it was arranged through the English manager of the railroad.

"Otis seems disliked and despised by all sides; still, McKinley keeps him on. All this he clearly explained in his report on his return. They all feel the uselessness of this taking places and giving them up directly again. He found the English houses of business most ready to help in every way, and with great knowledge of the country.

"Now, what to do? Can America withdraw? If so, it is only to make way for Germany and others to step in. This, I understand, England would not allow, and long ago, I believe, have indicated to the United States that if they go out, England comes in, but does not desire to.

"Further, it is a question here of whether the majority, who are 'Imperialists' - that is the name they give to those in favour of extension of outside territory - will prevail over the opposition.

"It seems a perpetual feeling of the pulse of the country, and that not to find out what is best for anyone, but what policy will keep the present men in power. It is the head seeing which way the tail will wag it! Everything is sacrificed to votes, office, *and* money!

"It is early days yet for me to have much opinion, but the impression I have is of everything being personal. Not policy, not measures, but men and men's personal interests. The papers are personalities from end to end. It astounds one to meet a man like General Wittier to-day, and then see the daily papers which represent a great nation.

"J. P. pretends that 'editorials', leading articles, are not the aim and object of a paper - thinks, or pretends to, little of them. *Head-lines* and sensation. He always wants the *Head-lines*, and seldom asks for the leaders to be read to him. Speeches - yes, but they are constantly very little but bombast and personal abuse of opponents.

"Of course, one hears endlessly of the next election. Bryan seems certain to be run, but it seems thought with no chance. J. P. and *his* hate him and his silver views even worse than McKinley, and so they are in a fix. J. P. is constantly in long-worded speeches inveighing against the corruption of the day, but he seems to do nothing with his powerful paper against it, but to go steadily on attacking McKinley and his party. He said one day: "I'll tell you what I'll do. I will run Dewey; I am sure I could get him in: he is the popular man", etc. And we heard a great deal of it, but I believe nothing would induce Dewey to stand.

"The Sunday papers arrived this evening, and after J. P. had gone up to bed, I was talking to Dr. Hosmer about them, and he expressed his contempt of it all. I asked him if there were no papers like the *Saturday Review*, *Spectator*, etc., and he said there had been, but were no more; that the papers were purely a money-making business, and no one cared to go into so little profitable a concern as high-class papers. It seemed to me a sad confession for a country where there is so much real intelligence and general knowledge.

"I hope to make out more the causes of it all, and, as a preliminary canter, I am reading Schouler's "History of the United States'. Dr. Hosmer tells me it is one of the best ones, and I am deep in Washington, Hamilton, and Maddison. I may come back with some general knowledge of the place and people, and that is an interest which helps to carry me through a lot that is tiresome and distasteful. I am getting to know Mrs. P. better, and like her. I think in the end we shall get on very comfortably, which will make a very great difference. Well, so far for to-day. I have not read this through again, but shall leave it, and go to bed with Mr. Schouler's work, and a slight indigestion from too much 'chicken fixings' at lunch, and a surfeit of 'frogs legs' at dinner! I would like a whisky-and-soda, but the grog has run out, and there are no spirits in the house. Quite right in the State of Maine.

"Monday.

"I have just been having a talk with a man named Leyman - who has just come up, on the *World* - as to the difference between English and American papers. He says the English papers appeal to, and are read by, a higher and more educated class than here. Here the papers are for the masses. Everyone reads them, and, as he says, commercially, it pays better to get a few cents from every housemaid, etc., than larger sums from higher-up people. That the papers read by that class in England appear once a week. Here it is every day, and the day's wares must be dressed up to suit the buyers, and to attract them. Hence the style. He is struck by the baldness and dullness of the news in England; I here, by its sensational style and frothy language.

"I do not understand the criticism of J. P. on the men now running the *World*: he seems to me to want it to be still more sensational, so far as I can make out. He and his men are much interested to see how Harmsworth's *Daily Mail* will get on, it being more of a "news-giving" paper than the older ones, and how Pearson's new paper, soon to come out to compete with the *Daily Mail*, will answer. All I can say is, I do trust they will fail to Americanize the English Press.

"The *World* to-day has a long account, with pictures, of the "snubbing" of W. W. Astor by the Prince of Wales - how the Duchess of Buccleuch had put W. W. Astor's name in the list of her house-party, and the Prince scratched it out, saying: 'Astor bores me'.

"Wednesday, 2nd August.

"I have not much to add in closing this letter. The weather is lovely, and things go on just the same. Mrs. P.'s brother, William Davies, came yesterday morning. He is a mining engineer in Denver. He is a remarkably good-looking man of about fifty, and I like what I have seen of him. When J. P. has gone to bed, we do a little cards - piquet and bridge - in the evening. Old Charley Fearing comes to-day. I cannot say I put up more easily with my life, and I feel that it would be impossible to take to it for any length of time. I am in too anomalous a position for a man of my age. It is an utter waste of life, and a loss of any individuality. However, here I am for the moment, and I must see my way before I drop this. It really was a pity I ever went to Egypt, but it looked a great opportunity. One could not tell, but it got me out of the way of things I knew about, and if I had made what I hoped, it would have been worth while. Of course, as you know, I took this as at the moment I had nothing else to do.

"When I read of the men who made the United States, it is hard to realize that politics have so hopelessly degenerated among their descendants.

"J. P. was so much interested by General Wittier's account of his experience in Manila that he was for a short time quite taken out of himself.

"He became quite conversational, said he wanted to know more, and talked of sending a correspondent to interview Aguinaldo. He asked me if I would go, as I knew Spanish well, was quite used to their ways and their colonies, and how the additional pull of having my brother just now Admiral out there, and a friend of Dewey, might help.

"For a brief space he talked of it as an actual possibility, and I had hopes of an escape from purgatory, and a most interesting journey and experience.

"However, it died out. I really don't feel sure that the eagerness with which I grasped the idea, and the pleasure which it would give me, did not weigh a bit with him on the opposite side. Not money, for he has the sense to spare nothing when he wants to gain what he thinks is a useful end."

"BAR HARBOUR,
"*11th August, 1899.*

"I find that five days have passed since my last letter to you, and I will send a few lines, though little enough to say.

"Last night we had a dinner-party, and I was amused to study the natives. One custom was new to me among Anglo-Saxons - that of leading the ladies back to the drawing-room after dinner, and then retiring to smoke. I much prefer the English way, and learn that this is a comparatively new idea.

"The women were well dressed, and the lively ones were much more so than those of England. I should say that the power of small-talk and saying chaffy nothings has been much more cultivated over here, and I think on the whole it is a good thing. The ice is broken more quickly. At first it sounds as though what is said means more than it does. Of course, all the people knew each other well, so that it was easy for them to have small-talk. I sat between a Miss Gray and Miss Wallack, the former a nice-looking, very fair damsel of some twenty-five years, with plenty to say and very white shoulders, which she gave us a good view of. From the amount of good turquoises she displayed, there must have been dollars about.

"Miss Wallack I liked much - small and round, not fat, pretty arms, and dark eyes which she had practised using, pretty teeth. Not quite pretty, but expression and go made up much for that. She comes from Washington, where she seems to have lived among the diplomatic set, etc. We rather made friends before the evening was over. But oh, their voices, both of them! I said to Fearing afterwards that I found her lively, and he said: 'You should see her at a Clam Bake; then she is in her glory!' There was a pleasant Adams there, very well-mannered, hardly any accent, a good specimen of an American well-bred gentleman in Congress, about thirty-six. The rest did not take my attention much. There was an insignificant man of about forty with his third wife; I did not make out if death or the courts had removed the other two.

"Those who have started on the matrimonial 'lay' seem, certainly about one out of three, to have tried divorce as a palliative to the dullness of the yoke. An incident before dinner will give you an idea of J. P.'s way of treating me. As we were riding in the afternoon, I reminded him there was a dinner-party which he had forgotten. And he said: 'You had better ask Mrs. P. if there is a place for you at dinner'. And when we got back he called his servant, and said: 'Send up and ask Mrs. P. if there are places at dinner for Mr. Seymour and Dr. Hosmer'. I suppose I was to have dined in the servants' hall. That will give you an idea of his views of the position to which he relegated his 'friend and companion' which he is striving to discover. Of course, it is only a matter of time and occasion when we part. I don't see how I can do it here, and also I want to see more of America and New York, but life is naturally a bore under the position, and for the first time in my life I have had to feel that poverty can be a disgrace.

"I honestly don't think he has a perception of there being anything curious in treating gentlemen like servants; he is so thinly veneered with anything of the gentleman that he cannot understand, so it would be useless to argue with him. I see that any question would end in my going directly, and I am not going to take the initiative in a parting at present.

"Fearing has a due appreciation of the thing, and makes use of a comfortable home, goes over to the club in the morning, and driving with Mr. P. in the afternoon, and only sees him at lunch and dinner. He said to me he used to wonder at times how Ponsonby could stand the way he would speak to him.

"Of course, I may find I cannot, and break out, but I think not till we get South, and perhaps are in England again. I will say for Mrs. P. that she makes it as pleasant as she can for me. I have given up any attempt to make friends here - it is out of the question - so I must go through my time in purgatory with the best patience I have. A story is told at which J. P. himself laughed. Someone met one of the *World* editors returning from Bar Harbour, and said: 'How long were you there?' 'As men count time, two days!'

"I was annoyed by a touch of sciatica, but it is better. I had to do an injection in the night, and just as I had got it ready the electric light went out, and there was no candle or matches, so I had to put it in in the dark, taking a little more than I wanted, which made me rather queer and jumpy next day.

"The weather here is dull and chilly - so cold at nights that we get round fires. They say it is unusual, but I would like a good sun-bake, and long for Ostend and its bright sun, etc.

"The war-ships have been, and are here, but I have seen nothing of them. I wanted to go to the big reception of the officers to which I was asked, but had to ride with J. P. instead. I don't think he would put himself out for a minute to oblige anyone. My word! I don't think I could imagine such self-centred want of any sort of consideration of anyone. Mrs. P. says his refusal to try to be pleasant to anyone makes it hard to do anything social of any sort. I can see that it is his having centred and concentrated his life and energy in one object which has caused his success in it, but he has left himself without a friend, and without the power of any interest or pleasure in life outside his paper, which is on a par with one or two English weekly papers, but much exaggerated! I find it hard to express the contempt I have for the whole thing. He reminds one in ways of Zola's man in 'La Terre', who had retired into private and 'respectable' life after keeping a maison tellier in his native town. I am quite sure neither of his boys will ever keep on that paper. This one, Joe, already fully appreciates his father. J. P. said to me: 'How quiet that boy is - not what I was like as a boy'. Quiet! he is exactly the reverse, but his father knows no more of him than of the nature of an elephant in the Soudan. Well, I won't begin another sheet, for my writings remind me of Ovid's 'Tristia', written from exile on the Black Sea".

"BAR HARBOUR,
"*Monday, 11th September, 1899.*

"I write you a few lines to catch the Wednesday boat. It is very probable that before this reaches you, you will get a wire to say I am on my way to England.

"In the Sunday edition of the *World* there was an attack on some of my nearest relations, the whole thing as bad as the lowest journalism could make it. I only saw it late to-day, and have not yet interviewed J. P. I was so angry I would not see him, in his blind condition, as I could not treat the head of such a paper as he should be. But to-morrow there will be an interview. I mean to ask him who is responsible if he is not, and then see what to do. The result you will learn in time. I have only seen Mrs. P., who is most angry and distressed, and has a letter from one of her dearest friends, who is bitterly complaining of abuse in the same copy of the paper. Of course, my remaining on after his publicly insulting my nearest relations is out of the question.

"Mrs. P. says he will say, *I know nothing about it; I am not responsible.* That is all very well.

"It is no use making a great fortune out of such journalism, and then saying 'I am not responsible'. You know I am not given to swagger, but I do wish I could have our old friend (a well-known old fighting Southerner) to send to the responsible party to-morrow, and give him the chance of standing up, a much greater privilege than he deserves. I want to do something, but not to make myself ridiculous by over zeal. It is vexatious, and very puzzling to know what to do. If there were the *story just mentioned* and *nothing more*, it would be unpleasant, but everyone knows the story was there; but this publication of alleged details is too much. It is only a few weeks back that he wrote to this very man, and he told that he had had a most polite reply to the letter.

"The next thing he may hear is this attack upon him in the paper of the man whom he had written to.

"It is obviously impossible that I can stay on with a man who can be made responsible for such an attack. If I felt myself I could, I don't see how I could face my relations again.

"If I can make it unpleasant to the so-called responsible party remains to be seen, and time will show. I only hope it is not one of the staff that I know, and all more or less like.

"There is a very nice fellow staying here – Ledley - who, while to a degree sympathizing with my feelings, says, over here they are all so used to it that they submit to it. How different to the days when they kept a *fighting* editor!

"Well, good-night; this scribble is rather different to my last one. Then it was the soft constellation Venus in the ascendant, now the red planet Mars. So we live".

"BAR HARBOUR,
"*Wednesday, 13th September.*

"You will have got my last letter, and so will not be so much surprised that I am shortly coming back to my native land.

"I wrote in a hurry to you that a story had been printed at large in the Sunday World, with untrue details put in the most offensive way, and pictures of everyone.

"Well, J. P. put off seeing me about it from Monday afternoon to Wednesday morning. However, the interview came. 'So distressed'. 'Know nothing about it'. 'Impossible to be responsible for all these things'. I told him that I knew that he personally did not write it, but his paid people did; that he was responsible for the system...

"They say he has not had such plain speaking for years, and he is a bit upset since. I asked him whether he thought I could remain with the man who had said in his paper that my nearest relation, whose letter he had in his pocket, had done such things. He seemed to find it come home to him, and he said he saw it was impossible. Therefore this act of the play is over, and the curtain will ring down to-morrow evening, when I depart for New York. I don't know which day and boat I come home by, but will let you know. I do wish I could have picked up a string of something to work at; I would have put up with a lot to have been a bit in New York to look about. I fear now that I cannot afford to remain on there, and have next to no friends and acquaintances in the place.

"It is unlucky that it has come so, though I feel like a prisoner escaping from the house of bondage; life was unbearable to me, and he grew more and more distasteful to me every day".

I left Bar Harbour in the evening, and stayed a day or two in Boston, as I wanted to see it. It naturally interested me very much; there is so much of the old-world England about it, but no one I knew had returned there yet.

I went to Harvard, which, of course, looked very new after colleges in England.

I found Charley Fearing in New York, and also Ledley, who were both most kind and hospitable; the one put me down as a visitor at the Union, and the other at the University Club.

Whatever mistakes we may think they make in New York, no one will say that they don't do their clubs well.

Nothing could be more comfortable and better done than these clubs are, and no dinner anywhere could be better cooked and served than that at the Union. The room, the waiting, and the wine were just perfect. I know of no club that is so well done.

Somehow the managers of the clubs quite overcame that great difficulty in the United States, domestic servants, for the club servants were as good as could be.

The University Club has below a Turkish and swimming bath; above, a barber's room, reading, writing rooms; a dining-room upstairs, with a fast lift, and a garden on the roof. The dining-room is wainscoted with English oak at a cost of fifty thousand dollars.

Nothing could exceed the attention and hospitality of the few men I knew who happened to be in New York out of season. Nearly everyone knows New York, so I need say no more about it.

I went to the office of the *World*, in the vague search for someone to make responsible for the story in the paper which had caused the ruction between me and Pulitzer, but it seemed impossible to fix it on anyone.

They laid it on a man who lived outside New York, and to him I applied, but, according to his story, he was as innocent as possible; it was the impalpable institution without a body to be kicked or a soul to be damned, but, of course, the man who raked in the dollars was the man really responsible.

They all seemed to think that the apology I had got inserted in the paper was such an unheard-of triumph that I ought to be more than satisfied, and that it was almost worth being libelled in the *World* to have the proud honour of getting an apology.

The *Oceanic* was just sailing on the return trip of her first voyage, so I shipped on board, and turned my nose towards home.

As she was brand-new, the boat was as stiff as possible - no vibration of any sort, even in a gale. I could not feel that the engines were working either in my berth or the writing-room. I hear now that she shakes so you can hardly write. She was rather empty, and I made hardly any acquaintances on board - none that I kept up - and we made a dull but good run home.

I was very sorry to hear, a few months later, that the house in New York was burnt down, and that the extremely nice Canadian lady who did housekeeper at Bar Harbour when I was there lost her life in trying to save Mrs. Pulitzer's jewels.

Chapter XXIX

ROUMANIA

Since I returned from Bar Harbour there has been little in my life to amuse or interest anyone.

My farthest expedition was to Roumania, to which I went, being interested in a company which had certain advantages given to it by the Government for the exportation of chilled and frozen meat, and a monopoly for exporting certain things to British possessions.

The importations of animals to improve breeding-stock was a part of the business, and there seemed to be every chance of a successful venture.

So far it has not been carried on to any advantage, through utter mismanagement.

There is a possibility of a very large business being done in pigs, and I saw the chance of a small Chicago on the Danube in the "hog" industry. But the man who the Board sent out proved that he knew no more about "hogs" than he knew about ostriches!

Roumania is one of the rising countries of the Near East, and has every prospect of a prosperous future, though how it will turn out, among that jumble of States which are struggling into independence out of the chaos of the break-up of Turkey, no one can yet tell.

Bucharest is interesting as a study of a newly-built capital city. A sort of miniature Paris or Brussels, streets and boulevards are springing up, but there is still rather a mixture of houses of the newest French style by the side of queer old shanties.

Some of the public buildings are really fine, and in course of time

284 Walter Seymour UPS AND DOWNS OF A WANDERING LIFE

it will be a well-built town of some importance. There is a river, which seems little more than an excuse for a good deal of banks to it with some adornment, and many bridges over very little water.

I am told that the inhabitants bathe in it considerably in hot weather, and that mixed bathing is the custom; also that dress regulations are not in force, and also are not in fashion. But it was cold when I was there.

Bucharest is hardly considered a model of social morals to the rest of Europe, but foreigners are most pleasantly received there, and very well treated, so that that does not matter to anyone.

French is the language of society, and everyone with any sort of education speaks it. Roumanian is a made-up language with a foundation of Latin of the old Roman colony planted there as one of the outworks of the Roman Empire.

I did not see enough of Roumanian society to be able to speak of it, but the books of my friends William Le Queux and Harry de Windt contain very lively descriptions of that part of Europe now causing so much interest.

I have in the course of this book had occasion to say something about the part which I have taken as an onlooker, and perhaps interested party, in one or two civil disturbances when what Mr. Gladstone called "struggling nationalities" have seen occasion to resort to firearms as a solution to the question of the moment.

Living a good deal in that sort of atmosphere has perhaps made me take a lighter view of fighting of that description than that generally taken by stay-at-home Britishers, and that, with natural taste - perhaps a touch of heredity as well - have made that sort of thing interesting and amusing to me.

I have had some small hand in one or two other affairs, which, however, I can only casually allude to for fear of causing harm or annoyance to people still living.

But to make the sum of my confessions more complete I will just add this much.

One affair in South America was naturally to displace the President then in power - that goes without saying. It was a work of some difficulty, which was originated in the Continent of Governments by revolution, and then financed on speculation in London.

Money was found, then arms, but the man? I suppose that I was looked upon as a professional filibuster, as I was asked to undertake the practical part of the job.

It is curious how many will risk their money, but their precious neck must be kept out of danger - quite willing to be accessories before the fact and gainers after it, but free to cry out that the whole thing was a shocking and immoral affair if it failed.

> "Treason does never prosper; what's the reason?
> If it does prosper none dare call it treason!"

The world is mostly made up of humbugs and hypocrites as well as Carlyle's fools.

But, poor dear things! very few realize what humbugs and hypocrites they are. They were born to it, and brought up to it. Retail killing is murder, and awful, haunting consciences, and ghosts, gibbets, etc., and Hell! Wholesale killing is war, is right and glorious, leads to wealth, honours, and Heaven!

A big revolution would be war; a little one very near murder. If only the President is wiped out, it would be murder. The line is drawn very curiously.

In this instance I was to go and be responsible for how most of the money was spent; natives could scarcely be trusted. There was a harmless-looking ship; men to be picked up - they were called navvies - for a line of railway; plenty of arms on board. All things seemed well arranged.

I was to land and confer with the local experts, and, when the train was ready for the match, the navvies were to disembark.

L'homme propose - but there were two conspirators in London who, as ill-luck would have it, both fell in love with the same fair lady.

The unsuccessful conspirator paid out his rival by giving away the whole show, and warning the President and Co.

I, luckily, got warning in time to save my skin, but there was an end of that performance.

The President was quietly knocked on the head at home a little later on, and some of them took the governing and robbing into their hands, but I and my pals had no hand or share in it.

It would amuse people if I could give the names of some of the subscribers in London. One great friend of mine always guarded himself by talking of it as the Duck-Shooting Expedition!

I was again asked to take a hand in a serious piece of business, which eventually involved our Government, but I saw everything to lose and nothing to gain, and declined the business.

I may remark that I knew something of the Young Turkish Party, as I was requested to help in not quite the peaceable way in which things have so fortunately turned out. I had got on some way in making various preparations and arrangements, and I liked very much of what I saw of the Turkish patriot; but, as far as I was concerned, it all came suddenly to an end by the sudden death of my friend in it all, for he died suddenly in the street in Paris.

He had always been very careful and nervous, and felt sure he was followed and watched. He may have been poisoned, but I do not think so; anyhow, there was no examination or inquiry, and he was quietly buried. I found out what I could when I got to Paris, which was very little, but I then dropped out of it.

I was rather astonished at the trust placed in me by some of the men in it. They knew me so little, and put their necks into my hands so absolutely confidently.

Having known for a good while more or less where most of the disused rifles in Europe were, I was approached on the subject by some of the purveyors of arms to the Carlists in the North of Spain some years back.

I had no political feelings, and looked on it simply as a matter of business, but it led me into some queer company, and I nearly got into trouble. I found the frontier on the North of Spain in a very disturbed state, and was warned to be very careful on the Spanish side of it, as no one knew who to trust, and the door of the Spanish prison was always half-open to those going in! One thing which puzzled me was how any man could risk his life for Don Carlos, for no pay and nothing whatever to gain. A popular idea, with about as much sense and reason in it as that which made the unfortunate rank and file follow those good-for-nothing, selfish, self-indulgent Stuart Princes once into England.

Almost recently I was asked if I was inclined for another South American adventure, but I said I was too old, and that, like Artemus Ward, "my professional career is over; I jerk no more!"

Chapter XXX

FINAL

I wish that I could tell whether the indulgent reader who has arrived at the end of the last chapter feels sufficient interest in the writer to care one rap about the conclusions and opinions to which he may have arrived after these many years of wandering ups and downs. Macaulay said of the "Faerie Queene" that few and weary were the readers who arrived at the death of the Blatant Beast, but only the stout heart of a commentator could survive to the end, and my readers may be only too happy to bury this Blatant Beast at the end of the last chapter.

However, he will try a few remarks as an "And now, my dear brethren, finally and to conclude!"

Ways and manners have much changed in my life. Children are brought up more indulgently, given more to eat at home and at school, and personal castigation has nearly died out. It may be a good thing, but I am old-fashioned enough to doubt it, and much believe in the old rough-and-ready way. The classics are still taught in the same slow, silly way as dead languages, but there is a possibility in most large schools of learning a modern language as a living plant, and not as a dead fossil, and some chemistry, mechanics, etc., may be picked up.

On the other hand, the extra twopence for "them as larns manners" is either not paid or is wasted. The manners of the youth of these days are deplorable: they cannot come into or go out of a room

288 Walter Seymour UPS AND DOWNS OF A WANDERING LIFE

with the dignity of a gentleman; their ways of offering a chair or doing any small service to a lady are those of a stableman; they invite their partners to the honour of a dance by saying, "Come on!" and all the amenities of life are on the same level.

As to their dress, fashions change, and the average boy and young man is neatly turned out; but the race of the dandies, some of whom survived in my boyhood, has quite died out, and has never been replaced. More's the pity, I think, for their elegance and punctiliousness about dress led to the same in manners, and their disappearance has led to the decadence of these.

Polite, polished manners indicated the polite, polished thoughts which prompted them, and showed a desire to please which is certainly now only too often absent.

Of the changes in the manners and customs of the young ladies I don't feel properly qualified to speak, as I only now meet a few of them; but, speaking for myself, I think that their greater freedom of life in every way makes the world easier to them, and they are more fitted to take their part in it, and I find that they have more to say.

As to their freedom, I remember in my youth seeing Lady Belinda Fitz-Battleaxe going out for an airing in the morning, with a tall footman with a big stick to guard her, and then forty years later seeing her youthful relative start out on her bicycle to join her "pals", and go out without male guardians for a jaunt of miles.

The American invasion has had much to do with this, but the independence of character and conduct which their example has made the rule now, and not the exception, has taught a greater self-respect and self-reliance, and has put the too-presuming and enterprising male animal into his proper place, and she need not say, "Unhand me, sir!" The young lady of the present day does not faint. One must suppose that she did some years ago, as in old novels every awkward situation was cut short by the young woman fainting.

I have spoken, in my account of my life in London as a boy, of the late hours we kept, and of the many places of amusement that have ceased to exist. Now half-past twelve sees the town shut up, and everything as quiet as if there was a curfew-bell rung. Are we the better for it? We are certainly the duller.

My memory does not go back to the hard drinking days, but in my youth much more was drunk at dinner-parties and at clubs, and in the country-houses many more bottles were emptied, than now. I remember once, at a very hospitable house, saying to one of the girls what good wine her father had, and she said: "Yes. We often wish it was not quite so good. The gentlemen seem to forget that when they join us after dinner they don't look quite the same as when we left them". That is quite ended. The horseshoe table, that was wheeled up before the fire after the ladies left, with its little silver train for the decanters, would only be seen now in a curiosity-shop; the pile of nuts and devilled biscuits is no more, and the taste of claret is forgotten; one glass of port is perhaps allowed before the tobacco begins. I don't mean to find fault altogether, for no doubt in the houses where coffee and cigarettes are brought in before the ladies leave the room the less prosy of the party are spared many a dull hour and half-hour. The present generation may be more outwardly sober, but I cannot see that they are more amusing, or even as much so. There is much more nipping at odd hours, with women as well as men, and gout and rheumatism are as common.

As to what are called their morals, I believe that the ways of society change little and slowly. There always have been faster and slower sets, prim and loose ones, frumps and frolickers, but at times one hears more about the doings of the more frolicking than at others. Kings and Emperors have never been expected to have morals, which are supposed to be most relaxed among the highest ranks of society. The Duchess of society is expected to be rollicking. Byron recognized that in "the Phantom of her frolic Grace Fitz Fulke!" the Marquis is traditionally "wicked", and so downwards. Are they so in fact? Well, very often they are. Country-house life is very often larky ; let those who run - or sit - read "The Visits of Elizabeth" and "The Hazard of a Die".

I have lived to see divorce become common, almost customary; one meets few families in which there has not been one. In old days it was the luxury of the great and the rich; now it is almost cheap, and it is generally very nasty as well. So expensive was it that the apologists of George Eliot and George Henry Lewes say that they would have obtained freedom to marry instead of keeping house together without any ceremony but that the expense of a divorce was prohibitory. My own opinion about it all is so without value that I spare my reader the expression of it; he is sure to like his own best, whatever mine may be. I look on, and am often amused, now and then shocked!

My experiences of life in South American republics have shown me that a republican government means a scramble for power, and for the money that clings to that power. In the Argentine tranquillity and turmoil - called revolution - are alternative states of government. There are no political parties as known in Europe; it is the party of the "Ins" or of the "Outs". Like boys who all want a ride on one donkey, they shout, "Get off. You have ridden him long enough; it's my turn", and if the rider won't get off he is chucked off, and the most active at the moment gets up, and puts the poor old moke through his paces, and is in his turn pulled off for another to have a ride.

How does the donkey, how does the country, like the change of rider? The country is never asked; the most astute, unscrupulous man of the moment rides: he fills his pockets, has a good time, lets his friends share more or less in his division of the taxes, and when they think he has had too much, the discontented join with the men left out in the cold, and down comes the giant tax-eater. Venezuela has been a splendid instance of this. Guzman Blanco scrambled into power, and paid his supporters so well that he had a good turn of it. His pile was big; he sent over to Europe some two million pounds, and enjoyed a dull life in Paris in the end as well as he could, and married his daughter to a Duke. His pocket was the treasury. His means were peculiar. Once he bought up a very large supply of brandy, and then put a prohibitive tax on the article. Then he made a corner in milk at Caracas. He forcibly acquired the cows within reach, and raised the price of milk. When the railway to La Guiana was made in which he was largely interested, he turned the traffic off the only road from the city to the port by decree, ruining hundreds of carters, and forcing everything to come by railway. Since his reign Castro has done very much the same, but he foolishly quarrelled with the rest of the world, and made nearly every country too hot to hold him when his downfall came. Blanco called himself the Liberator, Castro the Regenerator! In past days Rosas was the despotic tyrant of Buenos Ayres, and his blood-stained reign lasted long. Urquiza was the same in Entre Rios, and I have told the story of that ironhanded despot Francia in Paraguay already. The two Lopezes succeeded him, and their rule was despotic.

The question is asked: How does the country submit to it all? The answer is that a tyrant's hand is only hard on the "have-some-things"; it presses very lightly on the "have-littles" and "have-nothings". It was the same thing in Imperial Rome. The hand of Nero and those Emperors like him was little felt by the proletariat. They got their bread and circuses, and looked on with complacency and amusement at the robbery and throat-cutting of the rich upper classes.

Without exception, a republic in time has always led to a despotism. When liberty has become licence, when all social law and order have broken down, there comes a class longing for the return of some order, some law and police. They find a strong man, or, rather, he finds himself; he pays his followers, his soldiers, and his police well, first in promises and then in substance, and rules at first with absolute power, till it is modified by the necessities of the case. He may found a dynasty or he may not - that is not the question; but experience shows that a republic, whether a real or a paper one, always merges into a despotism, for one master has been found to be infinitely preferable to mob rule.

Socialism means a mongrel republic in which the State rules. In my republics the rider ruled the donkey, but the Socialists prefer that the donkey should rule the rider. The many-headed donkey is to kick and bite the would-be riders, but not to carry them till the society is sick of the donkey, and a strong rider is put on his back.

The State! It is such a splendid word, and means nothing. The other day I heard a spouter in the park say: "Now I have nine children. Who ought to keep them? Why, the State ought to keep them!" So I uplifted my voice, and said: "Well, I have ten; so as you and me and the others make up your State, you will have to keep half of one of my babies. It is rough on those who have none, or only two or three, but, of course, if you say so, we must keep each other's young uns, and those who have not indulged in a large litter must pay for those who have".

Of course, up to now no Socialist has formulated the scheme of a working Socialist State, so the anti-Socialists have only been able to attack an imaginary condition. However, anyone can fancy the delights of a society ruled by thousands of the class of men such as the Parish Guardians who have been "doing time" at the expense of the rest of the social community. But what are the Socialist tax-eaters to live on when the poor donkey has been ridden to death, and there is nothing left for him to eat, or the would-be riders either? The five per cent. tax, of course, will grow to twenty or a hundred, and what then? Who will pay the vast army of officials, and the still vaster army of incapables bred up by them, and who keep them in power?

In the countries from which I have drawn my object-lesson Nature has made life so easy that for those who are contented with just living along it matters little, but in a filled-up, hard-climated country what is to happen?

The population of the Southern Republics was drawn from countries almost despotically governed, so anarchy and despotism were the natural alternate outcome. The United States Republic so far does not acknowledge the Divine right of revolution. They had a serious attempt at it, but since it failed they have not repeated it. They have still plenty of space and untapped resources, but the time must come when the country is overpopulated and natural resources are overstrained. What will happen then? History so far repeats itself, and the future will see if it does not do so again in the North American Republic.

India must be more or less despotically ruled. If there is any order by rule there, it always has been, and always must be, despotic. An attempt at a constitution would be anarchy, war, and then despotism till the millennium. But the social economy of that Government has yet to be written.

In my wanderings I have always been much amused by the spouters of the rights of man. It was always their right to what I had, never my right to what they had.

I settled as an enterprising frontier settler on land to which I had no more right than the Government, who sold it to me at twopence an acre, or some such sum. The owners, the Indians, came and said: "Get out; this is ours!" So we shot them, and were called good frontiersmen. It was murder, of course, but the law, not made by the owners of the soil, said it was splendid enterprise!

It was simply the good old rule, the simple plan, that he should take who had the power, and he should keep who can. Right through it is nothing else. Each one of us wants to keep what he has got; the only question is how. Simply by a mixture of force made by combination of "have-somethings", and of humbugging the "have-nothings" by them. I pay so many police and soldiers to keep the poorer and more hungry from taking what I or my forbears have taken by force or by astuteness.

A few wolves are trained into a pack of dogs to keep the other wolves in order. A compromise is made. So much land and so much food is allowed to the poorer wolves on condition that they allow so much more of each than they have got to the masters. If they try to break through that condition, the trained pack make it very unpleasant for them.

But the "have-somethings" have another defence for their property besides the paid force of police to enforce the law they have made. They work the power of humbug to its utmost, and there are two weapons which they use. The first has some sense, the second none, but it is, and has been, very effective.

The first is to convince the " have-littles and have-nothings" that a community cannot go on without law and order, and as the "have-littles" want to keep what they have got from the "have-nothings", they grunt at the richer wolves, but accept their protection, while many of the poorer hope to steal or save something, and will want help to keep that when they have it. Hence the laws about property, and the institution of police to enforce them.

The second weapon is the religious one, by which they teach the poorer and the poorest that the Ruler of the universe made and sanctioned the different classes of mankind, and that rich, middle, and poor are a Divine institution; and, further, that the Divine wrath and punishment are sure to catch those who try to pull down the rich, and while the discontented will have a poor future time, the robbers of the rich will have a still worse one.

This works well so long as the poor are ignorant and superstitious, but as soon as they are educated up to having their doubts about bogy, and a future punishment for trying to get rich except in the regular ways laid down by the "have-somethings", that weapon of religious compulsion fails.

The Government of the "have-nothings" gives and promises as little as it can, but the sops to the "have-nothings" are a safety-valve, which is opened when the strain on the police driving-power becomes too great.

These are the conclusions to which I have come as to government and property in my wanderings.

Vanity of vanities - yes, but humbug of humbugs, all is humbug.

My prophet, perhaps the greatest writer in the world - Herbert Spencer - has convinced me that not only what we call the material world has been formed by evolution, but also the social world. Forms of government, social, ethical laws, and religions have all grown up gradually by evolution. The ruling power of the universe works steadily on, and various forms of governments, laws, customs, and religions have been evolved to suit the varied climates and varied necessities of the equally varied races of men in our world.

We in England have a very limited constitutional monarchy, which has the advantages of the freedom of a republic, and avoids the revolutionary, sudden changes of the monarch called a President. The safety-valve has often been opened by the "have-somethings" when they feel that the "have-nothings" are boiling over. So far this has been done only from time to time, so that social order has not been seriously upset, or only temporarily so; but we seem to have come to a moment when certain leaders who are in power are ready to sink everything in order to remain in power, and propose to remove the safety-valve altogether and let all the steam out. The "have-somethings" are to be legally robbed by the "have-nothings"; thus, the donkey is to mount the former rider, and the dismounted riders hope that the donkey will be so grateful that he will give them a good time, and, if not a permanent ride, a mount now and then. But will they? Well, those who live will see the result of this total removal of the safety-valve, if the present drivers succeed, as they are trying, in wrenching it off.

As to the various religions which have been evolved, as far as I have seen, they generally seem to suit the climate, race, and degree of civilization of races over the world.

Most men want a religion; nearly all women do. It has done, and does, much when gently used to soften manners and assist orderly government. When violently used, it soon degenerates into persecution and brutality. Its chief drawback is the invariable accompaniment of superstition, which narrows the mind and injures the limits of freedom.

The professional religious teacher may individually be an upright, charming man, but as he is briefed for life to one side of the question, he must be prejudiced and more or less narrow-minded, only too often very much so. Also his bread depends on it. An argument with him may be instructive, and at times amusing, but as his career and livelihood would be at an end if he were convinced, it can never be anything but a wordy passage of arms, ending in nothing, except now and then a loss of temper.

Personally, I should wish to give everyone a perfectly free hand in the choice of their religion, but social surroundings are greatly compelling to most, and to those who have exceptional ideas only too often amount to persecution. The religion of most people entirely depends on the chance circumstances of their birth and surroundings; that they should wish to have any choice about it afterwards strikes those about them as the most dreadful thing possible, and only a suggestion of the Evil One, and sure to lead to a place which, as the polite preacher said, "I will not name before ears so refined as those of my hearers".

And now how to express the philosophy I have learned, which has made me try to think with Plato's Sophocles and with Cicero that old age may be a pleasant thing. But first, do I think so? Pleasant it may be made, but as pleasant as young days by no means. Less strength, less health, less power to enjoy a dozen things does not make for happiness, but with fair health it may not be so bad. One great bother is as to friends and society. Most of my early friends are dead, and too many of those left are such growlers that I dread to meet them. Younger acquaintances are often civil and pitiful to me, and kindly patronize me; they think me an old fool, just as I think them younger fools, and I often wonder if I am as tiresome as so many that I meet.

The want of the occupations of younger days makes time hang, and few men of over sixty can take up a new line. Personally, I have done nothing but take up new lines all my life, so I have not found it so bad. I found a careful study of Herbert Spencer occupy much time and thought, but as I scarcely ever meet anyone who has done more than look into his works, it has not much helped conversation for me.

Then, by way of amusement, and being naturally argumentative, I took up the defence of the Emperor Julian, called by those who dislike his name the Apostate; they think it sounds nasty, though not one in ten thousand of them has the vaguest idea of what he thought, did, and wrote. The writing of that sketch killed much time, and caused

296 Walter Seymour UPS AND DOWNS OF A WANDERING LIFE

some reading of the history of those times and of neo-Platonic teaching and philosophy, as it is called, and a regular occupation for months helps one along over old age very much.

And now, having made some few remarks and reflections on what I have learnt from life, I leave my character and my credit in the hands of my reader, advising him to have as few personal habits as possible, and as few small daily necessities; it is the upsetting of these which makes half the misery of life; the big upsettings are rare.

If any younger readers wish to please and to be popular, let them forget themselves and the effect they are making, and think only of the pleasure and gratification of the other person; all study for effect is tiresome. Kind-hearted, unselfish desire to make another comfortable and happy will always produce the result they seek, and gain them popularity. There must be the will to please, not simply the desire to seem pleasing.

www.ingramcontent.com/pod-product-compliance
Lightning Source LLC
Chambersburg PA
CBHW030643270326
41929CB00007B/184